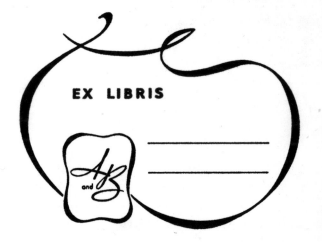

EX LIBRIS

_____

_____

Basic Dimensions of
ELEMENTARY METHOD

Basic Dimensions of

ELEMENTARY METHOD

George A. Beauchamp

Northwestern University

ALLYN AND BACON, INC.   BOSTON, 1959

FOR GEORGE AND ANNE

Preface

FOR SOME TIME it has been common practice in training elementary school teachers to distribute the problems, principles, and issues of method among a number of separate-subject methods courses. This approach has yielded two consequences. First, it has produced some duplication of effort for which our profession has received much criticism. Second, it has, in my estimation, tended to obscure a clear-cut interpretation of method itself. It occurred to me that it might be fruitful to examine the subject of method as it may be applied to teaching in the elementary school, in an endeavor to identify what I have come to call *basic* dimensions of method for elementary school teaching. The result of this examination is this book.

Believing that four basic areas comprise the essence of method, I have devoted an entire section of the book to each of these. Part I, of course, is introductory — it presents the scope of the problem, defines terms, and examines the setting in which method must operate. The theme of Part II is the study of elementary school children — why we study them, how we study them, and the implications of this study for teaching. Part III uncovers the basic approach that a teacher should have toward the organization of his teaching materials, derived from a discussion of the relative importance of content, method, and the learning experience. Part IV defines the actual teaching-learning process by integrating the fundamentals of teaching materials discussed in Part III, the essentials of child study presented in Part II, and the specific dynamics of the classroom situation — classroom groups, activities, routines, and discipline. Part V analyzes evaluation as it applies to several levels within the education

v

activity — those of the teacher, the individual, the group, and the process itself.

I wish to express my appreciation to those authors who have contributed their ideas toward the development of this work, to those publishers who have been kind enough to permit me to quote from their materials, and to Austin N. Stevens for his decorative illustrations. My sincere thanks goes to my colleagues Dr. John Lee and Dr. Joe Park for reading and criticizing all or parts of the manuscript. Finally, and especially, I express my very deep gratitude to my wife, Kathryn, for transcribing and typing the manuscript, and for her many fine suggestions for its improvement.

GEORGE A. BEAUCHAMP

Table of Contents

PART **I** Introduction
to Elementary School
Method

IT WOULD BE IMPOSSIBLE to begin a logical discussion of the basic
dimensions of elementary-school teaching method, without first
establishing a basis for identifying either those dimensions or
categories of dimension at least. Therefore, the first chapter will
be directed to an analysis of the various responsibilities and tasks
of elementary school teachers. The second chapter will be concerned with the meaning of method as an educational process.
An examination of this meaning in relation to the various tasks
of a teacher should give a conceptual framework for the discussion of the dimensions of method to follow.

CHAPTER 1

The Responsibility
of the Task

To UNDERSTAND FULLY the total responsibility of the elementary school teacher one must look at the teacher's position in terms of the forces that impinge upon it. The choice of frames of reference to describe this responsibility can be made in many ways. Most people consider the actual performance by a teacher in the classroom with children to be the most vital set of circumstances for which he is responsible. In this they may be right. However, it is unfair to the magnitude of a teacher's position to disregard his responsibility for those activities that precede and follow those of the classroom. In fact it is most difficult to interpret realistically classroom activities and the teacher's accompanying work without orienting these to the total educational activity.

In this chapter attention will be directed to the complete educational activity of the elementary school, and from analysis of that activity responsibilities of the teacher will be discussed from the points of view of the teacher as a social agent, the scope of teaching activity, and the uniqueness of teaching in the elementary school.

LEVELS OF EDUCATIONAL ACTIVITY

Modern education must expect to satisfy two demands. One of these has to do with the transmission of our cultural heritage;

the other has to do with providing for the educational interests and needs of children. Whenever social groups live together over continuous periods of time, the members of those groups learn ways of behaving as individuals and as group members. We generally speak of our learned ways of behavior as our *culture*. The longer groups live together the more complex and large their culture becomes. So long as cultures remain simple or primitive, the various elements can be transmitted to oncoming generations incidentally or by direct association with adult members of the social group. However, when a culture becomes complex, society has need for some formal means of transmitting it to the young. It is this need that causes societies like ours to establish institutions of cultural transmission; the elementary school is one of these institutions.

Most people accept the fact that the elementary school is an agency of cultural transmission, but they frequently disagree as to which elements of the total culture it should transmit. Problems in resolving this disagreement will be discussed later; the point of emphasis here is that the continuous generation of culture by a social group causes that group to demand a social service for the transmission of its culture. Part of that demand is focused upon the elementary school. A pointed illustration can be drawn from language as an element of our culture. Much oral communication is learned without benefit of formal instruction, and by the time children reach school age many oral language habits have been formed. Reading, on the other hand, is a different process, and it takes much skill, time, and patience to transmit this cultural process to the young. Because society considers the ability to read essential to our way of life, it stipulates that schools should provide this service.

The second demand upon modern elementary education is for services to elementary school children, designed to satisfy their interests and needs as the immature members of our society. It is part of our unique way of life to stress the development of individuality, and school programs continuously are called upon to meet the demands of individuals as they live in schools. Each person, young or old, is impelled into activity because of motives based upon his interests and needs. Some interests and needs are distinctly individual and others are somewhat common to people of equal age and similar cultural backgrounds. Nevertheless, each person must have opportunities to explore and satisfy these interests and needs. Perhaps it is correct to say that it is through recognition of the existence of interest and need patterns in school pupils that teachers are able to motivate pupils to work in learning activities. Thus there appear to be at least two good explanations for this demand upon the school. It is recognized that individuality needs to be fostered in school life, and that teachers must capitalize upon unique interest and need patterns as a motivational device in teaching.

These two demands upon schools need not be considered exclusive of one another. At one time in our educational history it was argued that school programs should be directed at the satisfaction of one or the other. On the one hand it was argued that it was the function of the elementary school to transmit the cultural heritage to the young in an orderly, systematic, and sequential manner, without too much regard for the unique interest and need patterns of the assembled pupils. On the other hand it was argued that the primary function of the elementary school program was to meet and satisfy the unique interests and needs of the children enrolled in schools. This argument no longer seems tenable. We have to recognize the concurrent existence of these demands. In modern schools the demands of interests and needs must be satisfied through, or in the process of, fulfilling the demands of society for cultural transmission. This is what might be called an interactive position, and it prescribes a dualistic responsibility for schools and their programs. We can return to the reading example to illustrate the spirit of this interactive position. The demand is made that the elementary schools teach children to read their language. Modern teachers recognize that there are various approaches that can and must be made to instruction in reading. Furthermore, there are innumerable sources of reading materials for various stages of maturity and on a great variety of topics. Children with different environmental backgrounds and unique personalities will seek interest and need satisfaction through selection of different reading materials. One child who has a deep interest and curiosity about automobiles, trucks, trains, or fire engines can utilize reading materials on these topics to develop reading skills. Another may select materials about animals, farms, or the zoo and develop similar skills. The selection of illustration is arbitrary, but it demonstrates that the interactive position provides a dualistic responsibility for elementary schools if they are to satisfy the two principal demands upon those schools.

The actual operation of the interactive position in the elementary school can be illustrated by the complete educational activity of the school broken down into various levels. This breakdown is illustrated in Figure 1. Three levels of the total activity are indicated: (1) the curriculum planning level, (2) the teaching-learning level, and (3) the evaluation level.

Curriculum planning level		Teaching-learning level		Evaluation level		Curriculum planning level
	Curriculum objectives		Planning and selecting specific objectives		Evaluative schema applied to objectives	
	Curriculum content		Planning and selecting content and activity		Evaluative schema applied to content selected	
	Curriculum organization		Planning organization for activity		Evaluative schema applied to organizational pattern	
	Curriculum evaluative schema		Planning and executing evaluation of activity		Appraisal of evaluative schema	

FIGURE 1. *The complete educational activity of the elementary school.*

The curriculum planning level

The first level of educational activity may be called the curriculum planning level, and in terms of the order of the three levels, should occur first in time. This is the avenue through which the demands of society for schools are indicated in light of anticipated capacities, interests, and needs of children who will attend those schools. Curriculum under this notion is *defined as the design of a social group for the educational experiences of their children in school.* Thus defined, the curriculum must stipulate the intentions of the social group in terms of the school's objectives, at least a broad outline of the content of the subject matter for the instructional program, the organizational arrangement of the content, and an evaluative schema. Curriculum thus defined is intended to be planned by the adult society under the leadership of the teaching profession prior to the assembly of pupils and teachers for the execution of an instructional program. In our school communities the cooperative interaction of members of the teaching profession and lay citizens is a process essential to insuring democratically that the two primary demands upon modern schools are prescribed by persons who have the authority and responsibility to do so.[1]

The teaching-learning level

The teaching-learning level is the one on which the teaching-learning classroom activity takes place. It is here that the problems of method become crucial. At this level the teacher becomes responsible for the adaptation of the results of curriculum planning to the classroom situations, and it is here that the teacher's professional training is put to its greatest test.

[1] For a full description of the meaning, significance, and application of cooperative, lay-professional curriculum-planning as briefly described above, see George A. Beauchamp, *Planning the Elementary School Curriculum* (Boston: Allyn and Bacon, Inc., 1956).

In adapting the planned curriculum for classroom use the teacher must do at least three things. First, the teacher must utilize his best professional skill in understanding the pupils to be taught. It is only because a teacher is thoroughly cognizant of the backgrounds, interests, needs, and capacities of his pupils that he can do a skillful job of modifying or expanding curriculum content for those pupils. The results of pupil study furnish the teacher with information about the range and character of individual differences in the classroom, and this information serves as a basis for decisions that must be made as teaching plans are formed. Second, the teacher must select from the curriculum (as formulated at the curriculum planning level) those areas of work that he expects will challenge the motivational patterns of the children and that will produce the maximum educational growth in those children. However, he can do this intelligently only because he has developed an understanding of his pupils. Third, the teacher must then develop resource materials around those areas of work selected from the curriculum, and with the resource materials formulate teaching plans.

Equipped with these materials and plans the teacher engages in a series of cooperative activities with his pupils. These are indicated in Figure 1. Via the avenue of teacher-pupil planning, a general topic from the teacher's resource materials and plans is selected, and specific objectives are formulated that are considered worthy of attainment by the classroom group. Through the use of the same cooperative process the group selects specific topics and activities by which it can achieve the planned objectives. The group then organizes itself to carry out those activities, and then it proceeds with them. During the pursuit of these activities the group will periodically evaluate its progress. Further evaluation will be done either at the conclusion of the activities or as a culmination of those efforts.[2]

---

[2] The writer recognizes that this description of such a complicated task as classroom teaching is in the briefest outline. However, the remainder of the book is dedicated to broad exploration of the problems of method that are so

The evaluation level

The third level of the complete educational activity emanates from the second level and points the way back to the first. This is called the evaluation level. Reference to Figure 1 again will indicate that an evaluative schema is called for at the curriculum planning level. In general, evaluation may be considered to be a triple-phased, circular process. The first phase of the process is one of determining whether sought goals have been achieved. A second phase is that of determining the adequacy of the means utilized to achieve the goals. The third phase is a matter of determining whether the achieved goals were, in the final analysis, worthy of the effort. This process assumes that activity or behavior has been directed toward the attainment of goals, and this is one of the reasons why objectives are stressed in the curriculum planning and teaching-learning levels. The matter of determining the achievement of the goals, of determining the adequacy of the method of achieving them, and finally, of determining the desirability of the goals, places into operation a cyclical process that keeps goals dynamically alive and the selection of content and method in harmony with them.

In this spirit evaluation becomes a means of keeping the entire educational program of the school dynamic. The purpose of including an evaluative schema at the curriculum planning level is to build into the curriculum-teaching operation a means of continuous, critical appraisal of the total activity. The function of the evaluation level is to apply the evaluative schema. It thus seeks to determine the success and appropriateness of both the curriculum and the classroom activity in producing desirable educational growth in boys and girls. The evaluative schema may call for such things as various kinds of educational measurement, the maintenance of historical and anecdotal records, specific reporting procedures, subjective types of appraisal, or the

---

crucial for this level of educational activity. The brief description is included at this point to orient the teaching-learning level.

use of systematic and over-all evaluative instruments. Whatever the schema may be, it becomes the responsibility of pupils, teachers, administrators, parents, and other lay citizens to apply it. Some application will be made after the teaching-learning activities have been completed, but a great deal can be accomplished while the activities are in process. In any case, the results of applying the evaluative schema provide bases for revising curriculum and classroom practices. This impels a return to the curriculum planning level, thus making the complete educational activity dynamic in nature.

THE TEACHER AS A SOCIAL AGENT

From this brief overview of the institutionalized educational activity we can look more pointedly at the responsibility of the teacher as a social agent. Since the teacher is one of a group of professionally trained people who bear many responsibilities for education, we will get a broader picture of this position in the educational system if we identify it within the broad organizational structure.

Public education in the United States is considered to be a function of the state. The Federal government has not seen fit to provide a legal structure for the organization of a public school system; therefore, it has been the obligation of the states to establish a mandate for the maintenance, organization, and support of the public schools. All states have fulfilled this obligation. To a considerable degree the states have delegated, or decentralized, control over establishment, program, and operation to local communities. The people of the local community, that is a county, a city, or a school district, select a board of education to establish policy and manage general school affairs for them. To give their work professional guidance and to provide a means for policies to be carried out, the board of education selects an executive officer who usually bears the title of superintendent of schools. The superintendent in cooperation with the board of education, selects school principals, supervisors, teachers, and other personnel to carry out the school activities. An elementary school teacher is assigned to a building under the leadership of a principal. In that building all of the teachers and the principal form an instructional unit within the total system of schools. The teacher, then, is one member of a large group of people who are concerned with the education of boys and girls. As a member of this kind of social group the teacher takes on a three-fold social responsibility: (1) responsibility to the school patron group, (2) responsibility to elementary school children, and (3) responsibility to the professional group.

Responsibility to the patron group

Because of the fact that lay social groups at either the state or local level (or both) have recognized and expressed a demand for educational programs for children in schools, and because of the fact that the organizational patterns are thereby structured, a teacher accordingly must accept a responsibility to the broad social or patron group. In a certain sense, the teacher becomes a social servant. This is not used in a servile or menial sense, but rather in a social and professional, in much the same sense that congressmen, mayors, presidents, or justices are servants of the people. More specifically, since parents and other school patrons have decreed that there shall be provided schools to help with the rearing of children, it becomes the task of teachers to carry out that decree. Not only must they carry out that decree through the instructional program in the classroom, but they also have the additional responsibility of keeping the patron group informed as to the success or failure of their efforts.

Concurrently the teacher must be a leader in society. In any changing society such as ours the needs for formal education are continually shifting. Scientific research is constantly bringing forth new information that affects the educative process. Members of the teaching profession must be willing to study these factors continually and exert leadership with the school patron groups so that they will recognize these changes and modify their expectations for schools. In many respects this is a teaching responsibility—a responsibility to educate adults concerning school needs and practices. A teacher who fulfills these responsibilities becomes a teacher of society in addition to being a teacher of children in the classroom.

Responsibility to elementary school children

If one had to select from the three categories of responsibility the teachers' greatest obligation, in all probability it would have to be their responsibility to the children they teach. It is in the fulfillment of this responsibility that teachers devote the majority of their time and energies. To be a successful teacher one must become adept at the many processes and skills which provide a productive learning environment for a classroom of pupils. The major function of this book is to probe the various problem areas related to this aspect of the teacher's work.

It is the teacher's obligation to be skillful in studying and diagnosing the various capacities, interests, needs, and motives of his pupils. A thorough understanding of these pupil characteristics is essential for purposes of adapting curriculum content and guiding pupil performance in selected learning activities. In fact this knowledge is basic to any teacher in respect to all of his professional responsibilities.

Obviously it is the duty of the teacher to select curriculum materials and adapt them to pupils' use. However, there is a unique function in this process that makes it a special service of teachers to students. Children of elementary school age are psychologically and socially struggling to interpret the complex world about them and to adapt themselves successfully to what too frequently appears to be an adult world. They must be helped to interpret their social and physical environments so that they can learn to behave in those settings. Furthermore, it is incumbent upon teachers to help boys and girls learn to behave in their environments in socially acceptable ways and with feelings of success.

Responsibility to the professional group

Too frequently the responsibility of the teacher to his own professional group is either overlooked or ignored. Because they cherish that status, teachers take pride in the fact that they belong to a profession, but too frequently they associate themselves with the profession only verbally. This kind of association tends to destroy a profession because professions depend upon their membership for character and perseveration. Therefore, if for no other reason than the fact that he is a member of a *profession*, it is the teacher's duty to ally himself personally with that group and do his best to make it a better profession because he is a member of it.

When an undergraduate student in a teacher-education institution elects to prepare for teaching, he makes his first move toward professional status. From that time on he obligates himself to professional behavior. The period of pre-service education is devoted to acquiring the necessary knowledge and skill for teaching. It is also a period during which an individual begins to formulate a philosophy of education and to accept the ethics of the profession.

A person officially becomes a member of the teaching profession when he receives his license to practice his profession, namely, his teaching certificate. But the thrill of membership in a profession is not felt to the fullest extent at this point. A teacher feels a greater sense of professional belonging when he becomes recognized by other members of the profession through his demonstrated competence in practice, additional growth due to in-service and graduate study, and contributions made through writing, research, and participation in activities of professional associations. A very old saying is applicable here; one gets from the profession in proportion to what one puts into it.

THE SCOPE OF TEACHING ACTIVITY

The concept of a complete educational activity and the inherent responsibilities of the teacher can be interpreted in terms of the scope of teaching activity or the action side of the teacher's job. The discussion can be organized under the same three general areas used in the previous sections, namely: (1) activities related to curriculum planning, (2) activities inherent in the instructional process, and (3) evaluation activities.

Curriculum planning

In an earlier section curriculum was defined as the design of a social group for the educational experiences of their children in school. Curriculum planning would then be a series of activities on the part of a social group aimed at producing that design. Theoretically at least, the social group for any elementary school would be composed of all the people who live in the attendance area of that school plus all of the professional personnel concerned with instruction and administration of the school program. Only because these people, or their representatives, participate in its planning can the curriculum really be called a design of the social group. This is the basic consideration behind a philosophy of cooperative lay-professional curriculum planning. Involvement in cooperative curriculum planning would require that the teacher work with other teachers, school administrators, the board of education,[3] and lay citizens.

Many people in education will not accept the point of view that lay citizens should be asked to work with members of the

[3] It must be remembered that curriculum planning is an aspect of board of education policy. Regardless of who may participate in curriculum planning, the results must be submitted to the board for its consideration and adoption as the policy of the school.

teaching profession in planning the school curriculum. For them the ideas expressed in the above paragraph do not represent the most desired course of action. They believe that it is the function of the professional group to plan the curriculum. Approval by the patron group of the school is sought through the acceptance of the curriculum by the board of education which is composed of representatives of the patron group.

Whichever viewpoint one accepts as to who should participate in curriculum planning, there are many common tasks that teachers must perform in the planning activity. These tasks are related to the processes used and the final results of the planning. If we follow the description of curriculum previously mentioned, the results of planning will have at least four parts: (1) a statement of the use to be made of the curriculum, (2) a statement of goal-direction for the school program, (3) an instructional guide, and (4) an evaluative schema.

More specifically, when a teacher participates in curriculum planning, he may become involved in writing, conferring, discussion, and studying. At various points in curriculum planning it is often necessary that records be kept of discussions, that notations be made of practices, and that actual writing of the several parts of the curriculum be accomplished. From time to time teachers have to confer with one another on an individual basis about the curriculum; frequently they will have to participate in group discussions. If they hope to elevate practices because of the new curriculum, teachers must become involved in study that will broaden their understandings and raise their insights.

As these tasks are performed, teachers may play any or all of several roles. They become *participants* in the planning process because it is their professional obligation to do so. As participants and as professionally informed people, teachers are *resource persons* in planning activities. Teachers have knowledge of the desirable content for elementary school programs. They possess knowledge and skill related to method, and they have knowledge and ideas about the application of considerations from fields of educational foundations to curriculum deliberations. It is because of such knowledge that teachers can be resource people for the curriculum planning process. Because many curriculum planning activities involve group work, teachers will often find themselves acting as *leaders* of discussions and planning sessions. The number of opportunities for teachers to assume leadership roles increases when they become involved in cooperative lay-professional curriculum planning, but even when the professional group does the planning alone, there are many occasions during which there is need for someone to play a leadership role.

Instructional activities

Once the curriculum is planned it becomes the job of the teaching staff under the leadership of the school principal to translate the curriculum into an action state. Each teacher is assigned a grade or a section of a grade, and he becomes responsible for the profitable interaction of the pupils in that grade with the appropriate portions of the planned curriculum. This is the second level of the complete educational activity, and it poses a multitude of tasks for the classroom teacher. At this point several of these tasks will be but briefly enumerated since the bulk of this book is devoted to problems inherent in this level.

STUDYING CHILDREN. One class of activity that will consume a considerable portion of a teacher's time is composed of the many things a teacher does to understand his pupils better and which put him in a preferred position to help them. One must familiarize himself with the kinds of background of the boys and girls. To do so may demand that the teacher accumulate historical information on their social backgrounds, the health records, economic statuses, and previous school experiences. Various kinds of measures of pupil capacity and achievement can be helpful. To get this sort of information the teacher may have to administer, or have administered, various standardized tests such as intelligence and achievement tests. On a more sub-jective basis there are a number of ways the teacher can acquire useful information about pupils, such as maintaining anecdotal records, making sociograms, assessing interests, testing ideas in practice in order to see which work under what circumstances, discussion of pupils' problems, and cooperative sharing of ex-periences and ideas.

DEVELOPING TEACHING AND RESOURCE MATERIALS. Clever de-velopment of materials for teaching in one sense is a time-consuming task, but it is one that will pay dividends in the form of good learning experiences for children and a successful teach-ing career. When a curriculum has been planned, a teacher must select from the instructional guide those areas of work appropriate for children of that grade, taking into consideration their readiness for that subject matter. This is the first step in planning for the actual task of classroom teaching. Then teach-ing plans need to be formulated around those areas of work. Such plans might include the setting of tentative goals, identify-ing some possible projects, thinking of possible organization of pupils, and selecting some culminating activities. In accordance with these plans resource materials for teaching and learning must be accumulated and organized. The resource materials may be books, paper, maps, construction materials, science equip-ment, community resources. It may even be desirable to identify resource people in the community. Obviously this kind of planning demands that the teacher project his thinking toward beginning and ending points as well as intermittant activities, but a teacher who takes the time to develop teaching and re-source materials carefully, frees himself for the leadership role that must be assumed in the classroom.

GROUP LEADERSHIP. When the pupils and their teacher are assembled together in the classroom, the teacher takes on the role of group leader. A major purpose of this leadership role is to help children impel themselves into constructive and productive learning activities. Modern educational theory, and in many cases classroom practice, indicates that a favorite technique for group leadership is teacher-pupil planning or group process. The technique is applicable to the various tasks the group must perform if the best learning situation is to result, and these tasks are similar to those performed by the teacher in his preparation indicated in the paragraph above. Using the planned curriculum and the previous work of the teacher as referent or beginning points, the group must decide upon the specific areas of work worthy of their attention. Once this is done they can move to establishing specific objectives to be accomplished and then proceed to organize themselves to do the work.

In the process of carrying out their activities, the pupils, as individuals and as groups, utilize the available resources for their investigations. There are innumerable kinds of things they may do in this process, such as reading, writing reports, holding discussions among themselves or with resource people, constructing models, drilling on needed skills, and so forth. From time to time as the work progresses, the teacher will help the group to pause long enough to make some evaluation or appraisal of their progress for purposes of modifying their directions or improving their method of attack. Finally, the group most likely will want to summarize their activities through some evaluative procedure or a culminating activity that will reveal what they have learned. Throughout all of these activities the teacher moves as a resource person and as one who helps with problems too difficult for the children. His principal function is to keep the activities continually moving in the direction of constructive learning.

GUIDANCE ACTIVITIES. As previously indicated one of the obvious responsibilities of the elementary school teacher is to the pupils. Since children are with the teacher most of the school day in the elementary school, the teacher in fulfilling this responsibility sees to their needs in the learning situation. One function may be that of advisor to individual children concerning their personal problems or those in their work. Another is that of pacing the kinds and amount of learning activity for individual capacities; this is a very important part of a teacher's work that calls for the best professional skill. If one thinks of discipline as a process whereby an individual proceeds from a state of dependency to a state of independency, this becomes an important guidance function of the teacher. This is a process that implies that an individual (the pupil in this case) must learn to accept greater responsibility for choosing his own problems to solve and finding ways to solve them, and be willing to accept the consequences of his behavior in doing so. The teacher is in a unique position to develop discipline in this sense.

Evaluation activities

Evaluation activities are an important aspect of a teacher's work, and too often they are slighted. Generally these activities should be performed as an application of the evaluative schema prescribed in the curriculum. In all probability the evaluative schema will require the teacher to carry on evaluative activities under several circumstances. Several of these have already been indicated, such as all those things that may be done in relation to studying children. On the one hand, we study children through testing and observation to ascertain their interests and capacities in order to facilitate the instructional program. On the other hand, we observe and test children to reveal the growth effect of the school program upon them. Another kind of situation calling for evaluation is that of the classroom procedure in which the main purpose is to improve the flow of activity and the quality of learning being accomplished. In these circumstances the principal evaluative techniques are observation, discussion, and measurement.

Another group of activities related to evaluation has to do with the maintenance of pupil personnel records and the reporting of pupil progress to parents. The tasks for the teacher in connection with maintaining pupil personnel records vary with the prescribed contents of those records and the uses to be made of them. One decision the personnel of every school must make is on the kind and amount of data that are to be maintained for children. Certain records such as attendance and health frequently are legally prescribed and the school must incorporate that information. Beyond that, the historical, anecdotal, and test data that are maintained are to be decided by local school authorities.

Reports of pupil progress to parents stem from the data described in the previous paragraphs. The purpose of reporting pupil progress to parents of children enrolled in the elementary school is to reveal to the parents the information known by school personnel about the effect of the school's program upon their children. There are many devices that are used for the purpose of reporting pupil progress. Among the more familiar are the letter-grade report card, a modified version of the letter-grade report card, the report letter, the parent-teacher conference, or some combination of these. Obviously the most desirable form of pupil reporting will be that which results in the clearest understanding on the part of parents. It is possible for the pupil reporting system to be a means whereby cooperative evaluation takes place between teachers and parents. Whatever technique is used, the tasks involved in progress reporting require expert professional skill on the part of the teacher if a clear and meaningful interpretation of pupil-growth data is to be made.

If the intent of the evaluative schema prescribed in the curriculum is to be fulfilled, the accumulated results of the various aspects of evaluation should provide information that is of material value in keeping the curriculum alive. The experience of pupils, teachers, administrators, and parents cooperatively focusing their attention upon a school program should bring to light needs for additions and modifications in the curriculum. The teacher must play a significant role in bringing these experiences to curriculum planning groups for their consideration in curriculum improvement.

Other activities

A description of the scope of teacher activity would not be complete without at least mentioning other functions in which most teachers engage, that are related to those described above but represent a slightly different type. For example, the teacher may be an active member of the local parent-teacher association, and it may or may not be affiliated with the National Congress of Parents and Teachers. As a member of a school staff the teacher becomes involved in the activities of that group. Moreover, there are other professional activities such as further professional study, writing, and active participation in professional and social organizations. All of these take time, but they tend to enrich a teacher's life.

UNIQUENESS OF THE TASK

There are several unique features of the elementary school that contribute to the nature of the responsibility for teachers in such institutions. For instance, most elementary schools are neighborhood schools. In many cases they serve groups of people who frequently meet in face-to-face social situations and who therefore tend to become a relatively homogeneous social group. Compared to other schools, the elementary school is usually the smallest. The combination of smallness and homogeneity of the neighborhood school places before the teachers and administrators of the school an opportunity to establish good lines of communication between the school and the community it serves. Good communication can lead to an educational program that is well supported, genuinely understood, and probably of high calibre.

Another unique feature of the elementary school is the self-contained classroom. There are elementary schools that are organized on other than the self-contained basis, but this is the most highly recommended. The self-contained classroom is organized so that one teacher becomes responsible for all teaching of pupils enrolled in that room. It does not necessarily require that the teacher do all of the teaching, but he does maintain responsibility for all instruction given. In most situations thus organized, the teacher actually does do all of the teaching. From an organizational point of view, the one-room rural school was, and still is in some places, an almost perfect illustration of the self-contained idea. The basic purpose or philosophy of the self-contained classroom for children of the immature ages, or elementary school pupils, is to provide one skillful person who is responsible for the total educational growth of boys and girls.

Fusion practices in the organization of subject matter have been utilized more widely in the elementary school than in the secondary school or the college and university. No doubt the existence of the self-contained classroom contributed to these practices. By fusion practices reference is made to the fusion or combining of two or more established subjects into one area of study. For example, the present-day social studies program is a fusion of subjects once separately identified as history, geography, and civics. At least two important purposes motivated fusion practices. One of these was the element of time. As the number of subjects required to be taught in the elementary grades increased, the amount of time allowable for each in the school day was reduced proportionately. Reduction in the number of subjects by fusion would allow larger and more flexible blocks of time in the school day. A more important purpose of fusion was to improve the psychological organization of subject matter, or said another way, to reorganize subject matter in the light of knowledge of how children can learn best. To return to the social studies illustration, it was found to be difficult for the immature minds of elementary school children to make desirable transitions between the separate subjects and thus come out with the most desirable attitudes, concepts, and skills as a social being. Part of these come from seeing relationships among historical fact, geographic circumstance, and civil organization. It can be speculated that fusion practices in organizing subject matter are in their infancy—we can expect many more in the future.

The nature of the elementary school program is principally one of general education. The subject matter is a cross section of our culture, and no effort is made to have pupils "specialize" in any phase of the program. The number of elective areas of study are few. In this setting the elementary school teacher is a generalist, and this is recognized in most teacher-education programs. It is a complicated task that confronts the elementary school teacher because there are so many dimensions of the position. Partially because it is so complicated, the work poses a very great challenge.

Summary

In this introductory chapter the general task of the elementary school teacher has been examined from four points of view. First, the setting for the teacher was examined in light of the complete educational activity of the school. Second, certain responsibilities of the teacher as a social agent were identified. Third, the scope of teaching activity was described in light of the complete educational activity and the various responsibilities of the teacher. Fourth, some unique features of the elementary school were noted.

In summary of these, several points should be stressed. At least three distinct levels of the complete educational activity can be identified: the curriculum planning level, the teaching-learning level, and the evaluation level. These levels are not independent of one another or unrelated. They tend to overlap, and they should. However, it is useful to us as professional people to be able to identify in our thinking reasonably discrete levels or phases of our total function so that each can be examined more carefully.

Schools are institutions established by society to perform certain cultural functions. Teachers are social agents since they are employed in those institutions. As social agents and as members of a professional group, teachers bear responsibility to their patron groups, to the children whom they teach, and to the profession to which they belong.

In recognition of the levels of educational activity and the responsibilities of teachers as social agents, various aspects of a teacher's work were identified. One of these was curriculum planning. Another consisted of various instructional activities such as studying children, developing teaching materials, group leadership, and guidance activities. A third aspect was related to evaluation activities. Such unique characteristics as the self-contained classroom, the homogeneous neighborhood, and subject-matter fusion practices were cited concerning the elementary school as a setting in which the various instructional elements of a teacher's work might be placed.

Thus the setting in which dimensions of elementary school method can be discussed is described. In Chapter 2 the meaning of method will be presented in the light of this setting. With the meaning of method established and the tasks of teachers identified, we can present the various dimensions of method in four areas or categories: (1) studying children, (2) organizing teaching materials, (3) directing classroom activities, and (4) evaluating.

Ideas for discussion and activity

1. Discuss with others interpretations of the tasks of teaching you held prior to reading this chapter. How have they been changed?

2. What in teaching motivated you to seek membership in the profession?

3. Write several paragraphs describing your concept of a teacher who is truly a professional person.

4. Discuss the kinds of knowledge an elementary school teacher should possess in order to teach in a self-contained classroom.

Suggested readings

Eye, Glen G. and Willard R. Lane, *The New Teacher Comes to School.* New York: Harper & Brothers, 1956, Chapter 1.

The title of this chapter is "Teachers for Our Schools." The authors discuss the many expectancies of the lay public for teachers, the pressures and demands upon teachers, and the social and professional setting for the teacher in modern American society.

Fox, Robert S., "Teaching *Is* Leadership," *Educational Leadership*, 14: 138-140; December, 1956.

In this article various leadership facets of teaching are stressed. The leadership roles are related to the professional and social functions of teachers.

Raths, Louis E., "What Is Teaching?" *Educational Leadership*, 13: 146-149; December, 1955.

In this writing Raths identifies a group of teaching functions and relates them to the promotion of learning that is focused upon values, thinking, and competency.

Rugg, Harold and B. Marian Brooks, *The Teacher in School and Society.* Yonkers-on-Hudson: World Book Company, 1950, Chapter 1.

This chapter imparts the enthusiasm of the authors for the adventure of teaching.

Witty, Paul A., "The Teacher Who Has Helped Me Most," *Elementary English*, XXIV (October, 1947), 345-354.

This article is a report of a study of good teachers as seen through the eyes of children. Responses are indicated in tables of traits or characteristics of teachers that were identified from the responses of children from all over the nation.

CHAPTER 2

The Meaning of Method

The MEANING and interpretation of method is a much debated subject in elementary education. For some people method is synonymous with simple, procedural, classroom techniques. For others method is very complex, in which case method becomes concerned with values as interpreted through means applied for achieving sought ends. In the thinking of many persons method is considered to be somewhere along a continuum between these two extreme points of view. However, method is principally thought of as a general process of providing interaction between pupils and school subject matter, and techniques are specific and subordinate acts within the general process.

The history of education reveals that quests for improved method and techniques of teaching are never ending. It seems as if our search for improved methods and techniques has become intensified with increased complexity in school programs. Possibly this is because many teachers see improvement in method as a hope for the dissolution of many frustrations of classroom teaching. For example, we frequently have searched for and found new approaches to the teaching of reading in the elementary school. In the hearts of many teachers has been the hope that with each improvement in procedure many problems of individual differences will be resolved, that cause so much difficulty in getting all children in the early grades to learn to read. Many of the improved techniques have helped, but we still have many problems in the teaching of reading. Similar illustrations could be given from other subjects in the elementary school program. It is sufficient at this point to emphasize that for many teachers the search for improved method is a continuous one.

It is the general purpose of this chapter to present the problem of method for the elementary school teacher. To do so, the various ways that method has been interpreted will be identified, and these will be directed toward contemporary viewpoints. The modern interpretation of method will then be related to the complete educational activity outlined in the previous chapter.

THE HISTORY OF METHOD

Space limitations of a single chapter preclude a complete review of method in the total history of education in the world. Besides, such coverage is more appropriately the purview of a volume on the history of education. Here we will try to concentrate on method as applied to elementary schools in our society. It will be necessary to refer occasionally to the influence of methods practiced in European countries because they have markedly influenced teaching practices in our country. The principal reason for illustrating various concepts of method that have been historically held is that many of them are still held whether they are now valid procedures or not.

Method in early schools

The early colonial schools for children were the dame schools, reading schools, and the schools of the three R's. The basic purpose of these schools was to teach what we would call today the fundamentals of communication. The dame schools and the reading schools were almost exclusively devoted to instruction in reading. The schools of the three R's offered instruction in reading, writing, spelling, and arithmetic. The methods in these schools were very crude. Method was principally a matter of hearing recitations on an individual and group basis. Most of the learning activities were a matter of memorization. The teacher's job was mainly one of assigning tasks to be done, hearing recitations, and keeping order.

A very important influence upon method in early schools was the attitude of adults toward children. The attitude is neatly expressed in the following statement:

> The most persistent and lasting concept of the child to be found in the colonial period was an outgrowth of the Puritan outlook that permeated much of the religious thinking of Americans for 150 years. It stemmed directly from the religious orthodoxy of Calvinism with its emphasis upon God's power and wrath, original sin, reverence and fear of God, obedience to His commandments, and obedience to the authority of parents and elders. An authoritarian education was seen as the only possible way to implement beliefs that the child's nature was inherently evil. Since the child was prone to sin, the best way to keep him under control was to instill in him a fear of breaking God's laws and a fear of the awful and dreadful consequences of sin. Fear, discipline, and obedience were the by-words of this conception of child nature. These formed the staples of educational method throughout the colonial period for those who fully accepted this view of religious orthodoxy.[1]

With attitudes like those described above toward children, schoolmasters were apt to be cruel in the administration of discipline to the girls and boys enrolled.

These crude methods, limited curriculum, and severe discipline contributed to making the school an unhappy environment for children. These things, coupled with the fact that the teachers were incompetent and untrained, produced a type of schoolroom environment that today would be considered completely intolerable.

Influence of the Enlightenment

The Revolutionary period was an inactive one as far as education was concerned. People were too busy with other things. During

---

[1] R. Freeman Butts and Lawrence A. Cremin, A *History of Education in American Culture* (New York: Henry Holt and Company, 1953), p. 66.

the nineteenth century there was a general awakening of educational consciousness. A part of this awakening was the trend toward emancipation of children from such complete adult domination. No doubt the spirit of democracy instilled in the common man during the Revolutionary War and the War of 1812 had something to do with this change in our country, but there were other influences of direct bearing stemming from Europe. A number of the ideas contributing to this influence were voiced in the seventeenth and eighteenth centuries. This was particularly true of what is called the Eighteenth Century Enlightenment.

EUROPEAN INFLUENCES. Some of the innovators in the seventeenth century led the way toward modern educational methods. Among this group, sometimes called the Sense Realists, were Frances Bacon (1561-1626), Wolfgang Ratke (1571-1635), and and Johann Amos Comenius (1592-1670). According to these men, learning proceeds from experience; that is, from the experience of the senses being activated by elements in the environment. These individuals actually began the teaching of what we now call the scientific method. They were interested particularly in the senses being aroused by experience in one's environment, the observation and collection of data for purposes of answering questions raised by experience in the environment, and reaching conclusions as a result of the collection of that data.

The Eighteenth Century Enlightenment was a period during which many great ideas in educational theory were brought forth. In fact many more ideas were voiced than were ever actually put into practice during that century. John Locke (1632-1704) did much to set the stage with his *tabula rasa* concept of the mind through which he anticipated faculty psychology which was to prevail in educational and psychological thought until the twentieth century. Method in elementary education was influenced by the rise of Naturalism in educational thought, lead by Jean Jacques Rousseau (1712-1778) and Johann Bernhard

Basedow (1724-1790). They postulated that, since all good comes from nature and everything degenerates in the hands of man, the process of educating children should be a return to nature. Learning should be built through experience rather than through the formalism of books and established postulates. Since everything was to be in accord with nature, emphasis was placed upon kindliness to children. They advocated studying children so that teachers might know them better, and advocated that learning should proceed around the interests of children. A good deal of stress was placed upon individual differences. In this sense Rousseau and Basedow were inspirers of modern psychology. Both of these individuals attempted to develop unique methods for different subjects. In a way, this began our modern concept of psychology of school subjects.

Johann Heinrich Pestalozzi (1782-1827), Johann Frederick Herbart (1776-1841), and Frederick Froebel (1782-1852) comprised a subsequent group who became known as the psychologizers. Many of their ideas stemmed from the Sense Realists and from the Naturalists before them, and they served as a transitional group from the eighteenth to the nineteenth century. These three individuals gave great impetus to improved educational method. From the teachings of Rousseau on the need to understand pupils came the psychological movement in teaching. For Pestalozzi, sense perception was the foundation for all learning. All subjects were reduced to their simple elements in order to give the perceptual processes the greatest opportunity to work. Following Locke, Pestalozzi sought to develop all the faculties of the mind. For Pestalozzi discipline was, of course, based upon love rather than cruelty.

Herbart placed method on a more specific basis. He particularly emphasized the scientific method. Herbart became well known for his five formal steps in teaching: preparation, presentation, comparison, conclusion, and application.[2] These five formal

[2] Originally Herbart described four steps: clearness, association, system, and method, but they became five among his American and German followers. See

steps played a significant role in subsequent teacher education. They became the bases for organized teaching method and they were vigorously taught in most teacher-education institutions. Like Rousseau, Herbart emphasized that good teaching starts with the interests of the child.

Froebel was particularly noted in connection with the kindergarten movement. In many respects, with his emphasis upon child activity, Froebel was the forerunner of the activity movement of the twentieth century. Activity was to stem from child interest. Considerable emphasis and time was spent on play, music, and construction. Froebel's greatest influence was in America.

Before looking at the effects of the beliefs of these individuals upon the practices in the United States, several important points need to be emphasized to contrast them with beliefs that prevailed in early schools in this country. First, a different concept of good learning is held from memoriter and often abstract learning from books. Sense perception is substituted, in which real objects are studied and the learner proceeds from the known to the unknown. Second, there is a shift from cruel discipline to kindliness to children. This is part of a recognition of children as children and not as miniature, sinful adults. Third, the act of studying children so that they can be taught better is emphasized for the first time, and fourth, the scientific method is advocated in teaching and learning.

INFLUENCE IN THE UNITED STATES. Americans visiting and studying in Europe observed the work and teaching of Pestalozzi, Herbart, Froebel, and their followers. They were profoundly affected by the ideas they encountered and, in turn, exerted leadership for modification of practices in this country. We should note several of these persons.

John Frederick Herbart, *Outlines of Educational Doctrine*, trans. Alexis F. Large and Charles De Garmo (New York: The Macmillan Company, 1904), pp. 53-59.

Horace Mann (1796-1859) has gone down in history as one of the greatest pioneers in modern education. Many of his ideas were influenced by European educators, particularly Pestalozzi. Since the time of Horace Mann's leadership there has been a continuous effort to improve instructional practices in schools in our country. Mann was most impressed with the freedom allowed children in many of the European schools and with the kindly attitude that teachers held toward them. This was strikingly in contrast with what he observed in his home country. Mann pioneered for the word method in the teaching of reading, and in other subjects strove to eliminate much of the formalism in school classrooms.

As superintendent of schools at Oswego, New York, Edward A. Sheldon (1823-1897) demonstrated Pestalozzian ideas to Americans. The methods of sense perception, reasoning, and judgment were emphasized. Object teaching, particularly in science, became an innovation. In fact, when the Oswego Normal School was established, object teaching was the thing for which that normal school became particularly famous.

On an even broader basis Frances W. Parker (1837-1912) was influenced by all of the psychologizers. Parker served as superintendent of schools at Quincy, Mass., and he later became principal of the Cook County Normal School at Chicago, which subsequently was incorporated as part of the School of Education at the University of Chicago. After Froebel, Parker was particularly interested in the principle of self-expression. For him, creative activity on the part of children was a necessity in the classroom. At Quincy, and later at Chicago, the number of subjects offered in school was reduced by combining them or by functional application of one subject in the teaching of another. For example, spelling was taught as a functional aspect of writing and reading. After Pestalozzi, Parker believed in the concentration of study in one area with other areas being correlated with it. In this respect Parker was a leader in the direction of the movement for correlation in curriculum organization of the twentieth century.

Another person who was influenced by the work of Herbart and Froebel and who has had the most profound effect upon education was John Dewey (1859-1951). At the University of Chicago he established the Dewey School in 1896 where many applications of his philosophy were demonstrated. Out of this early work came the activity program that Dewey conceived to be necessary for teaching young people to live cooperatively in a socially useful environment. He rejected some of the formalism of Herbart, and in his general attitude toward children he was much more like Froebel, with respect to creative activity, independence, and reflective thought. From the beginning, Dewey insisted that for succesful teaching, the teacher must study both the nature of the pupil's environment and the nature of the individual himself.

We can note here the same changes in the thinking of American educators as those that were noted in the previous section concerning the ideas of the European educators. We see greater application of the scientific method. We note the beginnings of the psychological study of children. Here were the beginnings of the activity concept with its inherent notions of activity stemming from interests of the learner and from the experiential environment of the learner. However, these ideas at the turn of the twentieth century were unique and were only practiced in places where a pioneering attitude was held. The following description of the elementary school in 1900 is indicative of the fact that these ideas were far from universally accepted at that time:

> A typical elementary school in 1900 was an eight-grade school, ordered and run in a cold, methodical manner. Boys and girls marched in and out of school in military fashion at the sign of the bell. The teacher ruled as master in the classroom. A bundle of switches stood in the corner of the room ready for use. Pupils recited by groups on a question and answer basis. The textbook was

used as a *Bible,* the sole source of truth and knowledge. Extra-curricular activities were confined to a few games at recess and lunch periods.[3]

Memoriter knowledge continued to be important. Faculty psychology and its educational counterpart in the form of mental discipline still predominated in curriculum and teaching. Nonetheless, the basic ideas for twentieth century concepts of elementary education and method had been laid down by these pioneers. These ideas were to have a profound effect upon the development of elementary education and method in elementary education in the United States during the twentieth century.

Method in recent times

Concepts developed in the twentieth century for the elementary schools stem from the teaching practices of the two previous centuries. The great spurt came with the progressive education movement, which probably had its source in John Dewey; the great leader of the movement was William Heard Kilpatrick. The general spirit of the progressive education movement was to apply the knowledge of science and the method of science to educational practices.[4] More than ever before during the twentieth century, method now came to have both a philosophical and a psychological basis. Or put in other words, there was both a philosophical and psychological notion of teaching method.

PHILOSOPHICAL BASIS. Method can be considered philosophically in the sense that it is concerned with relationships between ends and means. Here the question is raised whether subject matter used for learning really accomplishes the ends desired. Thus method cannot be considered in isolation from the subject

---

[3] William E. Drake, *The American School in Transition* (Englewood Cliffs, N.J.: Prentice-Hall, Inc., 1955), p. 454.
[4] For a larger treatment of this thesis the reader is directed to a little volume intended to explore the nature of progressive education: Carleton Washburne, *What Is Progressive Education?* (New York: The John Day Company, 1952).

matter being used, but rather, it must be selected in terms of its appropriateness for both that subject matter and the desired ends. For example, suppose one of the objectives of a unit in the social studies program to be improved citizenship behavior on the part of boys and girls; as far as method is concerned, the arrangement and use of the subject matter reaches its critical test at the point where an attempt is made to decide whether or not improved citizenship behavior on the part of the boys and girls actually does result.

PSYCHOLOGICAL BASIS. The psychological aspect of method is concerned with knowledge of the learning processes and the nature of subject matter. Man has accumulated a good deal of knowledge about how children learn and how they develop in the process of learning. We have previously indicated that a number of educational theorists prior to the twentieth century had advocated intensive study of pupils by teachers so that they might become more effective in teaching the children under their jurisdiction. As the psychological laboratory has furnished more information about how children grow and develop and how they learn, the process of child study has become both facilitated and complicated. It has become facilitated because we have learned how, but it has become complicated because the novice has so much to learn about the process. Method has also become psychological because we have studied appropriate means of organizing subject matter in harmony with what we know of the learning process and what our experience has taught us with boys and girls in the elementary school with those subjects. For example, it is possible to spend a considerable amount of time studying what frequently is called the psychology of elementary school subjects. In the fields of reading and arithmetic alone the amount of research that has been done in the quest for better methods of teaching and learning is monumental.

APPLICATION IN PROJECT METHOD. There were a number of unique applications of these notions of method in actual practice.

Of particular significance was the project method that was advocated by Parker, Dewey, Meriam and others, although Kilpatrick was its outstanding advocate. For Kilpatrick, a project is a life-like activity in which pupils are self-impelled toward solving a problem that they accept as being their own problem. The project must be an activity in which the learner is self-motivated and has the opportunity to make choices in action. It must further make provision for the application of good principles of learning; and a third important principle is that the individual learner must develop a sense of responsibility for the project and for his efforts within the project. It was not intended that the project would eliminate all traditional subject matter of the elementary school; the project was another way of organizing subject matter for purposeful learning. In fact Kilpatrick enumerated four classes of projects: (1) the creative project, (2) the appreciation project, (3) the problem project, and (4) the drill project. An important distinction between project method and the ordinary school subject is that the organization of the latter is a logical one, whereas that of the project is psychological.

OTHER APPLICATIONS. There were a host of plans and schemes that were a part of the progressive education movement in addition to the project method, such as the unit method, the Dalton Plan, the Winnetka Plan, the Platoon system, the contract plan, the child-centered school, ability grouping, homogeneous groupings, and the activity program. Two principal purposes motivated these schemes for the improvement of instruction in elementary schools. One was a conscientious endeavor to provide a curriculum that was more in harmony with the changing needs of society. In this connection educators were also concerned with the changing needs of children in a dynamic society. A second stimulus behind these plans was the hope to solve some of the problems of individual differences among pupils enrolled in schools. Contributing to these problems, of course, were different rates of educational growth, variable environments, different interest patterns, and different social stratification. These concerns were originally raised when it was suggested that teachers should study children; the study of children had simply become more complicated. From these ideas and efforts we have developed the modern concept of method.

NARROW AND BROAD
CONCEPTS OF METHOD

The student of education will discover that a distinction is made in modern educational literature between what is called a narrow and a broad concept of method. Some discussion of these two will help to clarify a modern interpretation of method.

A *narrow concept*

Usually a narrow concept of method is considered to be one that is concerned only with the manipulation of school subjects in the form of "successful" or "time-proven" techniques. The following statement from Wingo and Schorling is illustrative of the emphasis that often has been placed upon the narrow concept of method:

> In the first chapter of this book, during a discussion of the elements of successful teaching, we took occasion to suggest that it is not possible to relate success in teaching to the use of specific techniques. Yet, within a generation, many members of the teaching profession have grasped at a dozen widely-advertised "methods" which were going to solve once and for all the fundamental problems of teaching. Most, if not all, of these were administrative plans involving such techniques as grouping of pupils or the preparation of some kind of standardized teaching materials. No doubt every one of these procedures made some contribution to educational method, but it is doubtful that any teacher should ever have limited his operations in the classroom to any single one of them.
> There is a curious notion abroad that there is only one good way to teach, if it can only be found. In fact, the history of education is replete with instances of the unending search for this "philosopher's

stone". No search of the ancient alchemists for a formula to trans-
mute base metals into gold was more futile than the effort to develop
a foolproof formula for teaching.[5]

A person who holds a narrow concept of method places his
emphasis only upon teaching the school subjects. He is concerned with the transmission of the subject matter and has
little regard for ends in view. Furthermore, one who accepts
this point of view is prone to believe that once a successful
technique has been found, it will be good in all circumstances
under which that subject is taught. In this sense, one who holds
a narrow concept of method tends to disregard individual differences among the learners in the classroom and different
temporal circumstances.

Occasionally in our discussions about procedures that can be
used in classrooms, we confuse method with specific techniques.
It should be pointed out that specific techniques of teaching,
such as the administration of tests, the use of workbooks, the
class discussion, the use of bulletin boards, and so forth, become
important in method, but they are not broad enough to be
considered method itself. A good caution is to beware of any
technique that is advertised as a cure-all for teaching problems.

A broad concept

The broad concept of method is the one most appropriate
for modern educational thought. As previously suggested, a
broad concept of method will have both a philosophical and a
psychological base. It is philosophical in the sense that method
becomes concerned with the ends or the objectives to be achieved.
As Dewey states it: "Method means that arrangement of subject matter which makes it most effective in use. Never is
method something outside the material . . . Method is not antithetical to subject matter; it is the effective direction of subject

[5] G. Max Wingo and Raleigh Schorling, *Elementary School Student Teaching,*
2nd Ed. (New York: McGraw-Hill Book Company, 1955), p. 202.

matter to desired results."[6] Under this interpretation, the use of subject matter is that of a vehicle toward some desired result. In contrast to a narrow approach then, the transmission of subject matter becomes important only as it contributes toward the desired results. In the selection of ends or objectives, values are indicated and translated for school use.

A broad concept of method has a psychological aspect because method is concerned with the learner, the learning process, and the psychology of the subject matter. If method becomes a process of arranging subject matter so that it can be effectively used by the learner, there is an obligation placed upon the teacher to become so familiar with the learners under his jurisdiction that he can effectively make that arrangement of subject matter. Obviously the techniques of child study are of crucial importance here as tools for the teacher to execute this dimension of method. Similarly, in order to be effective methodologically, it becomes important for the teacher to have a knowledge of the learning process and the means of observing changes in learners' behavior. Much of the research of modern times has indicated that there are certain unique characteristics of different kinds of subject matter, that have implications for the teacher in the arrangement of subject matter so that learners might profit from their experiences in the classroom. A very good illustration, of course, is the volume of knowledge that has been accumulated about the organization and arrangement of reading material for children in the elementary school.

When the broad concept of method is interpreted in terms of what it means for the classroom teacher, three specific obligations fall upon the teacher's shoulders if he is to carry out this concept of method in his teaching. In the first place, the teacher must at all times be aware of and familiar with the ends in view or the objectives sought in classroom teaching. Secondly, a

[6] John Dewey, *Democracy in Education* (New York: The MacMillan Company, 1916), p. 194. Used by permission.

broad knowledge of the subject matter of the elementary school must be maintained by the teacher. It is difficult to see how a teacher can be effective in arranging subject matter for constructive use unless that teacher is reasonably well grounded in the subject matter itself. Thirdly, the teacher must have as part of his behavior repertoire an adequate body of techniques; that is, techniques that will help him to fulfill the psychological and the philosophical aspects of the broad concept of method. This is why aspirant teachers frequently are required to take courses in the philosophy of education, educational psychology, and methods of teaching. There is no question but that the broad concept of method places a large burden of responsibility upon a teacher, and certainly it increases the complexity of teaching if it is applied properly. The broad concept of method has developed because man has learned more about man and man's social processes. A complex, dynamic society such as ours is more difficult to maintain and manipulate than were primitive, simple societies. Similarly, the educative process is more difficult to manipulate in a complex society than in a simple, primitive type of culture.

CURRICULUM AND METHOD

It would not be wise to complete a discussion of method without relating it to the school curriculum. Too many persons think curriculum and method are one and the same thing. In the author's opinion, the failure to keep method and curriculum separate or in their own relative positions, has contributed to a good deal of confusion in educational thought. There is no question of whether or not there is a relationship between curriculum and method. They are closely related. The problem simply is one of making a distinction between method and curriculum as different levels of a complete educational activity.

Meanings of curriculum

Part of the difficulty here rests with the fact that various curriculum theorists have held different concepts of the meaning of curriculum. It is possible to identify at least three rather distinct definitions of curriculum in contemporary literature. Probably the most commonly accepted definition of curriculum is that which considers it as all the learning experiences that children have under the jurisdiction of the school. One of the major difficulties with this definition is that it is possible to interpret the precise nature of curriculum in many different ways and still hold to the definition. If one were to review many modern books on curriculum planning that foster this definition, it would be observed that the issue as to the precise nature of the curriculum itself is avoided. Few writers specifically describe the concrete nature of the curriculum, and when they do, it usually is described in terms of a statement of objectives, an instructional guide, or some combination of those two. The author believes that the real problem here is an unwillingness to be decisive as to whether the curriculum is a real thing such as a written document that can be described, or a psychological phenomenon described in terms of changes in behavior of boys and girls. At the base of this is the interpretation of "experience." If by experience (as far as the definition of curriculum is concerned) is meant a description of activity, one can visualize a plan for it. If by experience is meant a psychological change in a child, it is difficult to visualize a structure. This difference will become clearer when the psychological notion of curriculum is examined, but the point here is that we need a concept of curriculum that will serve as a point of departure for an understanding of method.

A second mode of describing curriculum is to consider it as a psychological process. It becomes a process of an individual interacting with his school environment, in which changes occur in the individual's behavior. Curriculum in this sense becomes an individual thing that can only be registered and stored in the mind of the learner. Advocates of the emergent type of curriculum are especially prone to accept this notion. For them the curriculum is an individual thing that emerges from the school environment because of the activities that go on there. Again it is difficult to find a point of departure for a distinction between curriculum in this sense and the application of method to school business. In fact under this notion there probably is more method than there is curriculum. Much more emphasis is placed upon the processes and results of pupil behavior than upon subject-matter organization. It should be noted that these comments are not made for the purpose of criticizing these notions of curriculum, but rather, they are made for the purpose of illustrating some of the present difficulties in communicating about curriculum and method in modern education.

A third way of considering curriculum is in terms of some structure that will represent a design, a social design if you please, *for* educational experiences of children in school. This design should take into account all the demands upon a school program. Such demands include the needs of the social group, the individual needs of children as anticipated by adults, the requirements of custom, and the peculiarities of the school as a social institution. Curriculum thus defined represents an interactive approach to the concept of curriculum. It attempts to recognize that there are peculiar reasons for the establishment of elementary schools in our society and that it becomes mandatory that the program of the elementary school attempt to fulfill those needs. At the same time we recognize today that children are individuals. They are reputable citizens of our society and worthy of the dignities normally accorded to other citizens. Their interests and needs must be satisfied at the same time that the social needs for the institution are being satisfied. It becomes the function of the curriculum to fulfill this interactive requirement.

In a previous writing the author has suggested that curriculum under this notion may be considered an actual written document and that it should contain at least four parts. The first part would be a descriptive statement indicating the nature of the curriculum and the intent of curriculum planners for the use of the document. The second part would be a statement of goal direction or objectives for the elementary school program. A third part would be an instructional guide which would contain a broad, flexible outline of the total subject matter of the elementary school, organized in terms of the administrative organizational segments of the elementary school. A fourth element of a curriculum might be a statement of the intentions for evaluation and subsequent modification of the curriculum.[7]

When curriculum is thus specifically considered and identified, it is possible to think of method as a process of putting the curriculum to work in a classroom. As indicated in Chapter 1, this level of method, or the teaching-learning level, is the one at which the curriculum is put to work in the classroom. Dimensions of method become significant when a teacher attempts to arrange subject matter that has been prescribed by the curriculum, so that the pupils will interact with the subject matter and socially useful changes in their behavior will result. Under this notion of curriculum it is easier to see the precise relationship between curriculum and method. Curriculum may indicate the ends or objectives, and it may indicate subject matter to be used to achieve those ends or objectives; but it becomes a problem of method actually to put curriculum to work with boys and girls. *Thus curriculum becomes a description of intent, and method is a process of carrying out that intent.*

Method and the levels of activity

If the reader will refer again to Figure 1 in the preceding chapter he will note that the complete educational activity of the ele-

[7] George A. Beauchamp, *Planning the Elementary School Curriculum* (Boston: Allyn and Bacon, Inc., 1956), Chapter 3.

mentary school was divided into three phases or levels; the curriculum planning level, the teaching-learning level, and the evaluation level. The discussion of curriculum and method can be illustrated perhaps a little more vividly from this frame of reference. According to that arrangement of levels, curriculum planning becomes a process of preparing a design or structure for the educational program of the elementary school. At this level the only consideration of method that would enter into planning deliberation would be questions as to the feasibility of teaching certain kinds of materials to boys and girls at the various ages. Curriculum must be planned with method anticipated, but method does not need to be, nor should be, prescribed at the curriculum planning level. At the teaching-learning level, however, real problems of method become most apparent. It is here that subject matter is arranged and presented in accordance with the peculiarities in the interests and capacities of the boys and girls of each specific classroom, in order to carry out objectives that have been delineated. It is here that both the philosophical and psychological aspects of method reach their greatest significance for teachers. Evaluation is closely entwined with method and curriculum, because at the evaluation level an attempt is made to determine both the adequacy of the curriculum including its objectives, and the adequacy of the techniques that were utilized in the teaching-learning process for the purpose of achieving those objectives.

Summary

Since method has been a topic of serious concern in elementary education, the purpose of this chapter has been to examine the nature of method as a problem in elementary teaching. We have taken a brief look at the changes in people's notions of method throughout our history, and at some of the sources of influence that brought about those changes. Principally, there have been two things at the heart of these influences that caused dramatic change in the concept of method of teaching in elementary schools. One of these is a change through history in the attitude of adults toward children. From a somewhat cruel attitude toward children as being sinful and miniature adults, we have shifted to the humane approach that children are children and hence different from adults, but at the same time, citizens of our society and therefore worthy of recognition. The second basic influence has been the increased knowledge that has come to us concerning human growth and development, and the learning processes.

The modern broad-concept of method refers to the arrangement of subject matter (and/or activities) in school classrooms so that pupils can and will interact with that subject matter in such a way that there will be socially useful changes in their behavior, in accordance with the objectives of the activity or activities that were launched. In other words, method produces a means for a learner to profit usefully from learning tasks. Thus method is related to ends, to means, to subject matter, and to the learner.

A distinction has been made between curriculum and method for the purpose of clarity in communication about educational matters. If the terms curriculum and method are to be used synonymously and interchangeably, there is no need for both concepts, but as professional people we should be able to make a distinction between them. This chapter suggests that it is easier to make this distinction if we consider curriculum as a design of a social group for the educational experiences of its children in school, and consider that design as a realistic document having a specific structure. If this is accepted, method then becomes a process of putting that curriculum to work in the classroom with groups of boys and girls assembled there for purposes of instruction. With curriculum thus established as a specifically real instrument, we can use it for our purpose here to discuss the various dimensions of method for putting curriculum to work with children in elementary schools.

Ideas for discussion and activity

1. Investigate one of the following and report your findings to the class:

> The Dalton Plan
> The Winnetka Plan
> The Platoon System
> The Contract Plan

2. How has the study of this chapter changed your thinking about teaching method?

3. Formulate in your own thinking a distinction between curriculum and method. Where possible consult references with conflicting viewpoints.

4. Compare the approach to method made by writers of an earlier era, such as David Perkins Page or Herbart, with that of more modern theorists.

Suggested readings

Bartky, John A., "The Nature of Teaching Method," *The Elementary School Journal*, 57:199-203; January, 1958.
A slightly humorous slant is taken toward certain teaching practices. Direction, permissiveness, and *laissez-faire* attitudes to teaching method are analyzed.

Broudy, Harry S., *Building A Philosophy of Education*. Englewood Cliffs, N. J.: Prentice-Hall, Inc., 1954, Chapter 8.
A philosopher discusses the rationale of method, relates method and learning, and describes the classical methods used throughout the history of education.

Butts, R. Freeman and Lawrence A. Cremin, *A History of Education in American Culture*. New York: Henry Holt and Company, 1953.
The index cites 69 pages opposite the heading "Methods of teaching". Various periods of time in our history are indicated so a student can see the changes in method through time.

Dewey, John, *Democracy and Education*. New York: The Macmillan Company, 1916, Chapter 13.
The entire book should be read by every student of education, but at least this chapter on the nature of method is a "must".

Kilpatrick, William H., "The Importance of Good Teaching Methods," *Frontiers of Elementary Education, I*. Edited by Vincent J. Glennon. Syracuse, New York: Syracuse University Press, 1954, pp. 37-41.
A very famous American educator discusses the importance of good teaching methods. The relationships between ends and means are stressed.

Page, David P., *Theory and Practice of Teaching*. Edited by E. C. Branson. New York: American Book Company, 1899.
A student of method should read at least part of this methods book written in the nineteenth century.

Washburne, Carleton, *What Is Progressive Education?* New York: The John Day Company, 1952.

This little volume is a simply stated analysis of the meaning of progressive education. The reader will be impressed by its obvious implications for teaching method.

Wingo, G. Max and Raleigh Schorling, *Elementary School Student Teaching*. Second edition. New York: McGraw-Hill Book Company, Inc., 1955, Chapter 8.

This chapter is a fine analysis of a broad concept of method written for the particular attention of the student teacher.

PART	III	Dimensions of Method in Studying Elementary School Children

IN MODERN ELEMENTARY SCHOOL TEACHING one category of dimensions of method is the studying and diagnosing of elementary school children. This is a major area of work for all elementary school teachers. It is of cardinal importance that they become competent with the tasks involved, for this competence is a large factor in teaching success.

The psychological laboratory has taught us a large and variable number of techniques for studying children. Problems center around the appropriate choice of technique and the interpretation of technique used. Nevertheless, it must be recognized that intelligent application and interpretation of these techniques are first steps in the solution of the multitudinous problems of individual differences among children in schools.

For these reasons Part II will focus upon dimensions of method related to studying and diagnosing elementary school children, as essential factors in elementary school teaching. The presentation will fall within three chapters devoted to this category. In Chapter 3 we will examine the basic purposes of pupil study and diagnosis as a dimension of teaching method. In Chapter 4 some of the important techniques of pupil study will be discussed in connection with situations appropriate for the use of those techniques. Finally, in Chapter 5 we will examine the problem of individual differences as it creates teaching problems for the elementary school teacher.

CHAPTER 3

The Purpose of
Pupil Study and Diagnosis

MANY PROSPECTIVE TEACHERS, as undergraduate students, wonder about the need for extensive pupil study by the teacher. It is often difficult for them to foresee the need for constant and complete pupil diagnosis for successful teaching. It is the function of this chapter to present the significance of pupil study and diagnosis in the hope that it will motivate teachers to become competent in this area.

For the purpose of clarity in communication it would be wise to identify the meaning of the terms "study" and "diagnosis" as used here. By study is meant any activity in which a teacher engages for the purpose of acquiring data of any kind about pupil characteristics and behavior. By diagnosis is meant organization of the data accumulated in pupil study, for a course of action by a teacher working with a particular pupil or with a group of pupils. In diagnosis then, the teacher relates the data of pupil study to the course of his work in classroom teaching. For this reason studying and diagnosing pupils is a basic dimension of teaching method.

The principal intent of this chapter is to indicate some of the basic purposes that impel teachers to study their pupils and make diagnoses as a result of their study. We will examine these purposes in the light of the following activities that are an integral part of an elementary school teacher's function: assessing readiness, judging capacity, becoming aware of interests, noting growth in pupils, using knowledge in guidance activities, using knowledge to select resource units and plan activities, and using knowledge for grouping and work division. It is obvious that most of these topics are closely related to one another. The reason for separate presentation is to emphasize differences in functional concern; that is, differences in concern that teachers may have relative to studying and diagnosing children.

ASSESSING READINESS

One of the most difficult tasks of the elementary school teacher is to determine the readiness of school pupils to profit from instruction, so that teaching might be started. This statement sounds very simple for a very complicated task.

The meaning of readiness

Readiness as used here refers to the condition of the learner in terms of his capacity or ability to profit from instruction at any given time. Readiness is very closely related to the concept of maturation if we conceive of maturation as the achievement of functional capacity. Maturation in this sense is a general term referring to the condition of any organism to perform a specific act. We use the term readiness as a special case of maturation when the task is to learn a given concept or skill, or group of concepts and skills. Readiness in this sense refers to a psychological condition of an organism in its totality. One of the most familiar illustrations of the concept of readiness for learning for elementary school teachers is readiness for reading in the first grade. Reading readiness is a problem of considerable concern for all first-grade teachers. We have learned that children who have not achieved reading readiness cannot profit from reading instruction. Wise first-grade teachers find other activities for children who have not achieved reading readiness, but they are alert constantly to the emergences of readiness so that the child in question might begin reading activities.

There is some possible source of confusion with respect to the term "readiness" as it is used here. As previously indicated, readiness refers to a total psychological condition of an organism, in which it can learn and thereby profit from instruction. For a number of years now, people interested in the subject of reading in the very early elementary school grades have discussed an activity called the reading readiness program. This program is one designed in some cases, to accelerate reading readiness in the psychological sense, and in other cases it becomes a vehicle by which the teacher can watch for the emergence of psychological readiness. For example, one feature of most reading readiness programs is the improvement of vocabulary. This is most effective in those circumstances where children have come from linguistically poor environments and, therefore, do not have the necessary vocabulary background to profit from reading instruction.

Components of total readiness

In spite of the fact that we have been able to identify some of the components of total readiness, many still are a mystery to us. Some children can learn to read at six years of age and others cannot. What makes the difference? Generally speaking, girls mature socially more rapidly than boys, even though their environmental backgrounds may be quite similar. Characteristics can be thus identified, but the results in individual behavior are not so predictable because we are not aware of many readiness components for behavior. Because of this kind of observation we tend to consider it important to study many aspects of human growth and development, and further study may lead to greater understanding. Thus far we have been principally concerned with physical growth, intellectual growth, social and emotional growth, and educational growth.

PHYSICAL GROWTH. We have all seen large children in elementary schools who have had difficulty in learning various things of an academic nature, such as reading and arithmetic. On the other hand, those same large children might learn skills in physical education or skills in art and music with great facility. We also have seen small individuals who had difficulty in learning such things as skills in physical education, but who had great facility in learning skills in the academic world. We have often seen the reverse of both of these cases. From observations such as these we have concluded that physical growth is a component of readiness for learning, but only to the extent that some degree of physical growth is prerequisite to the learning.

INTELLECTUAL GROWTH. By intellectual growth we usually refer to growth in mental age. Intelligence sometimes is expressed in terms of a ratio between the individual's mental age and his chronological age. This ratio is called the intelligence quotient or I.Q. There has been a good deal of debate about the interpretations one should make of the results of mental measurement as a feature of readiness for learning. Nevertheless, other factors being equal, the magnitude of one's intellect in many learning situations affects readiness for learning. For example, for a number of years we said that a child should have a mental age of six years and four months before we could reasonably expect him to profit from instruction in reading. Today we accept a very flexible interpretation of this critical point.

SOCIAL AND EMOTIONAL GROWTH. One's social and emotional growth is an important component of readiness. A learner can best profit from experience if he perceives himself as being capable of coping with the learning situation, if he feels that the learning situation is non-threatening, and if he desires to learn. Whenever a learner comes to a learning situation, he brings his entire past experience with him. Particularly important are the social and personal experiences that contribute to his concept of himself as a behaving mechanism and as a social being. It is extremely difficult to separate social growth and emotional growth because they are so interactive. One's emotional structure is based upon his success or failure in acceptable social growth and, conversely, one's social growth is inhibited because of emotional bias or emotional immaturity.

We cannot expect, for example, that an individual who is essentially a selfish person, or one who refuses to be cooperative with others, can be ready to profit from an experience in which team play or cooperative work would be learned. Such an individual carries a psychological barrier to this kind of learning situation. It is unreasonable to expect a child to learn the complexities of government until he has had sufficient social experience to recognize the need for the existence of government and the need for his understanding as a citizen, of the processes of government.

EDUCATIONAL GROWTH. Like social and emotional growth, educational growth is a function of one's past experience. Broadly interpreted, all learning acquired can be considered educational growth. The educational growth that can be attributed to schools, however, is a function of the experiences that children have had in school under the school's curriculum. It is very important to recognize that the experiences which result from the curriculum will vary for different pupils, and this complicates the problem of determining educational readiness. Nevertheless, a number of things that we ask children to do in school have educational prerequisites. For example, the usual logical organization of the subject matter of arithmetic implies, if not overtly states, that each step in the process is a prerequisite to the next. Addition is a prerequisite to subtraction; addition and subtraction are prerequisites to multiplication and division. In this sense one's educational growth is a highly important component of total readiness for learning.

Significance for teaching

The significance of pupil readiness for teaching is probably already obvious to the reader. This significance is twofold. First, the determination of readiness for learning is important in order that the teacher may teach. Second, it is important so that we may examine the results of teaching.

The idea that readiness must be determined so that a teacher may teach appears to be very simple. It is obvious that before a learner can learn he must be ready to do so. In spite of this, there have been entirely too many circumstances in elementary school classrooms in which learners were expected to perform prior to the achievement of the capacity to do so. We cannot expect a learner to begin at a level higher than his present level of attainment. No one would expect a newborn baby to walk within the first twenty-four hours of his life. Similarly, no one should expect an individual to begin to read until he has achieved readiness to do so. The principle of readiness for learning is so important that the determination of readiness should be axiomatic for all teachers.

The second significance of readiness for teaching is the fact that the results of determining readiness become a means whereby we may examine the effect of teaching upon the learner. If the status of the learner is not determined prior to instructional activity, there is no basis for the accurate determination of effective growth that takes place because of the instructional process. Actually, a point of readiness can be considered a point of achievement, so that any subsequent achievement measure might be compared with the initial status.

Never-ending search for readiness

The concept of readiness discussed here is a continuous concept. In other words, one state of readiness leads to another state of readiness so that at every point of instruction the determination of readiness becomes significant. Therefore, no teacher can consider his problem of readiness determination ended so long as he and his pupils are assembled in the classroom.

Readiness is a function of growth if we consider growth as any organismic phenomenon that is characterized by change. It is not always possible to identify the specific kind of growth that contributes most to readiness at any given time. Furthermore, all aspects of growth, or all kinds of growth, rather insensibly lose their separate identities as they result in total organismic development. The fused result of all specific kinds of growth that have taken place is what the learner brings to each situation. It becomes the problem of the teacher to somehow appraise readiness in the light of this wholistic development. When we speak of "the whole child" we refer to a complex, but yet single, organism that is the result of all of his past experience and maturity. It is from this whole child that readiness determinations must be made.

In the preceeding paragraphs of this section devoted to the purpose of assessing readiness, we have attempted to deal with readiness as a large, complex picture. Throughout the remaining sections of this chapter more specialized aspects of assessing readiness will be treated. This does not mean that they are different from total readiness, but rather that they are identifiable aspects of total readiness.

JUDGING CAPACITY

One of the purposes in studying and diagnosing children is to place the teacher in a position where he can judge the capacities of the learners both as individuals and as a group. Like readiness, capacity is a complex phenomenon. In its most general sense capacity refers to the total ability of an organism to learn, and this total ability would include intellectual, social, and physical characteristics. It is in this sense that capacity is used here. Frequently, however, people when speaking of capacity refer only to the individual's intellect. Furthermore, they usually refer to intellect in a special way, namely as measured by an intelligence test.

Significance for teaching

When the significance of student capacity for teaching is re-
viewed, other purposes for determining this capacity become
evident. In the first place, the capacity of the pupil is indicative
of the level of work that a teacher might expect him to do. For
example, every third-grade teacher has the experience of having
children assembled in the same room who read at several different levels. The instructional process is hereby complicated
but, nevertheless, in order for teaching to be successful, these
various levels must be recognized and the work of the teacher
modified accordingly.

Another purpose that can be served by having information
available concerning student capacity, is the amount of work
that a teacher might expect the pupils to do. In a fourth grade,
for example, a teacher might reasonably expect that all pupils
could handle problems involving arithmetic skills. However,
the quantity and quality of problems to be handled by different
children in the classroom would vary. Thus knowledge about
the level of work and the amount of work that has been done
by individual pupils becomes a means by which teachers establish
their expectancies for the behavior of boys and girls in the classroom. A teacher who formulates realistic expectancies for the
performance of his pupils and who adjusts his practice in the
classroom accordingly, is apt to be a more successful and certainly a happier teacher than one who fails to do so. One of
the frustrating experiences of a teacher is to look for a certain
caliber of work from pupils and then to be disillusioned because
that caliber of work does not emerge. Nearly always this dis-
appointment comes because a teacher has failed to make adequate judgments about the capacity of his pupils.

Some cautions

Some cautions in respect to judging capacity are warranted, and
they will be repeated later. Often teachers are prone to judge

capacities of pupils in terms of intelligence quotients or mental ages, as the result of administrating an intelligence test. This single criterion is not adequate for judging capacity. No single criterion will serve this purpose. This is especially true if the results of only one intelligence test are procured. It may be necessary to couple with the results of intelligence testing, the results of achievement testing, physical measures, and indications of interest, because all of these things have some bearing on the total capacity of the individual to perform in the classroom. But again for emphasis, it is repeated that the principal purpose in judging capacity is that a teacher may adjust his expectations for pupils and accordingly modify his behavior as a teacher.

DISCOVERING INTEREST AND NEED

A third purpose in studying and diagnosing school pupils is that a teacher may become aware of interests and needs of pupils. We have long recognized the significance of both interest and need as motivating factors for boys and girls in learning situations. It is completely unrealistic to expect healthy learning on the part of boys and girls unless learning experiences are well motivated and intrinsically so. The prime factors in self-motivation are need and interest.

The study of interest and need is both an individual and a group problem. Certain kinds of interest and need may be common to groups of boys and girls, whereas others are unique to individuals. Interests that are common to groups are culturally motivated more often than not. The interest of young boys in cowboys and Indians is a function of our culture. In societies having a different culture one would not find boys of this same age interested in this phenomenon. In fact many boys and girls in the world have never heard of cowboys and Indians. Some group-needs seem to be culturally generated. An example might be the need for peer group status by the adolescent youngster.

On the other hand, several kinds of interest and needs make boys and girls unique within a group that may have some common interests and needs. One fifth-grade boy who has a common interest in and need for peer group status may be highly interested in mechanics and aviation while others may be much more interested in art, music, or literature.

Because of differences in environmental circumstances, the needs of boys and girls can vary markedly. In discussing needs it is helpful to think of the specific nature of different kinds of need. To speak of needs-in-general is to perpetuate confused conversation. On the other hand, we can speak of biological needs; we can speak of psychological needs; we can speak of social needs; and we can speak of educational needs. Here is one place in education where we can and should be more specific.

Thus far in discussing this topic we have been thinking in terms of becoming aware of interests and needs as a means of facilitating or improving instruction. It is important to note, however, that the satisfaction of pupils' interests and needs is more than the facilitation of method. The satisfaction of interests and needs is a function of both curriculum and method. Because the teacher has a responsibility to the pupils as individual citizens and as members of the classroom group, he is obligated to insure that the curriculum utilized and the classroom program satisfy their interests and needs.

NOTING GROWTH IN PUPILS

Another facet of studying elementary school pupils that has significance for the classroom teacher is to note child growth that takes place during the elementary school years. The primary purpose of any elementary school program is to produce educational growth in children. In order to be aware of growth that takes place while children are under the jurisdiction of the school, it obviously becomes necessary to make observations of some kind.

Growth may be defined as any organismic phenomenon that is characterized by change. Organismic phenomena that may be characterized by change fall into several categories. These were previously identified under the topic of assessing readiness as physical growth, intellectual growth, social and emotional growth, and educational growth. Our principal concern here is for educational growth attributable to classroom experience.

The noting of growth that takes place in boys and girls becomes particularly significant when we attempt to evaluate the elementary school and its program. For instance, as teachers we wish to know quite specifically what growth has taken place in the skill subjects — reading, arithmetic, spelling, and other forms of language arts. The exhibition of improved behavior in these skill areas is truly a growth phenomenon. Therefore, in order to appraise for our own satisfaction as teachers, the amount of growth that has been produced because of activities performed in our classrooms, notation of growth becomes an important criterion for determining the effectiveness of our work.

One of the more difficult and significant aspects of the teacher's work is the interpretation of educational growth to parents. If this growth is to be interpreted to parents by teachers, then teachers must be aware of the nature and magnitude of the growth that has taken place. Without this information it is impossible for teachers accurately and concisely to report educational growth to parents.

Growth is the end product of education. It is the desired outcome of all of our instructional efforts. As an end product it is related to the objectives established for the school program, the subject matter selected to fulfill those objectives, and the means or methods by which that subject matter is organized to fulfill those ends. This significance of growth is extremely important as a justification for the study and diagnosis of pupils.

A BASIS FOR GUIDANCE ACTIVITIES

Another purpose in studying and diagnosing children in the elementary school is that the knowledge acquired can be used by the teacher in pupil guidance activities. By pupil guidance activities are meant here those means that help each pupil to fulfill his potential to the greatest possible degree, considering all of the limitations of the classroom. These guidance activities also become a means whereby a teacher assists pupils in character and personality development.

There are innumerable reasons for this purpose to be fulfilled by teachers; character and personality development is a process whereby an individual is helped to become more accepted by his social group, because his social group sees worth and dignity in him. This development is also a means whereby the individual perceives himself in proper focus with his environment and his social groups. In school life and outside school an individual's character and personality development are affected to some degree by his cumulative past experience. Part of his cumulative past experience is that acquired in school. This past experience causes an individual to have a set of attitudes toward schools and school work. If these are a desirable set of attitudes, they become an asset in a teacher's work, and conversely, if they are negative or undesirable, they become an inhibition to a teacher's work in the classroom. One can readily appreciate this difference for the work of a teacher of music. The content of the program and the teacher's approach is entirely different with a boy who thinks of music as a sissified preoccupation, from that with a boy who has lived in an atmosphere of music appreciation.

In modern education it is no longer sufficient to say that we are interested in character and personality development solely for the purpose of facilitating an instructional program. Objectives related to character and personality development have become an integral part of the school program. Therefore, these guidance activities become mandatory because they are an aspect of the school's total job. Furthermore, these tasks are a part of the teacher's responsibility to school pupils as individual citizens who have been placed in the teacher's hands for personal and educational guidance.

SELECTING RESOURCE UNITS
AND PLANNING ACTIVITIES

The selection of resource materials and the planning of activities for boys and girls in the classroom is an important dimension of a teacher's work that gives further purpose to studying boys and girls. This is one of the critical aspects of any teacher's work. It is here that a teacher selects materials from the curriculum to be implemented in his classroom and does the tentative planning of activities to be carried out by the pupils. It is only because a teacher knows the capacities, the interests, the readiness, the educational level, and so forth, of his pupils that he can expect to be successful in selecting units of work and planning activities.

Furthermore, if we accept the need for intrinsic motivation in learning, we have to recognize that a teacher must know his pupils and know them well in order to select with any degree of accuracy the kinds of materials, the kinds of topics, and the variety of activities that can be arranged that will challenge the interests and curiosities of the boys and girls. This is the point at which the subject matter and the learner must be compatible. They can only be compatible when a teacher skillfully adapts learning materials and activities in accordance with accurate and full information about his pupils.

Obviously, the selection of resource units and activities is related to the character and quantity of growth that may be expected in pupils. As previously indicated, it is the responsibility of the teacher to produce the maximum growth. Similarly, these activities are related to the fulfillment of the prescribed objectives of the curriculum as well as those selected by the boys and girls in the teacher-pupil planning procedures.

GROUPING AND WORK DIVISION

It is possible to indicate as a purpose of studying and diagnosing school pupils, the use of that information for grouping children in the classroom and for the division of work among individuals and groups in the classroom. In modern education we have placed a great deal of emphasis on individualized instruction. In some cases we are prone to be so extreme in the problem of individualized teaching that we forget that groups may be taught as well as individuals. If, however, groups are to be taught in the various grades of the elementary school, it must be remembered that these groups should be flexibly organized within each classroom and organized for specific kinds of activities. A good example is the first-grade teacher who organizes boys and girls into reading groups according to the level at which they are reading. In a good situation of this kind pupils move in and out of these various groups. Occasionally the groups are completely reorganized in order to introduce greater flexibility. It is possible that this kind of grouping can be extended to other subjects and activities in all grades of the elementary school. However, such grouping can only be done if a teacher is aware of the present state of readiness, the capacities, and the educational level of the pupils under his jurisdiction. He can only change groups and move pupils from group to group because he is constantly aware of changes in the status of his pupils.

In any classroom a division must be made of the total work effort to be performed. This can be done several ways. One is to assign persons to groups and assign tasks to those groups in accordance with the groups' interests. Another example might be organizing persons to do a similar task but at different levels. A third variation is to assign pupils to groups deliberately, in order to have each group represent a range of capacity as well as of interests, and then to let each group select its activity within the total program of the classroom. More will be presented on this subject in a later chapter. This much is presented here for the purpose of demonstrating that before these various activities can be carried out by a teacher, it is essential that he become aware of the total status of the pupils in his classroom. The teacher can do this only when he has made a systematic study and diagnosis of his pupils.

Summary

In this chapter we have attempted to outline the major purposes of pupil study and diagnosis as a basic dimension of elementary method. These purposes have been presented in the hope that they will help teachers to see a need for becoming familiar with and skillful in the use of techniques of studying and diagnosing pupils, because this is a professional aspect of the teacher's work.

One group of purposes have been outlined in terms of the kind of information a teacher should acquire about pupils and the reasons why he should acquire that kind of information.

Another group of purposes belong in the category of facilitation or improvement of a teacher's work as a classroom technician.

Basically it can be said that the major purpose for studying boys and girls is that a teacher can do a better job. To do a better job the teacher must become informed as to the readiness of his pupils, their capacities, and their interests and needs. It was further indicated that once the teacher has this type of information available it becomes useful in several respects. It is helpful to a teacher in judging whether any change has taken place in the individual while he has been under that teacher's jurisdiction. The knowledge to be acquired from studying pupils is extremely useful in helping a teacher adapt curriculum materials to the particular group of children in his classroom. This information is useful to the teacher in guidance activities designed to foster good character and personality development. Finally, the information helps the teacher manipulate individuals and groups in their tasks in the classroom. Most of the topics discussed in this chapter are closely related. The differences that have been dealt with have been discussed for a functional purpose; that is, for the purpose of interpreting them in terms of specific kinds of operations that teachers must perform.

Ideas for discussion and activity

1. From your study of this chapter and other readings, list as many specific purposes for studying children as you can.

2. Show why each item on the above list must be considered to be part of the professional work of the teacher.

3. Discuss relationships between the concepts "growth" and "learning."

4. How are intelligence and capacity related?

5. Why is readiness on the part of the pupil so significant for the teaching act?

Suggested readings

Beauchamp, George A., *Planning the Elementary School Curriculum.* Boston: Allyn and Bacon, Inc., 1956, Chapter 6.
     This chapter draws implications for curriculum planning from an overview of purposes and techniques of child study.

Ilg, Frances L. and Louise Bates Ames, *Child Behavior.* New York: Harper & Brothers, 1955, Chapters 1, 2, and 3.
     These passages describe the basic philosophy, assumptions, and techniques used by one of the outstanding child study centers — the Gessell Institute of Child Development.

Lane, Howard and Mary Beauchamp, *Human Relations in Teaching.* Englewood Cliffs, N. J.: Prentice-Hall, Inc., 1955, pp. 3-83.
     This book is dedicated to the task of helping teachers understand that all human behavior is social in origin and purpose and that, therefore, teachers must study and reflect upon observed behaviors in terms of human motivation. The pages recommended are devoted to the question, "What Does It Mean to Be Human?"

Millard, Cecil V., *Child Growth and Development*. Boston: D. C. Heath Company, 1951, Chapters 1 and 2.

Chapter 1 presents the origin and philosophy of the organismic view. Chapter 2 establishes basic principles of growth and development and points up their implications for teaching.

Olson, Willard C., *Child Development*. Boston: D. C. Heath and Company, 1949, Chapters 1, and 15.

The first chapter of this book presents a description of growth and development concepts, and general methods of studying growth and development. The final chapter contains a series of rating scales intended to help one appraise his own philosophy of growth.

Prescott, Daniel A., *The Child in the Educative Process*. New York: McGraw-Hill Book Company, Inc., 1957, Chapters 1, 2, and 3.

In these chapters Prescott relates purposes of child study to the educative process. The nature of the teacher's task and basic assumptions about human behavior are pointed toward the advantages of a clinical approach to child study.

Theman, Viola, "Emerging Concepts of Child Growth and Development: What They Suggest for Classroom Practice," *The American Elementary School*, Harold G. Shane, editor. Thirteenth Yearbook of the John Dewey Society. New York: Harper & Brothers, 1953, pp. 57-86.

This presentation summarizes concepts of growth and development and relates them to classroom practices.

CHAPTER 4

Techniques
of Studying Children

THE PURPOSE of this chapter is to help the reader see how children can be studied from several frames of reference to result in broad understanding by the teacher. In the elementary school teachers work so closely with children that they have an opportunity to take the broader view of child growth and development. However, they can only avail themselves of the broader view of growth and development if they are skillful in the use of the appropriate techniques. This is why use of the techniques of pupil study constitutes a basic dimension of teaching method.

The selection or order of presentation of these techniques is quite arbitrary. For this presentation the following topics will be discussed: (1) gathering historical information, (2) determining capacity, (3) assessing interests and needs, (4) accumulating behavior records, (5) assessing growth and learning, and (6) checking on pupil adjustment.

GATHERING HISTORICAL INFORMATION

Historical information is gathered for one of three reasons. First, it may be mandatory to do so by law, such as in the case of immunization records against communicable diseases, birth data, or attendance records. Second, certain types of historical records are considered to be useful by a school system, and therefore it is the policy of the Board of Education to obtain this information on a regular basis. Examples of this type of information are those indicated above when not required by law, records of height and weight of children while they are enrolled in schools, and family records indicating names of parents, brothers, and sisters. A third reason is that certain types of information are deemed worthy because they are useful for teachers in adapting educational programs to individual children. For example, many teachers in the very early grades like to know about certain time elements in the development of their pupils, such as the age at which a child walked and talked. They believe that the rate of growth in these functions may be related to rate of growth in school functions. Many teachers consider it helpful to be informed about serious illnesses, injuries, or malformations which may demand unique adjustments in the school program.

The methods by which historical information is gathered depend upon the nature of the information wanted and the resources available to school people for procuring that information. Obviously all of these cannot be cited because of diversity of practice; however, a few can be indicated for the specific records that usually are maintained.

The health record

The health record usually is initially acquired by means of a form prepared by the school system to be used by the family physicians in a pre-school physical check-up. This form generally contains birth information, records of communicable diseases that the child has had, and immunization history. In addition it may call for the customary opinions of the physician as to the general physical condition of the child, his vision, his hearing, and recommendations as to limitations to be placed upon a child's activity. This record is maintained by means of an annual physical examination by the family physician. In those cases where children cannot be examined by their own family physician, arrangements often are made whereby local health authorities provide these services. Sometimes there is a periodic check made on the immunization record by the school nurse or the local health authority. Records of height and weight are kept in most elementary schools. Again local policy determines which of these records will be maintained. They are also maintained in various forms. The Wetzel Grid (Figure 2) is an interesting device that can be used for purposes of maintaining records of height and weight which, in turn, will also provide another kind of information. The Grid is designed to reveal graphically the relationship between height and weight for an individual. Each person maintains his own unique relationship between his height and weight. So long as the individual maintains good health, the relationship between his height and weight remains constant. A change in this relationship often is indicative of another kind of physical disturbance such as caloric deficiency. The Grid is a reasonably simple device to maintain and it does provide the additional service of a health check.

The preschool experience record

The preschool experience record is the type of historical information that is considered to be desirable by school teachers, because this information will help them in bringing a child and his educational program together more successfully. Several different kinds of information are collected here that are different from the health record. For example, the birth certificate frequently is required to be presented by a child's parent at the time of initial enrollment in school. The presentation of the birth certificate accomplishes several things. It serves as a check upon the accuracy of the child's age for the purpose of determining if he is old enough to be enrolled in school. It can provide the school with accurate information as to the legal parentage of the child. It also can serve as a record to establish the child's citizenship. For the most part, presentation of the

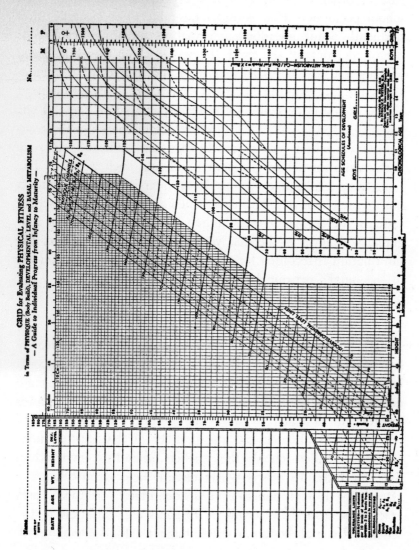

FIGURE 2. A *Wetzel Grid*.

birth certificate is a matter of routine formality. This is not so true of other types of preschool experience information that school personnel often consider desirable. For example, they frequently want anecdotal information revealing peculiar or persistent habits of the child, the age at which the child began walking and talking, particular likes and dislikes of the child, and some indication of his travel experience. This information can be acquired by sending a form to parents that they fill out and return to the school. This only works, of course, in those circumstances where parents are literate and sufficiently in sympathy with the school program to fill out such a form. The same thing can be accomplished by an interview with the parents during preschool round-up days which are held by many school systems the spring before children enter kindergarten or first grade, whichever is the first year of school. In any case, the information is recorded for the teacher's use and placed on file in the pupil's personnel record.

The attendance record

The attendance record is another form of historical record. Usually the maintenance of attendance records is required by law. In many states and communities the attendance records become the basis by which schools and school systems are determined to be qualified for state financial aid. Attendance records are designed to show the number of half-days and whole-days of absence and the number of days of tardiness. In some smaller schools the teachers keep their own attendance records. In others where clerical help is provided, the attendance is maintained by a school office. In those cases teachers send a daily record of absences and tardiness to the school office, and they are incorporated in the total school record.

The total school record

In a sense, the total school record is a historical information record. This includes all growth and behavioral data maintained by schools on children while they are enrolled. It particularly has to do with the amount of learning that children have acquired and the ways in which children have demonstrated they can use the learning acquired. The accumulation of this type of information is of such magnitude, however, as to demand major treatment in subsequent sections of this chapter.

DETERMINING CAPACITIES

When we speak of capacity, we must be extremely careful because there are various interpretations of that term. We should therefore take time to note different meanings that are applied to the capacity of a pupil to perform in school functions.

Interpretations of capacity

The most usual interpretation of capacity is that of intelligence. In a very general sense, intelligence is thought of as a basic capacity for learning or problem solving. Psychologists have spent a good deal of time trying to identify this capacity and to measure it. There seems to be little doubt that intelligence as we now think of it is a peculiar integration of one's biological capacity plus the effect that environmental nurture has had upon that capacity. We are forced to accept this concept of intelligence because of the nature of the instruments that have been used in attempts to measure intelligence. Modern intelligence tests try to measure performance in activities closely related to those performed in schools, and so they become useful in anticipating pupil performance in school. Whatever it may be that is being measured by intelligence tests, we may be reasonably confident that both an individual's biological capacity and the environment in which he has lived play a significant role in determining the results he achieves on an intelligence test. The measured results represent a configuration of capacity and the effect of environment upon that capacity. This result we speak of as a measure of intelligence.

The raw score from an intelligence test is converted to months of mental age. Mental age is the growth increment of intelligence measurement. Another expression of intelligence is the intelligence quotient. It is computed by dividing the number of months of mental age by the number of months of chronological age of the pupil as of the date he took the intelligence test. This ratio is multiplied by 100 and the result is the intelligence quotient. Briefly this formula is expressed as:

$$I.Q. = \frac{MA}{CA} \times 100$$

Another way of interpreting capacity is in terms of readiness. Readiness refers to the condition of an organism for learning a new concept or skill. The best example of readiness that we have in modern elementary education is reading readiness. We have found that instruction in reading in the early grades of the elementary school is unprofitable in those cases where children are not yet ready to read. We are not sure of all the reasons why children achieve reading readiness at different ages, but the fact that children develop at different rates physically, mentally, emotionally, and socially, is one of the reasons. Another factor in reading readiness is the amount and kind of language experience that children have had prior to coming to school. Most school programs now provide a reading readiness program in the first weeks of the school year for first-grade children. This program attempts to do two things. Through the use of devices such as the reading readiness tests, an attempt is made to form a prognosis as to the time at which each child will profit from reading instruction. Secondly, activities are fostered that provide for social and language experiences assumed to be prerequisite to reading activity. In elementary education more emphasis has been placed upon reading readiness than any other kind of readiness, but it is also a factor in other areas of elementary school life. The principal thing to keep in mind about readiness is that it is used in reference to a specific kind of activity.

A third interpretation of capacity is the total ability of the organism to function in a social setting. This can be called functional capacity. Functional capacity is thus a generalized concept of one's total ability to function upon demand. It can be noted that readiness is a special case of total functional capacity, and obviously this is much greater than an interpretation of intelligence alone as capacity. Intelligence becomes one factor in functional capacity. In elementary schools it is this total, functional capacity that we are primarily concerned with in diagnosing and interpreting children's behavior or their abilities to behave. In pursuit of this concern we endeavor to acquire indices of this capacity.

Determining mental age

Mental age is one form of capacity index. It is one that is more commonly used than any other. There are three principal devices that are used in elementary schools to determine mental age: the group intelligence test, the individual intelligence test, and the performance scale.

The group intelligence test is one that can be administered to an entire group of children. Of all the intelligence tests the group intelligence test has the least validity; there are several reasons for this. In the first place, the group intelligence test nearly always involves reading on the part of the pupil who is taking the test. Should the pupil be a poor reader, his reading ability rather than his intelligence may give him a low score. Conversely, if the individual is an unusually good reader for a child of his age, his mental age score may be higher than it really is. Because the test is administered to a group of individuals, the examiner is unable to note carefully the condition of each pupil during the examination, and to observe unusual frustration or lack of attention to the examining situation.

On the other hand, the group intelligence test has the advantage of being administrable to groups of individuals, thereby saving a considerable amount of time. The group test also can be administered by classroom teachers if they take time to study instructions carefully and follow the test manuals; and because it does not take specially trained personnel to administer it, the group intelligence test can be given in any elementary school in the country. The tests themselves are quite inexpensive and they will give the teacher an indication of a child's mental age. If the test is administered every two or three years and consistent results are obtained, more faith can be held in the results.

The individual test of intelligence must be administered to one person at a time, and it must be administered by a specially trained individual. This type of intelligence test tends to accent verbal ability and performance. Reading ability is thus brought under greater control. The trained examiner is expected to note the kind of examining situation that has prevailed and to indicate whether in his estimation the testing situation has been a good one. If the testing situation has been a good one, greater faith can be placed upon the results. The strength of the individual intelligence test lies in its greater validity. Since it requires specialized personnel to administer the test, its principal weakness is that it cannot be used in schools where trained personnel are not employed.

The performance scale is similar to the individual intelligence test in that it is singly administered by specially trained personnel. The language factor is reduced and emphasis is upon perceptual and motor performance.

Other forms of capacity index

As previously indicated, a measure of mental age is but one index of capacity. There are many others, among which one may include interest patterns, educational growth, emotional and social growth, and personal adjustment. These factors, however, are of such magnitude that they will be treated under separate headings.

ASSESSING INTERESTS

Modern elementary education places a good deal of emphasis upon the interests of children and the effect these should have upon school programs. Many persons advocate that the entire elementary school program be adjusted in terms of the interests of the children enrolled in elementary schools. Others feel that children's interests should be taken into account along with other factors such as the social demand upon schools in determining the content of the school program.

Regardless of which of these two points of view one holds, the interests of children are important in relation to teaching method. For example, the kinds of interests children hold tend to give direction to teachers in selecting specific activities for use in the classroom and in adapting curriculum materials for use there. Interest is an important factor in motivation. In fact, it may be *the* most important factor in motivating students to learn. Not only is interest significant in impelling a learner to release his energy into productive activity, but also it is of particular importance in the selection of activities. Teachers who fail to take the factor of interest into account in their teaching are ignoring the lessons they learned from the psychological laboratory. The mandate is entirely too clear. To expect productive learning in classrooms without interest and understanding is like expecting to make an appetizing cake without the proper ingredients.

Unfortunately we do not have good measures of interests for children of elementary school age. Specific interest measurement has been restricted mainly to adolescents and adults, for the purpose of vocational guidance. Interests of children have been observed, however, and by systematic means even though widely used standardized measuring devices have not been created. Children have been systematically observed by researchers in such places as child development laboratories, so that we are informed as to general interest patterns of children in our society. Individual research persons have attacked such problems as reading interests, hobby interests, or play interests. In either case, careful records have been kept of observations by such devices as check-lists, interview forms, anecdotal recordings, and pictures.

By these same means teachers can study the interests of children in their classrooms even though concrete measures do not result. No doubt the most useful means whereby a teacher becomes aware of the interests of children in his classroom are observation and keeping records of those observations. Inferences must be made from those observations for the purpose of adapting curriculum materials and motivating pupils. To some degree this can be done casually, but casual observation should be supported by systematic approach. Here is an instance where the behavior journal or anecdotal record becomes so useful. If over a period of time a teacher notes the kinds of activities a pupil selects or the ways in which he elects to perform activities, that record should reveal a persistency from which can be inferred kinds of pupil interest. Careful observation of the kinds of materials that children select to read, the kinds of radio or television programs they watch, or the things that they do at home and in the neighborhood outside of school, help to unfold before the teacher the child's selective world. When the selective world of the child is revealed, rather good inferences can be made of the interests held.

BEHAVIOR OR ANECDOTAL RECORDS

The behavioral or anecdotal record has been mentioned several times. Obviously, the behavioral record is more subjective than such instruments as the standardized test that have substantial reliability indices. However, in dealing with complex human beings it is not always possible or desirable that we be completely objective. Much of the school classroom is a subjective world and many of the interpretations that must be made in that world are subjective in nature. One reason for recommending such record-keeping is to introduce some element of self-control in this matter of subjective interpretation of pupil behavior. Like anyone else's, a teacher's memory over a period of time tends to distort past occurrences. The advantage of the anecdotal record is that notation is made of behavioral occurrences at the time they happen and in many cases an interpretation is made at the same time. With this record, a review of occurrences and interpretations of them can be made periodically.

The behavioral journal or the anecdotal record has some clinical use in diagnosing behavior characteristics. For example, the child who is basically an aggressive person frequently becomes involved in instances in which he commits aggression against someone else. A record of the regular occurrences of this individual's aggression against others or his environment would be kept in the behavioral journal. Such information if known by the teacher is helpful in guiding the pupil in the classroom environment.

The manner in which anecdotal records are maintained and the extent to which they are maintained vary considerably. In some schools the maintenance of these records is left to the discretion of the individual teacher. In this case each teacher maintains the records in the manner with which he is most familiar. On the other hand, there are elementary schools in which all members of the teaching staff have agreed to maintain anecdotal records in a systematic manner because they as a group have deemed it desirable to do so. Of course there are schools in which no anecdotal records are maintained at all.

A rather popular form for keeping records of pupils' behavior is for teachers to make notations on three-by-five cards of be-havioral incidents. There usually is entered upon these three-by-five cards information that describes the incident, the cir-cumstances, and the teacher's interpretation of those circum-stances. These are then filed according to use the teacher intends to make of them. A poor use of these is to allow them to accumulate in the teacher's desk drawers with little reference made to them unless an emergency arises. A good use is for teachers to keep them filed chronologically by date under each pupil's name. Occasionally the teacher will summarize or generalize from these accumulated records, and that generaliza-tion is filed in the pupil's personnel folder.

Some authorities introduce into the maintenance of anecdotal records some specific characteristics. For example, Prescott indi-cates that a good anecdote should have the following character-istics:

> 1. It gives the date, the place, and the situation in which the action occurred. We call this the setting. 2. It describes the actions of the child, the reactions of the other people involved, and the response of the child to these reactions. 3. It quotes what is said to the child and by the child during the action. 4. It supplies "mood cues" — postures, gestures, voice qualities, and facial expressions that give cues to how the child felt. It does not provide interpretations of his feelings, but only the cues by which a reader may judge what they were. 5. The description is extensive enough to cover the episode. The action or conversation is not left incomplete and unfinished but is followed through to the point where a little vignette of a behavioral moment in the life of the child is supplied.[1]

A narrative description of incidents thus patterned reveals a substantial body of information. It does pose one difficulty and that is the amount of time it takes for the teacher actually to write out this type of record. Obviously a teacher would not be able to do this during the course of a school day and, therefore, it would have to be done after school hours. In spite of the fact that the actual writing of the record is done after school

[1] Daniel A. Prescott, *The Child and the Educative Process* (New York: McGraw-Hill Company, 1957), pp. 153-154.

hours, the teacher will have to make some notation within the temporal proximity of the incident in order to leave as little to memory error as possible. This is one systematic and thorough approach to the maintenance of anecdotal records.

Another type of behavioral or anecdotal record is what Olson refers to as the behavioral journal.[2] The behavioral journal is a ledger form prepared for each child using paper with vertical ruling. The journal should indicate the date on which the incident occurred, a description of the incident, and the initial or name of the person recording the incident. Thus maintained, the behavior journal presents a chronology of typical behavior on a single sheet or a series of sheets. These sheets are more easily filed in cumulative records than are three-by-five cards. Periodically, a teacher should summarize the journals for two reasons. One is to cut down on the volume of records, and the other is to give the teacher an opportunity to review behavior patterns.

There is often a tendency for busy teachers to make reference in behavior records only to negative behavior. This is wrong. The anecdotal record should reveal *typical* and persistent behavior and changes in it. If a child is a perfectly typical child in most every respect, the behavior record should reveal it. Only when both positive and negative types of behavioral incidents are recorded can the record serve its many purposes.

ASSESSING GROWTH

We have considered growth as any organismic phenomenon that is characterized by change. This admittedly is a broad interpretation of growth but it lends greater meaning to the kinds of things that are attempted with children. Some interrelationships among the various kinds of growth have been established. In fact there appears to be homeostatic relation-

2 Willard C. Olson, *Child Development* (Boston: D. C. Heath and Company, 1949), pp. 389-397.

ship among the various kinds of growth within the same organism. The principle of homeostasis is that a living organism tends to maintain a state of balance or equilibrium; in the process of striving to maintain balance, the organism is constantly shifting to and from the balanced state. It is the existence of these interrelationships that furnishes justification for teachers to be concerned with some of the characteristics of physical growth. It is a generalization of these interrelationships that causes us to say, "The child grows as a whole." In studying pupils all facets of growth need to be taken into account.

Intellectual-educational growth

Learning may be defined as a change in one's behavior because of his experience with his environment. If this definition is accepted, learning may be seen as a growth phenomenon. It becomes the basis for intellectual and educational growth.

The measurement of intellectual growth has been previously discussed under intelligence testing. It will be recalled that most of the measures used for this purpose involve both performance in certain basic motor functions and performance based upon previous cultural learning.

The principal means of measuring educational growth is the achievement test. For children of elementary school age, standardized achievement tests have been devised with good indices of reliability, and they can be used with assurance. However, as in the case of all tests, the interpretation of test results must be mellowed with good judgment. The instrument that is most commonly used in the elementary school for measuring educational achievement is the standardized achievement test battery. Four of these that are used widely are the Stanford Achievement Test, the California Achievement Test, the Metropolitan Achievement Test, and the Iowa Every-Pupil Test.[3] The achieve-

[3] These tests are published by the following companies respectively: World Book Company, the California Test Bureau, World Book Company, and Houghton Mifflin Company.

ment test battery will give measures of achievement in arithmetic, language arts, social studies, science, and in some cases study skills.

An achievement test battery provides teachers with information that serves three very useful functions. One of these is to give teachers an indication of the magnitude of educational growth as of the date of the test. More specifically, it may reveal the amount of educational growth, as measured by the test, between the present and any previously administered test. A second use for the achievement test, which is as important as the first, is to provide the teacher with a substantial amount of diagnostic information about the kinds of things their pupils have learned or failed to learn. Such information is invaluable in adjusting the instructional program. The third use of achievement test data lies in using the information for purposes of reporting pupil progress to parents.

Sometimes people argue about the most advantageous time to administer achievement tests. Some would prefer that they be administered in the spring, such as in the month of May. Others would prefer that achievement tests be given early in the fall (September or early October) so that the new teacher has the most recent information at the beginning of the school year. Others prefer to see achievement tests given twice a year — once in the fall and again in the spring, or once at mid-year and again at the end of the school year. The decision as to which of these plans is to be followed should be a matter of policy cooperatively determined by teachers and administrators.

But standardized measurement is not the only means whereby educational growth can be observed. Teachers will construct their own informal tests, or they will devise projects intended to reveal the child's understanding or skill. Not to be overlooked, too, is the possibility of self-evaluation by pupils. This is a device that is used too infrequently by teachers. Children should be given an opportunity to make an honest and open appraisal of what they have learned, for the reason that it gives them an opportunity to become more consciously aware of what they have learned, the meaning of what they have learned, and a sense of satisfaction derived from that learning. Certainly the teacher living in the classroom daily with a group of elementary school pupils observes changes in performance by the kinds of things and the quality of things that pupils are doing. The anecdotal record is useful for keeping track of these observations. Many persons believe that these kinds of appraisals have greater significance in assessing the educational growth of boys and girls than the standardized measuring instruments.

Social-emotional growth

For a long time we have recognized the significance of social and emotional growth in boys and girls, both as a by-product of what happens to them in schools and in terms of the effect that such growth has upon what may be done with them in school.

Unfortunately we have very few measures of social-emotional growth. The Vineland Social Maturity Scale [4] has norms that can be interpreted in terms of growth increments. However, the authors of this scale recommend that the persons using and interpreting it have clinical training. Most of the devices intended to interpret emotional maturity or emotional stability are highly clinical in nature, such as the Rorschach Test, the Thematic Apperception Test, or the Children's Apperception Test, and require specifically trained personnel to administer and interpret them. Furthermore, they are not scaled to reveal growth increments and they are used principally to appraise personality adjustments.

The sociogram is a device that is very useable for teachers to ascertain the social status of pupils in the classroom and to become aware of some of the social fields of force at work among the children. A sociogram is illustrated in Figure 3. To accumu-

[4] Published by the Educational Test Bureau, 720 Washington Ave., S.E. Minneapolis 14, Minnesota.

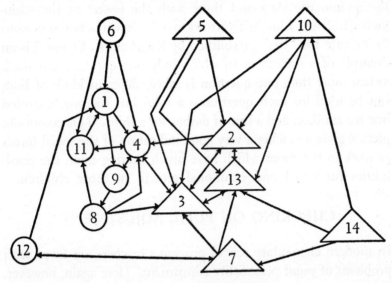

FIGURE 3.   A *Sociogram*

late data for a sociogram every pupil in the classroom is asked
to respond to one or more questions having to do with his
choice of a person with whom to associate in some activity.
Such questions might be asked as: "With whom would you like
to share your table? With whom would you prefer to play?
Whose home do you like to visit best?" It is also possible to
give the pupils an opportunity to list three choices for each
question in order of preference. Pupils in the classroom can
then be assigned a sociometric score on the basis of the number
of times they were chosen. A sociogram can be made by using
one question or more depending on how much social information
is sought. The data can be plotted in graphic form as illustrated
in Figure 3. A different symbol should be used to identify boys
from girls in the sociogram. Those receiving the greatest number
of choices should be placed near the center of the diagram and
those having the fewest choices, toward the extremes. We
speak of those who receive the greatest number of choices as

the sociometric stars and those with the fewest as the socio-metric isolates. Lines with arrows may be drawn between persons to indicate the "ties" established by the choices. Figure 3 is an example of a sociogram in which only one question was used. When more than one question is asked, different kinds of lines can be used for each question — a solid line for one, a dotted line for another, and a line of dashes for a third. This composite picture gives a teacher a very good indication of the social forces at work in the room which have much bearing upon the possi-bilities for social and emotional growth in those children.

CHECKING ON PUPIL ADJUSTMENT

In modern elementary school programs teachers are faced with problems of pupil personality adjustment. Here again, however, it must be emphasized that we are concerned with the problems of pupil personality adjustment not primarily because adjustment is a specified and delegated function of the school, but rather because adequate pupil personality adjustment is necessary in order that curriculum and method in the classroom can be effective. More often than not, the maladjusted personality calls for different methods from those for the normal personality. The choice of method that a teacher might anticipate to be successful with most boys and girls may fail dismally with a maladjusted child.

It should be stated emphatically, however, that there is a danger in too much clinical diagnosis by most classroom teachers. Axline strongly warned us about this practice by calling much of it "pseudo-psychiatric diagnosis." [5] We are warned against making inaccurate value judgments and statements based upon inadequate information, lest we damage the well-being of school pupils. Teachers should take heed of this warning. They are

[5] Virginia M. Axline, "Meeting the Crisis in Educational Leadership Today," *Educational Leadership*, 14: 330-335 (March, 1957).

not adequately trained to make clinical diagnoses of children's personality disturbances. When teachers become aware of unusual circumstances of behavior, they should solicit specially trained help.

Nonetheless, teachers must be sensitive to the possibility that failure to perform or to learn may be attributable to factors other than capacity. In those cases the causes of failure to perform must be attacked before the expected, realistic learning can take place. For example, there have been any number of cases in our elementary schools, in which children in the early years at school develop a reading block for one or more of many reasons. These are circumstances in which individuals do not read even though to all other appearances they should be reading. We are not sure of the many factors that contribute to this problem, but we have a hunch that some of them are caused by attempting to force reading upon children before they are ready to read. However, the point is that whatever its cause, the reading block must be removed before a child can profit from reading instruction. The lesson to be learned from this kind of thing is that teachers should not be hasty in reaching such conclusions as "the child is lazy," or "the child is stupid." In most cases there are other causes for failure to learn to read; such condemnation would never be made by a teacher who had carefully studied the child.

Most of the techniques whereby teachers can check on pupil adjustment are subjective and clinical in nature. One is the anecdotal record that has already been discussed. The persistence of unusual behavior as revealed through the behavior journal is an indication that the pupil is not properly adjusting to the classroom environment. Another is the sociogram. The sociogram reveals to us the degree to which an individual is accepted or rejected by other members of his group. Teachers can acquire a great deal of information by conferences and interviews with parents, the pupils themselves, and others who may have close contact with the pupil. Comparisons can be made of the behavioral characteristics of a pupil in school and in other circumstances. Naturally the most thorough assessment of adjustment can be made by clinical psychologists, psychiatrists, or psychoanalysts. The services of trained personnel like these are not available in very many schools, and referral to qualified people for help is restricted to extreme cases.

There are some standardized instruments available for personality appraisal, such as the California Test of Personality and the Mental Health Analysis (both available from the California Test Bureau). These instruments attempt to indicate degrees of adjustment under several headings. Probably the best use teachers can make of tests like these is to support their own observations.

Some schools are sufficiently concerned about pupil adjustment that they will make case studies of pupils whose adjustment they question. In those cases a large amount of data is collected by persons with specialized training. Information is gathered from the classroom teacher, school administrators, the school nurse, the school psychologist, and in some cases from a psychiatrist in the school or school system. These persons pool their information and their opinions and collectively attempt to make recommendations for a course of action to help the pupil's adjustment.

Summary

This chapter has been concerned with techniques of pupil study and diagnosis. Essentially, the discussion has revealed six principal techniques that an elementary school teacher might use. The historical record is maintained to note the chronology of events and the presence or absence of prerequisite information for teaching. The direct measure, such as height and weight, is obtained to satisfy legal requirements or to be used in growth appraisal. The test is used to determine capacity, adjustment, or growth. The interest inventory is administered to assess interest patterns. The anecdote is maintained to observe typical behavior and changes in behavior. The case study is used for special cases needing concentrated attention.

The teacher is directly involved in the collection and use of this information. That is why the study and diagnosis of children can be considered a basic dimension of method. The teacher collects the vast majority of the data; occasionally he is helped by special personnel. The information is used by the teacher in adjusting curriculum materials for individuals and groups, and in arranging the classroom so that pupils and subject matter can come together effectively. Thus the emphasis here is upon the teaching-learning situation, and the big question for pupil study and diagnosis is, "What do I need to know about my pupils so that I can help them learn better?"

Ideas for discussion and activity

1. Compile a useful list of intelligence, achievement, and personality tests that you can use as an elementary teacher. Be sure to include the title, authors, and publishers (with addresses). Indicate opposite each its principal use.

2. If you have access to school classrooms, practice making anecdotal notations about children as you observe them at work. Share these with one another and criticize one another's work.

3. Discuss thoroughly the uses a teacher may make of such information as the intelligence quotient, the grade achievement level, and behavioral information.

4. The class will profit from reports of collateral readings on techniques of studying children.

5. Check your understanding of the following concepts:

> learning
> growth
> intelligence
> educational achievement
> readiness

Suggested readings

Blair, Glenn Myers, R. Stewart Jones, and Ray H. Simpson, *Educational Psychology.* New York: The Macmillan Company, 1954, Chapters 17 and 18.

Here are two chapters focused upon testing. Chapter 17 discusses various diagnostic tools available to teachers, such as intelligence, achievement, and interest tests. Chapter 18 stresses the use and interpretation of test results.

Brown, William H., "Behind the Test Score," *Educational Leadership,* 15:161-165; December, 1957.

A plea is made for the use of good judgment in the interpretation of test scores. The need for cooperative work by teachers and psychologists is emphasized.

Cronbach, Lee J., *Educational Psychology.* New York: Harcourt, Brace and Company, 1954, Chapters 6 and 7.

Cronbach approaches the study of school pupils from the viewpoint of assessing their readiness to perform. The first of these chapters deals with personality and motivation; the second presents ways and means of assessing abilities.

Hansen, Alice F., "How the Teacher Collects and Uses Evidence," *Educational Leadership,* 13:430-434; April, 1956.

A practical and specific scheme for use by teachers in collecting and using evidence for the purpose of solving classroom problems is presented. The following steps are advocated and illustrated: (1) the establishment of criteria, (2) the collection of data, (3) the interpretation of data, and (4) planning for a course of action.

Morse, William C. and G. Max Wingo, *Psychology and Teaching.* Chicago: Scott, Foresman and Company, 1955.

Here is a fine presentation of the basic principles of growth and development, coupled with suggestions to teachers for classroom practice.

Prescott, Daniel A., *The Child in the Educative Process.* New York: McGraw-Hill Book Company, Inc., 1957, Chapter 6.

In this chapter Prescott discusses ways teachers can obtain anecdotal information. The chapter is richly illustrated with examples.

CHAPTER 5

Recognizing
Individual Differences

I<small>N THE PRECEDING CHAPTERS</small> we have discussed the purposes of pupil study and diagnosis and a number of techniques for carrying out pupil study. The very existence of such purposes to be fulfilled and supported by these techniques indicates that the problem of individual differences is one of critical importance for members of the teaching profession. An attempt will be made in this chapter to present the nature and significance of the problem of individual differences as it affects the thinking and behavior of the elementary school teacher in the classroom.

The fact of individual differences presents a two-fold problem for teachers. First, it is because children are different that we must study them. Second, we must use the results of our study as a basis for our teaching. At first glance these two statements appear to be extremely simple. However, in actual operation it becomes very difficult to live up to these demands. In the following pages we will try to examine the two-fold problem for teachers posed by individual differences, by analyzing the following topics in terms of their implications for the thinking and behavior of classroom teachers: (1) children are different, (2) children are alike, (3) the large range of individual differences, (4) conflict between knowledge and practice, and (5) a modern philosophy of individualization.

DIFFERENCES IN CHILDREN

Elementary school children are different in many ways. In fact we still are discovering new ways in which they differ. Several of these need to be discussed because of the interpretations teachers make of these differences, and the attitudes they hold toward these differences are critical for success in teaching.

Physical differences

One has but to walk into any elementary school classroom in which a single grade is found and he will be struck by the obvious fact that children in the same grade and of approximately of the same age differ widely in their physical characteristics. In comparison with the group as a whole, some of the children seem to be tall and others appear to be short. Some children tend to be very slender; others may be quite obese. Some have black hair; some have very blond hair; some may be red heads. Some children may have white skin; other children may have black skin. All of these physical differences have some effect upon the persons who bear them. However, physical differences are only one of the major and noticeable differences among children.

Mental differences

Children also differ mentally. Some children have the capacity for rapid and extensive mental growth. Mental growth in other children is slow and limited. Unlike differences in physical growth, differences in mental growth are not readily observable by looking at children in a classroom. To be at all exact, measurements of mental age are taken initially to determine the mental level of the child, and then at intervals to determine his rate of mental growth.

It is not possible to predict relationships between mental growth and physical growth. We have all seen the highly gifted individual who is tall and slender as well as the highly gifted individual who is short and obese. We have also seen children with less fortunate mental capacity bearing these physical charac teristics. The existence of these differences requires that teachers help pupils in different ways with their problems of learning; and they must expect learning on the part of these pupils to be different in quantity and quality.

Cultural differences

Elementary school children differ culturally for several reasons. One of these is the home environment. Of particular importance in the early school years are differences in language backgrounds, language habits that are fostered in the home, and the amount of cultural enrichment that is provided there also. These things teachers can do little about. Nevertheless, they affect the behavior of children in school, and teachers must take them into account in working with the children.

The kind of community in which children live effects differences in children's cultural backgrounds. Children who have lived in an urban environment have assimilated cultural elements different from those of children who live in rural areas. The availability of cultural advantages to both of these environments tends either to magnify or reduce these differences. To illustrate, television as a mass medium of communication is one avenue by which these differences are being reduced rather sharply where it is available to both groups. Where television is available to one group only, the differences are magnified.

Added to these differences in cultural opportunity are differences in physical and mental growth that affect the degree of cultural assimilation that children can make. Two children may have lived in highly similar environments, but because of differences in capacity they may have profited from that environment in divergent ways.

Growth pattern and personality

Each child establishes his own growth pattern and rate of growth in the various human characteristics. The principle of wholism in growth is well established; it teaches us that, although the same child may have a different rate of physical growth from that of mental or educational growth, all aspects of growth become somehow fused into a total, regulated, unique pattern of growth and development for that individual. It is this interaction of all the characteristics of growth within the same individual that causes us to say, "The child grows as a whole." It is homeostasis at work.

Because of physical, mental, and cultural differences children develop different personalities. These different personalities cause individuals to act and react in unique ways within and outside their school. These unique ways of acting are the individual's discovered means of adapting his own differences to the environment in which he finds himself.

All of these things most teachers know. Furthermore, most teachers will accept these facts as being true. The difficulty for teachers, however, occurs with the problem of what to do with this information. How can a teacher cope with all of these differences at the same time with so many children in the classroom and so much to teach? This is a question that perennially plagues teachers.

SIMILARITIES IN CHILDREN

In spite of the many ways that children are different, there are some common denominators of child life that cause them to be alike in certain respects. The fact that we can find some common characteristics for children of similar ages gives schools and teachers certain possibilities for children that would otherwise be impossible.

Personality traits

From the viewpoint of the schools, the principal cause of likeness among children is a common culture that envelops their daily lives. Culture refers to the configuration of our learned ways of thinking and behaving that have been generated by our social groups living together. All persons living in the same culture tend to assimilate these ways of behaving, and in the process their personalities become affected by this assimilation. Now if the various individuals living in a common culture have their personalities affected by the same culture, then in certain characteristics those personalities should be alike. This configuration of common personality characteristics for a society has been referred to by Linton as *Basic Personality Type*.[1] When we say that an individual is typically American or typically Parisian or a typical New Yorker, we refer to learned behaviors that have been observed with regularity in individuals from particular social groups.

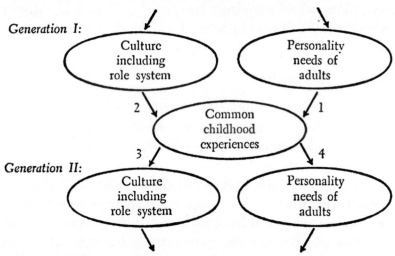

FIGURE 4. *Common Childhood Experiences in Relation to Culture and Personality. Adapted from Theodore M. Newcomb,* Social Psychology (New York: Henry Holt and Company, Inc., 1950), p. 448.

[1] Ralph Linton, *The Cultural Background of Personality* (New York: D. Appleton-Century Company, 1945), p. 129.

A more specific application of this for children lies in the number of common childhood experiences they have as they live in our various social groups. These common childhood experiences to some extent are prescribed by both the culture in which the children are living and the personality needs of the adults, and they in turn lead to further generation of culture and new personality needs of adults. Figure 4 diagrammatically represents this process by showing how at any given time a group of personalities, indicated as Generation I, are in interaction with their culture. Because of the needs of adult personalities and the demands of the culture, children are subjected to many common childhood experiences. These common childhood experiences link the culture and the adult personalities of Generation I with those of Generation II, and the similarities should be great. It should be noted that in our society where we have compulsory school-attendance laws for all children of elementary school age, the elementary school is one block of common childhood experiences for our children.

Interests and needs

In all of this very complicated social-cultural process there is a tendency to generate among persons with similar backgrounds, certain common interests and needs. Now these common interests and needs are not held by all peer members of a social group at the same time, nor to the same degree. They exist rather as a central tendency of that group. For years the Gesell Institute of Child Development has been studying the stages of development of children and the accompanying behavior.[2] The very fact that these researchers have been able to identify similar behavior characteristics of boys and girls at similar ages is indicative of the fact that the common culture in which our children

[2] Arnold Gesell and Frances Ilg, *The Child From Five to Ten* (New York: Harper and Brothers, 1946), or Frances L. Ilg and Louise Bates Ames, *Child Behavior* (New York: Harper and Brothers, 1955).

are living tends to generate common behavior patterns that stem from interest and need.

Implications for schools

It is these common elements in the behavior of most children at given ages that allow us to create a curriculum for the children who will attend the elementary school. When the pediatrician is able to predict from his knowledge, he can prescribe to mothers and potential mothers, infant and child care. Similarly, from the knowledge and experience of psychologists and educators we can predict some elements of structure for a school program. To use a very simple example, we know better than to expect the seven-year-old second grader to deal with historical relationships. He is not yet ready nor able to cope with the space-time concept. On the other hand, the fifth- and sixth-grade child has reached sufficient maturity so that he can deal with this relationship. The lesson for curriculum planning is very simple. Delay the introduction of any complicated study of history until the upper grades and beyond.

In the early years of the elementary school we try to deal with direct, firsthand types of experiences. We do not do this only because we believe the firsthand experience to be the most desirable. We can do little else. Until a child can read with a reasonable degree of independence, we cannot expect him to profit from vicarious experience. Thus we can see that there are certain elements of our total social-cultural pattern that appear to be fairly orderly and sequential. It is these elements that allow us to do curriculum planning within a broad framework.

It is these common elements that make it possible for us to work with groups of children in schools. When classes in school range upward from 25 children per teacher, the notion that completely individualized instruction is possible becomes less practicable. Perhaps it should not be recommended. The fact that children, within limitations of course, have some common interests, needs, and behavior patterns furnishes teachers with bases for grouping them within the classroom. Certainly there are advantages from an educational point of view to having children grouped together for purposes of work and study. Very important is the fact that children working together in groups can learn a good deal from one another. Secondly, when children are grouped and a teacher then divides her time among the various groups, the individuals tend to receive a larger proportion of the teacher's time and attention. In many respects it can be said that because of common knowledge, common interests, common needs, and common behavior patterns, teachers can, through the process of grouping, better provide for individual differences within their classrooms.

RANGE OF INDIVIDUAL DIFFERENCES

Regardless of the number of elements we may find common to children, the range of individual differences within any given classroom is large. The largeness is attributable to the combined effect of the ranges of many personal characteristics and variables of behavior. It is large because the same children differ with respect to two or more variables in different ways. Consequently each of the differences we are able to identify becomes compounded when we think of the combined complex effect upon the behaviors of a group of human beings.

Most of the measures that we take to describe pupil growth, either in a physical sense or an educational sense, tend to distribute themselves for a random sample of pupil population in accordance with what we call the normal probability distribution, or normal curve. For example, if it could be assumed that the pupils in one fifth grade were a typical sample of all fifth-grade pupils in the country, it would be expected that their performance on a standardized reading test or arithmetic test would be distributed in accordance with the laws or principles of normal probability distribution. Thus we would expect our scores for that group of pupils to cluster around some average and then taper in both directions toward fewer numbers of pupils' scores at the upper and lower limits of the distribution of scores. The pertinent fact here to be noted by teachers is that this distribution under average circumstances will be maintained. The distribution may move up or down the total scale of educational achievement, but the distribution will still be there. *There is little the teacher can do about the distribution other than to learn to live as a teacher within the story it tells.*

To some degree, flexible grouping of pupils within the classroom tends to reduce the range of the total distribution of pupils. If pupils are grouped only in accordance with their abilities to cope with a specific activity such as reading or arithmetic, the grouping reduces the total range of individual differences for that particular variable. At other times an individual teacher may group pupils within the classroom deliberately so that a wider range of individual differences is present in the group. The subject of grouping will be taken up in greater detail in Chapter 10. The purpose of mentioning it at this point is to note that grouping does not eliminate wide ranges in individual differences within a single classroom.

The range within any one classroom widens as children become older. In a certain respect then, this complicates the work of the upper-grade teacher. However, this does not mean that the task of teaching upper-grade children is more difficult than that of teaching younger children. As the children mature, they are able to assist teachers greatly in ways that tend to compensate for the wide range of differences. When they are older, children can do a better job of planning activities that are commensurate with their individual abilities. They are also able to work more independently on the activities that they have planned for themselves. Thus, self-guidance and self-direction on the part of pupils is an asset to the teaching task with respect to individual differences. Furthermore, the shift of responsibility from the teacher to the pupil for the selection, execution, and evaluation of learning activities is a desirable and educative transition to be made within the school environment.

CONFLICT OF KNOWLEDGE AND PRACTICE

At least within the elementary school, the real problem of individual differences lies in the conflict between knowledge and practice. One normally expects there to be some gap or variation between theory or knowledge and practice, but one should not expect them to negate each other. In the case of the conflict under discussion there tends to be too much variation. Several points will help illustrate this.

In the first place, education should tend to widen the range of individual differences. In fact it must, if we are to call it education. We know, for example, that because of differences in ability some children can learn more and faster than others. The fact that they learn more and faster than others should cause their rate of educational achievement to exceed the rate of those who have less capacity. This increased rate causes the differences between these individuals to fan out rather than to follow a single straight channel. Furthermore, most of the measures that we use to determine individual differences are directly and specifically affected by the things that we ordinarily expect children in school to learn. Again there is a direct relationship between the educational program and modifications of individual differences among children in school. This is in harmony with the nature of the function that we should be performing.

On the other side of the picture, many school programs have tended to restrict this range of expansion. Various endeavors have been made to have school children behave alike with respect to some of their academic activities. Several illustrations of this could be given. Some schools have accepted the notion that the elements of a planned curriculum are elements that should be transmitted to all school pupils and to quite a common degree, or so they assume if not directly state. This notion of a rigid curriculum tends to deny the existence of individual differences. For instance, to assume that all fifth-grade children should learn to cope with the mathematical processes that are usually taught in the fifth grade, to such a degree that they could pass a standardized achievement test at the grade-level norms for the fifth grade, is a denial of what we know actually happens. The norms themselves are established on the basis that somebody will be below them, otherwise the norm could not be. It simply represents typical behavior. To expect all children to achieve the norm is an unrealistic attitude.

Similarly, the idea of grade standards or minimum essentials is also a denial of our knowledge of individual differences. In most cases when teachers and administrators speak of minimum essentials, they do not mean what they say in the most absolute sense. They do not mean that they expect all pupils in the grades for whom these essentials are established to achieve them. What they usually mean is that they believe teachers should work with these essentials in the classroom because it is important that children be exposed to the opportunity to learn about them. The important thing to note here is that there is not an absolute denial of our knowledge of individual differences, but rather a certain amount of carelessness in the use of language. Rarely do we find school teachers and administrators who establish minimum standards for all children at specified grade levels and then adhere to them rigidly. In few schools are children regularly failed because they do not achieve their grade norm on a standardized achievement test or by other criteria. In those few circumstances where such practices have been followed, some of the children in grades five and six approach the maximum age of compulsory school attendance, and they leave school as soon as that age is reached.

The self-contained classroom of the elementary school complicates method with respect to individual differences, but at the same time it facilitates instruction because of individual differences. This is one of the unique features of the elementary school. The self-contained classroom is designed so that one teacher can be responsible for all of the educational activities of the boys and girls. This kind of organization allows the teacher to become familiar with the capacities, interests, needs, and motivations of the pupils, but it does complicate the scope and magnitude of individual differences because of the many elements of the school program for which the single teacher is responsible. The fact that the teacher in the self-contained classroom has the children under his jurisdiction all day long allows that teacher a good deal of flexibility in the arrangement of activities that the pupils will undertake, in regard to both content and time spent. At the same time it allows the teacher to manipulate pupils in and out of work groups so as to give them the best opportunity to learn. If teachers do not take advantage of the strong features of the self-contained classroom, they tend to weaken the type of instruction for which it is designed.

Entirely too frequently we have raised the wrong questions about our problems of individual differences. We seek ways to eliminate them rather than ways to capitalize upon them or to proceed to cope with them. Consider as an example, the attempts that have been made to assign children to classrooms in accordance with their intelligence quotients. In its most reduced form this has been an endeavor to reduce the range of individual differences, thereby to facilitate the teaching act and be productive of more homogeneous results among the children in the respective rooms. Apparently these efforts did not accomplish the desired ends. Another illustration is that we have often sought a report card or a grading system that would resolve the problem of individual differences or at least report pupil progress without regard for individual differences. The results of this search in many cases have been quite disastrous. More frequently than not with our five-point grading scale, A, B, C, D, E, we have simply labeled a gifted student as being so on his report card, and conversely we have labeled the dull student as a dull student. In both cases the students may have been living up to their capacities, and so the report card is absolutely meaningless; it only labels the differences.

In the foregoing paragraphs, several illustrations have been given of discrepancies between our knowledge of individual differences as they relate to the educative process, and some of the things we attempt to do about them. It seems only reasonable that each teacher should think through a philosophy by which he might guide his behavior in the classroom with respect to this important dimension of teaching method. Perhaps the following paragraphs will be helpful in summarizing constructive ideas, and at the same time serve as a summary for this chapter.

A MODERN PHILOSOPHY
OF INDIVIDUALIZATION

From our present knowledge we should be able to formulate a modern philosophy for dealing with problems of individual differences. The reason for using philosophy as a concept in this sense is purposely to avoid giving the reader the impression that any single bag of tricks or single list of methodological manipulations will furnish teachers with ways and means of solving the kinds of problems under discussion. Teachers must become familiar with the facts and the assumptions about individual differences in the classroom and then apply their creative intelligence to the application of these facts and assumptions to their daily work. Several guideposts for developing this point of view might be suggested.

Teachers should realize that *no* administrative organization can be provided for them that will solve the problem of individual differences. Whenever administrative attempts are made to group children in classrooms according to some criterion such as intelligence, this grouping has produced a wide range of individual differences in other human characteristics. Parenthetically, the age-grade system of assigning children to classrooms for purposes of instruction seems to be about as effective as any other means that has thus far been designed. *Individual differences are an instructional problem, and an instructional problem they must remain.*

Thus far we have been unable to find a grading system that would eliminate individual differences in the classroom, or at least some of the problems inherent in individual differences. Grading and reporting pupil progress must be done in harmony with a sound philosophy of individual differences. Advice to teachers in this connection is very difficult to give. Grading systems vary somewhat and local interpretation is of critical importance in many circumstances; a grading system is something that teachers may have to live with for some time to come. The best we can do is to recognize them for what they actually are and not try to relate them to some function for which they are not appropriate.

One must relate the curriculum pattern of the school in which he teaches to this philosophy. Again, there is no curriculum pattern that will resolve individual differences for teachers. Whether a curriculum is organized by separate subjects or whether it is organized under broad problems of living, the organization pattern itself will not do the job for the teacher. Whether the curriculum be detailed and rigid or broad and flexible, in itself it cannot resolve these teaching problems. The problem of individual differences must be taken care of by the teacher's creative abilities to adapt the curriculum materials and manipulate the school pupils and those adapted materials so that profitable learning results. This should not be interpreted to mean that the organization of the curriculum is not an important thing. Every school needs to have a design for its operation in terms of the goals it sets out to achieve. If we call that design the curriculum, then it does not become an end point in teaching, but rather it becomes a point of departure for teaching. It becomes a point of departure for teaching, and teaching requires the exercise of careful judgment because that curriculum must be adapted to the individuals who must work within its framework.

Another critical point in building a philosophical attitude toward individual differences in the elementary school, is the uses to which textbooks will be put. Like everything else, textbooks can be used well or they can be used poorly. When a textbook is used in such a way that all pupils in the classroom begin on page one of the book and laboriously plow their way through page by page until by the end of the school year they have at least turned over the last page, the textbook becomes a stifling approach to learning, and this indicates that the teacher chooses to ignore individual differences among his children. On the other hand, when a teacher uses a textbook as a source for materials of instruction, patiently guiding the less gifted to those things they can profit from and allowing the more gifted to explore broadly the textbook as well as many supplemental materials, that teacher truly uses the textbook as a resource for selective learning rather than a rigid dictum to be followed by all. He recognizes individual differences and is willing to do something about them.

Teachers can do well to improve their use of professional language with respect to individual differences, so that communication about many of the important activities of our classrooms can be improved among members of the profession, as well as between members of the profession and their patron groups. An illustration of this has already been offered in the case of our talking about minimum essentials or grade standards when these are not quite what we mean. When we communicate about such things as grade standards, our listeners assume that this becomes a standard that all must achieve. In many cases in the elementary school we do not mean this at all. It is also incongruent to talk about providing a program for the interests and needs of children and to expect children of different interests and different needs and different abilities in the same classroom to perform the same activities with the same degree of motivation. To speak of pupil growth in one breath, and in the next to call report grades as we ordinarily know them an expression of growth, is inaccurate. Grading systems must be interpreted as grading systems. Indices of growth should be used to reveal magnititude of growth. We need to practice the accurate and precise use of our professional language.

We must be willing to accept the thesis that education should attempt to broaden the range of individual differences rather than to restrict it. A teacher who accepts these facts in this way welcomes a wider range of individual differences because that wider range probably indicates good teaching. Conversely, one who accepts this point of view eliminates from his thinking any reference to channelling all children in the same classroom within meager, specified limits, because to do so would be a denial of what he believes. To carry out this principle places obligations on teachers. They must foster educational growth in all children regardless of capacity and experiential background. This means that teachers must be concerned with children at either extreme as well as those in the middle. Emphasis here has already been placed on the broadening of individual differences by encouraging more rapid growth on the part of gifted children. On the other hand, serious educational attention needs to be given to those at the opposite end of the ability scale. No child can begin to learn at some point or level above his present stage of readiness. To place him in a position where he must attempt to do something that is beyond his present state of ability is knowingly to commit that pupil to failure. Thus in many cases for the slow learner, a teacher fosters the broadening of the range of individual differences by permitting and encouraging pupils who do not have ability to do rapid and high caliber work, to work at their own pace and at their own level. Furthermore, these pupils of varying abilities must be evaluated in terms of their own potentials and in terms of the growth that has taken place with respect to those potentials. It is incongruent professional behavior to provide classroom activities appropriate to individual differences and then constantly evaluate by other criteria. Actually, a modern philosophy may be representing a shift from an attitude of forcing pupils to do those things that all children are expected to do, over to an attitude of having pupils work as much as they can at what they can do.

Lest the foregoing comments be interpreted to mean that we should emphasize individual differences to that point where we do not conceive of any structure to our educational program, but are only concerned with a complete laissez-faire exploration of environment on the part of children, a caution must be inserted. We dare not forget as members of the teaching profession that the elementary school has a unique role to play in our society. The curriculum that we use and the methods that we use in adapting that curriculum to pupils in the elementary schools must be developed to fulfill that unique role. This then means that we must emphasize differences in education, but they must be based upon a common structure and this common structure is the school curriculum. However, a teacher in adapting the curriculum materials to the individual pupils must uniquely enrich them for the gifted and uniquely modify them or restrict them for those who are less gifted. In other words, the designing of a curriculum for the elementary school indicates that the institution is created to fulfill certain purposes. We dare not relinquish this obligation. We simply must carry it out intelligently.

When reduced to its simplest terms, the problem of individual differences lies in the *expectancies* that teachers have for the performances of youngsters. We get into our most severe problem situations when teachers expect children to do what they cannot do. For this reason the author is prone to suggest that the real problem of individual differences lies in the attitudes of teachers and other adults toward the behaviors of children. When we learn to adjust our attitudes (expectancies) in accordance with careful appraisal of our pupils' capacities and motives, we will lick the issue of individual differences.

Finally, a person who accepts the professional responsibility of developing a philosophy of individual differences, by which he lives as a teacher, takes on another obligation. That is to communicate this philosophy to the patron group of the school so that the school program operates in an atmosphere of sympathetic understanding. It is fairly safe to say that most school patrons at this point in our history do not understand the significance of individual differences for method in modern elementary school classrooms. One of the reasons why this misunderstanding, or lack of understanding, exists is because members of the teaching profession have not been successful in communicating the significance of these problems to the patron group. We cannot sensibly report our efforts to parents nor can we expect our patrons to maintain sympathetic attitudes toward schools unless they understand the basic philosophy under which the schools are operating, and accept that philosophy. Thus we have an educational problem with the patron group as well as among ourselves, regarding individual differences. However, education is our business and if we can intelligently apply our present and future knowledge about individual differences in school, we can teach patron groups to understand and appreciate our problems and our actions.

Ideas for discussion and activity

1. Discuss your reaction to the final section of this chapter devoted to a philosophy of individualization.

2. How can you reconcile in your own thinking the facts of individual differences with the desirability of grade standards in the elementary school?

3. Investigate ways in which ranges in individual differences in elementary schools have been appraised. For example, see page 382 of Frandsen listed in the suggested readings.

4. Visit an elementary school classroom and observe as many differences in the behaviors of boys and girls as you can. If you can, concentrate on observable differences in ways of attacking school work, attitudes toward school work, and kinds of work attempted.

Suggested readings

Frandsen, Arden H., *How Children Learn*. New York: McGraw-Hill Book Company, Inc., 1957, Chapters 12 and 13.

These two chapters review ways of appraising individual differences in ability and contain suggestions for providing for those differences. These chapters are well documented with research and other references.

Hightower, Howard, "Individual Differences," *Educational Administration and Supervision*, 41:458-461; December, 1955.

This is a study of individual differences among seventh graders. It is concluded that we should teach to increase the range of individual differences rather than reduce it.

Ilg, Frances L. and Louise Bates Ames, *Child Behavior*. New York: Harper & Brothers, 1955.

Consult the index of this book for a number of references to individual differences in behavior of children of different sex and at various ages.

Olson, Willard C., "Individual Differences: A Precious Asset," *Educational Leadership*, 15:142-143; December, 1957.

Olson presents an editorial as the lead presentation to a volume of *Educational Leadership* entirely devoted to individual differences. His theme is the need to maintain the realities of individual differences because they are an asset to progress in education.

Rudolph, Orville G., "A Study of Recent Practices in Providing for Individual Differences at the Elementary School Level," *Pittsburgh Schools*, 28:110-112; March-April, 1954.

The article reports a study of practices in providing for individual differences in elementary schools, with emphasis upon tendencies in curriculum practice.

| PART | **III** | Dimensions of Method in Organizing Teaching Materials |

A SECOND CATEGORY of basic dimensions of teaching method revolves around the organization of teaching materials. At the moment we have the greatest wave of curriculum-guide production ever noted in the history of education. The basic hope of such effort is that the instructional guides produced will help teachers gain greater insight into the total instructional program as well as improve their individual organization of teaching material. Most prospective and in-service teachers need help in seeing the relationships between the instructional guide, the textbook, and other instructional materials on the one hand, and the teaching plan on the other. These relationships become more complicated when such ideas as unit, resource unit, and teaching unit are added to the discussion.

The basic purpose of Part III is to help the reader understand the various complications and to become aware of proper sequence in the organization and selection of teaching materials; namely, from curriculum to resource materials and from resource materials to the teaching materials actually to be used in the classroom. The dimensions of method center around the selection of materials, the organization of materials, and the use of materials. These are to be expressed through chapters on the separate-subjects approach, the experience approach, instructional materials, and planning for teaching.

PART II.

Dimensions of Method in Organizing Teaching Materials

CHAPTER 6

The Separate-Subjects Approach

IN CHAPTERS 1 and 2 a distinction was made between curriculum and method. It will be recalled that the distinction goes somewhat as follows. The curriculum is described as the design of a social group for the educational experiences of their children in schools. Such a design should include at least a statement describing its intent and function, a statement of goals expected to be achieved because of the creation of that design, an instructional guide, and an evaluation schema. The curriculum thus conceived is an instrument or a document that is constructed prior to the act of instruction in the classroom.

It becomes the function of method to arrange the content of the curriculum, particularly the instructional guide, and the school pupils in such a way that learning can take place and the goals of the curriculum can be achieved. Furthermore, it becomes a function of method to apply the evaluation schema of the curriculum to the processes that were utilized in carrying out the instructional guide, to insure or to make judgments about the effectiveness of both the method and the curriculum itself. In other words, method becomes a critically serious consideration at the point at which a teacher attempts to put the curriculum to work in the classroom.

In those school systems where a curriculum as described above or an instructional guide has been prepared, the instructional guide reveals some sort of organizational scheme. In the actual world of practice only two kinds of organizational scheme can be found. The one that is most prevalent is to have the instructional guide organized by the various and separate subjects that are taught in the elementary school. The other type can be described as the attempt to move away from the separate-subjects organization through arranging the subject matter of the school around units or themes in which the separate subjects tend to lose their individual identities.

Since a most important aspect of method is that of providing a transition between curriculum and classroom activity, it would appear reasonable that the efforts of teachers in making this transition should be along the same basic organization pattern as is utilized in the instructional guide. Because the most prevalent theme is curriculum organization by separate subjects, our attention in this chapter will be directed toward problems involved in organizing teaching materials under the separate-subjects approach.

CHARACTERISTICS OF THE SUBJECT

In order for one to understand the subject approach, a careful distinction needs to be made between *subject matter* and *subject*. The subject matter of schools is selected from the total configuration of learned behavior, or the results of learned behavior that is generated and transmitted by members of a social group in the process of living together. In a sense, all of our culture constitutes all of the potential subject matter of schools or any other institution dedicated to processes of cultural transmission. Historically, as cultures became more complex, institutions needed to be created to transmit some of the culture to oncoming generations. This is especially true in the case of schools. Schools were orginally created for the purpose of transmitting to the young, certain elements of the culture, because it was felt that this was the best way or the only way to have that culture transmitted. Those elements of the culture intended to be within the jurisdictional framework of schools can be called the total subject matter of schools, in our case, of the elementary school.

The total subject matter of the elementary school is divisible into several homogeneous parts. That is, certain classes or elements of the total subject matter are very closely related to one another. We call these homogeneous parts *subjects*. A subject then becomes an arrangement of homogeneous elements of our culture. As subjects, these homogeneous parts have been arranged in vertical order assumedly proceeding from the simple to the complex, with the assumption made that each step is a prequisite to the next. Once these parts were arranged in this kind of order, they were then divisible into parts that could fit within the administrative organization of our school systems, or more specifically, within the graded system of the elementary and secondary schools. It should be noted that so long as instruction goes on in schools and so long as learning takes place in schools, *instruction and learning must be about something and that something is the subject matter of the school.*

DEVELOPMENT OF SUBJECTS IN AMERICA

In America we have a long tradition of separate subjects in the elementary schools. In fact our earliest schools were single-subject schools. The earliest colonial schools were established for the purpose of teaching children to read. In those, reading was the sole subject of instruction. Later writing was added to the curriculum, and still later, arithmetic. In fact the school of the three R's (reading, writing, and arithmetic) emerged as a distinctly American school. Its curriculum was limited to reading, writing, and arithmetic; it also included spelling and catechism.

To these early colonial beginnings a number of new subjects were added to the elementary school curriculum during the nineteenth century. Figure 5 shows the evolution of the elementary

1775	1825	1850	1875	1900
READING	READING* Declamation	READING DECLAMATION	READING Literary	READING* LITERATURE*
Spelling	SPELLING*	SPELLING	Selections	Spelling
Writing	Writing	WRITING	SPELLING	Writing*
Catechism	Good Behavior	Manners	PENMANSHIP*	......
BIBLE	Manners & Morals	Conduct	Conduct	ARITHMETIC
Arithmetic	ARITHMETIC*	MENTAL ARITH* CIPHERING	PRIMARY ARITH. ADVANCED ARITH.	
	Bookkeeping GRAMMAR	Bookkeeping Elem. Language GRAMMAR	...... Oral Language* GRAMMAR	...... ORAL LANGUAGE Grammar
	Geography	Geography	Home Geography* TEXT GEOGRAPHY	Home Geography TEXT Geography*
		History U. S.	U. S. HISTORY Constitution	History Stories* TEXT HISTORY*
		Object Lessons	Object Lessons* Elementary Science* Drawing* Physical Exercises	Nature Study* Elem. Science Drawing* Music* Play Physical Training*
	Sewing and Knitting	......	......	Sewing Cooking Manual Training

CAPITALS = Most important   Underlined = Subjects of medium
        subjects.   importance.
Roman = Least important   * = New methods of teaching
        subjects.   now employed.

FIGURE 5. *The evolution of the elementary school curriculum,
and of methods of teaching.* Adapted from E. P. Cubberley,
Public Education in the United States *(Boston: Houghton Mifflin Company, 1934), p. 473.*

school curriculum from 1775 to 1900. It should be noted that
the development of the curriculum from 1775 forward was an
additive process, and very little subtracting was done. It can also
be noted that at the beginning of the period covered by the
chart the essential elements of instruction were reading, spelling,
arithmetic, and grammar, but by 1900 the essential subjects were
reading, literature, arithmetic, oral language, geography, and

history, with many other subjects listed as subjects of medium or of lesser importance. These major subjects have continued to be integral parts of the elementary-school curriculum up to the present time.

The pattern of separate-subjects organization was disturbed somewhat by the progressive-education movement during the second, third, and fourth decades of the present century. Leaders of the progressive-education movement reacted to the formalism and the rigid boundary lines established among the various subjects. It was their claim that such organization was contrary to what man had discovered regarding better ways to teach and organize learning materials. In spite of this movement away from the subject-centered approach, the contemporary scene indicates that the separate-subjects approach is much entrenched in educational practice.

There are a number of factors that contribute to the persistence with which the various subjects in the elementary school have maintained their separate identities. In recent times there has been a shortage of trained persons to teach in our elementary and secondary schools. Persons with little professional training tend to teach as they themselves were taught, which of course was under the subject-centered approach. There has been a wave of criticism of the public schools. Under this wave, people, method, and curriculum have been under severe public attack. All of these factors tend to cause more conservative behavior on the part of school personnel. Conservative behavior, of course, can only be reflected in what people generally think to be a return to the fundamental subjects that have long been a heritage of our elementary schools. One can also couple with these thoughts the fact that publishers and authors collaborate to produce teaching materials for teachers to use in the classrooms. Virtually all of these materials are organized around a separate-subjects approach. Materials are organized for teaching individual subjects and are therefore much more readily available to teachers. In fact there are very few published materials for any other type of organization.

SCOPE OF THE USUAL SUBJECTS

It is possible to break the modern aggregation of separate subjects into two categories. These are illustrated in Figure 6 as the subjects having to do with the skills of communication and

Areas of Living	Skills of Communication

1. Social Studies
  Geography
  History
  Civics
2. Science
3. Arts and Crafts
4. Music
5. Literature
6. Physical Education
	1. Language Arts
	  Reading
	  Spelling
	  Grammar
	  Composition
	  Handwriting
	  Listening
	  Speaking
	2. Arithmetic

FIGURE 6. *A breakdown of school subjects into areas of living and skills of communication*

expression, and those having to do with what might be called areas of living.

Skills of communication

Our basic skills of communication involve arithmetic and the language arts. Arithmetic is a subject that has maintained its own unique identity in educational practice. The language arts, on the other hand, are organized in various ways. Generally, the language arts are composed of those subjects that have been called reading, spelling, grammar, composition, handwriting, speaking, and listening. These may be organized in various ways, but the acts of reading, writing, and speaking and their concomitants of spelling, composition, and grammar are skills that must be taught. In many cases reading is maintained as a separate subject and the remaining language arts are taught together. In other schools, reading, spelling, and handwriting maintain their separate identities in the early grades, with grammar and composition being added in the later grades. Regardless of the various types of organization, these are referred to as our basic skills, or sometimes they are called the tool subjects.

Like other subjects they are arranged to proceed from the simple to the complex. The skills of communication and expression are organized so that children in the elementary school will pass through three rather distinct phases: (1) one of readiness; (2) one in which the pupil builds up power to utilize and progress in the development of skill on his own initiative; (3) one that might be called a tool phase—the phase in which skill becomes a means whereby the individual increases his own living power through explorations in his environment, that he can make only because he has available to him these tools of communication and expression.

READINESS PHASE. The concept of a readiness phase is based upon recognition of the need for functional capacity before learning can take place. There are two primary ways of considering the concept of readiness. One way is to think of readiness as a point in the total development process, or a maturative stage. The other way of viewing the concept is to consider the various activities that children might perform in order to provoke the desired development or maturation. The concept is extremely important for the elementary school curriculum and particularly for the tool subjects, because of the wide ranges in the stages of maturity of children who are enrolled. The readiness phase of skill learning is accented in the early years in school, as in the case of reading readiness; but throughout the elementary school the vertical arrangement of content in the separate subjects implicitly assumes that each stage in skill development is a prerequisite for the next stage and therefore constitutes an element of readiness.

POWER BUILD-UP PHASE. If we are concerned with developing

the communicative skills as tools, it is only logical that once the stage of readiness is passed and a child can profit from instruction in that particular skill, we should help him to develop power in the use of it. The basic assumption behind tool instruction in the elementary school is that it will provide children with the ability or power to utilize the skills in solving realistic problems. It is during this phase that children are taught to use the skills independently. For example, in reading this is the phase in which children are taught independent attack upon words and sentences. With this help they can grow beyond the sight-vocabulary level and become able to progress in the use of the reading skill on their own initiative. The same thing is true in arithmetic. This is the time when children learn the basic arithmetical functions and develop skill in the manipulation of these various processes. Thus the power build-up phase of skill- or tool-learning is that aspect of the program that takes the individual learner from a state of readiness to the point where he is quite independent in his use of the skills concerned. This type of emphasis usually is prevalent in the middle grades of the elementary school. However, the concept of building power permeates all levels of an instructional program because of the range of individual differences in children, as well as a constant need to increase power and fortify that which has already been developed.

TOOL PHASE. It is toward the tool phase of learning that most skill instruction is directed. The real meaning of tool usage refers to the communication of ideas through speaking, writing, and listening. In this phase the skills become a means by which an individual explores his environment further and in a more independent manner; they are a means by which ends are attained, and are not ends in themselves. This is an important aspect of our instruction in the skill areas or subjects of the elementary school that is sometimes overlooked. There is some tendency to get so involved in the readiness or the power build-up phase that we fail to remember that our principal objective in teaching the tool subjects is to make our learners independent and good users of these tools of communication.

Areas of living

The second category into which the various subjects of the elementary school program can be identified may be called the areas of living. The subjects most frequently identified under this category are indicated in Figure 6 as the social studies, science, arts and crafts, music, physical education, and literature. With the exception of physical education, these are sometimes called the content subjects because they tend to furnish the substance or knowledge that is manipulated by the skills of communication and expression.

Like the skill subjects these usually proceed from the simple to the complex. They begin with the familiar and proceed toward the unfamiliar, and they also tend to begin with kinds of direct, contactual experience and move toward vicarious experiences. This organization can be illustrated by the general scope of these various subjects.

SOCIAL STUDIES. The social studies organization specifically exemplifies the notion of proceeding from direct experience toward vicarious experience and from the familiar to the unfamiliar. In discussing trends in the organization of the social studies program of the elementary school, Hodgson makes the following statement:

> There is considerable consistency among the various city school systems and state departments of education regarding topic selection for grades I-III. There is also general agreement among the social studies specialists that the topics currently taught are both desirable and recommended: e.g., grade I-Pets, Our Homes, Our Schools; grade II-Community Helpers, Life on Our Farm, and Pets; grade III-Food, Shelter, and Clothing. In grades IV-VIII, there is less agreement, but the following topics are found most frequently: grade IV-World Folk, Local Community, Pioneer Days, Indians, Eskimos; grade V-U.S.

History and Geography; grade VI-Europe and Asia, Our American Neighbors; grade VII-Europe and/or United States, Local Community, Local State; and grade VIII-United States, Local Community, Local State. A sharp difference in suggested topics is found in grades IV and VII. City school systems are currently placing emphasis on World Folk in grade IV while the state departments recommend the study of the local or state community.[1]

It can be seen from this summary that the social studies program for children begins with those things with which they are usually most familiar in their home, in their neighborhood, and in school. The program then expands outward, supposedly as the individual's ability increases to cope with an expanded environment. Furthermore, it can be noted that in the earlier grades many of the experiences or activities of children can be direct, contactual experiences in the community, whereas most of the experiences for children in the upper grades must be vicarious in nature.

SCIENCE. The science program of the elementary school is somewhat similar to the social studies program, at least in some of its basic assumptions. As the social studies program is composed of excerpts or pertinent information from the various social sciences, the science program is a general or generalized science program containing selected and appropriate elements from the various sciences. For example, in a recent review of research on the subject of science in the elementary school, Craig described the scope of the science program as follows:

> Science instruction should be broad in scope to provide for growth in learning about all the major aspects of the environment — the sky, the atmosphere, the earth (including rocks, soils, and minerals) — conditions necessary to life, other living things, energy and forces (physical, chemical, and biological), and the inventions and discoveries of mankind.[2]

[1] Frank M. Hodgson, "Trends in Social Studies in the Elementary School," *School and Society*, Vol. 80 (September 18, 1954), p. 86.
[2] Gerald S. Graig, *Science in the Elementary Schools*. What Research Says to the Teacher Series No. 12, Department of Classroom Teachers and American Educational Research Association, N.E.A., 1957, p. 7.

In the organization of the science program in the elementary school, these major aspects of environment are distributed through all grade levels. The children study them at various levels. The problem of repetition of topics is not serious because of continued emphasis upon investigation of these major aspects of environment at different levels of complexity.

MUSIC. The music program in the elementary school is regarded as a desirable cultural experience. It is designed to include such experiences as singing, listening and appreciation, creative activity, expression through rhythm and dance, and in many schools, the playing of instruments. A great deal of emphasis is placed upon enjoyment and creative expression. Technical elements such as note-reading and part-singing are introduced in the program as they become important elements to increase the listening, appreciation, and participation skills of the student. Instrumental music, of course, involves specific instruction in technique from the outset.

ARTS AND CRAFTS. Like music the arts and crafts program is intended as cultural enrichment. The great emphasis of the modern arts and crafts program is toward creative expression on the part of children in a variety of ways. Particular emphasis is upon providing children with a wide variety of media for expression of thoughts, feelings, and ideas. Among the media that are used are finger painting, painting with oils and water colors, clay modeling, block printing and textiles, and various crafts such as basketry, weaving, and papier-mâché. The important idea is to provide children with opportunities to learn various ways in which they can express their feelings and ideas in their own creative manner.

LITERATURE. The literature program of modern elementary schools is based upon two objectives. One of these is to help children find enjoyment in reading and thus use reading as an avenue for the worthy use of leisure time. The second objective is to acquaint the young with the literary heritage of the race. Many of the great ideas and morals of man that need to be transmitted to our young are found in good selections of literature for children. The literature program contains opportunities for children to have reading experiences in adventure, biography, legends, moralistic fables, and serious issues of life. These are available to children in both prose and poetry.

PHYSICAL EDUCATION. The physical education program incorporates body-building activities, rhythms and dance, and simple and complex team games. Much stress is placed upon body development, physical coordination, and in the team games, such concepts as cooperation and sportsmanship. When health and physical education are considered as one subject we must add to these instruction in personal and community hygiene, first aid, health, and communicable diseases. Sometimes the health aspects are incorporated in the science program, but more frequently one sees reference to the health and physical education program of the school.

Method and separate-subjects

There are a few basic assumptions behind the separate-subjects approach to curriculum organization that have significance for method. One of these is that the subject is regarded as an ideal in the philosophic sense. It becomes an ideal because it is an organized package of our total culture, that we deem significant to be transmitted to our children and youth. This cultural transmission becomes an ideal of education. Furthermore, for the idealists the subject is of more significance for teaching than is the learner, because the elements of the subject must be transmitted regardless of the learner. Now it must be noted that even the most extreme idealists, in this sense, would still take into account the fact that all learners could not learn subject matter to the same degree nor at the same rate, but they are convinced that attempts must be made to transmit the various elements of subjects to children wherever possible.

It is further assumed that the homogeneity of subject matter in each subject is highly desirable for learning. In this connection, many believe that the great strength of organizing the subject matter into separate subjects to be transmitted to children, lies in the assumption that this homogeneity produces greater simplicity for the pupil and thus facilitates learning.

In addition to the homogeneity of the subject matter in each subject, the subject matter is also vertically organized in what is called a logical and sequential manner. In this organization the initial subject matter to be taught in the lower grades is assumed to be the most simple elements of that subject, and as children progress through the grades in each subject, the subject matter becomes more difficult. In this manner a system of prerequisites from grade to grade and almost from month to month in each grade are built into the subject organization. This is illustrated well in the mathematics programs of our public schools. Addition and subtraction are considered to be prerequisites to multiplication and division. Counting precedes both of these. These fundamental processes are considered to be prerequisite to the manipulation of fractions, decimals, and percentage. Arithmetic is a prerequisite to algebra and algebra a prerequisite to geometry. The importance of this assumption is that it is believed children can learn best in this way.

Finally, there is the assumption of transfer of training among the various subjects. It is taken for granted that when children learn the subject matter they will either consciously or unconsciously be able to relate what they have learned in one subject to what they have learned in other subjects, and what they have learned in all subjects to more complicated living problems. At a number of times in our educational history this assumption has been vigorously challenged, and perhaps some advocates of the separate-subjects approach would deny the existence of the transfer assumption. There are some indications that the assumption is being denied. Reference here is made to the fact that in many elementary school programs the various elements of language arts instruction are fused together, and it is rather common that the social studies program is a fused program rather than several subjects such as history, geography, and civics. One of the principal reasons for the fusion of these subjects is the recognition of certain weaknesses in the transfer assumption.

When one understands the nature and scope of the separate subjects along with the basic assumptions behind them, the inferences for the organization of teaching materials become quite apparent. Each subject is to be treated individually even though the contents of different subjects may be correlated. All pupils are to study the same subjects at the same times of the school day. The implications here for the organization of the daily class schedule are obvious. The day is broken up into as many parts as there are subjects, and pupils work on those subjects during the delegated times. The degree of rigidity with which any individual teacher follows a daily class schedule depends upon the teacher and the supervisors and administrators under whom he works. Teaching materials must be organized so that they lead pupils from the familiar to the unfamiliar in harmony with separate-subjects organization. Taking all of these things into account, teaching materials must be organized so that differences in individuals and groups are anticipated by the teacher. This may result in flexible assignments for pupils with different abilities, or it may result in organizing groups within each subject being offered. Usually the textbook becomes the principal instructional tool for the teacher. This is so not only because it is the most readily available tool of instruction, but also because its organization is completely in harmony with the separate-subjects organization. The textbook is also the major source of information for pupils in most schools. It may be that pupils will investigate other sources of information relative to the various topics under discussion, but the textbook is the reference point. The teacher is obligated to develop plans and select materials of instruction that are in harmony with the basic assumptions of the separate-subjects approach; this includes treating each subject separately and following a predetermined order of topics within each subject.

One can see from these inferences that it becomes a problem for the classroom teacher to plan for a transition between the various subjects in the curriculum and the working activities of boys and girls in the classroom. This is the problem of lesson planning prior to teaching. The subject of planning the lesson is discussed in a later chapter and will not be discussed here. However, the point has been made that separate-subjects organization, because it has certain characteristics and assumptions, forces classroom teachers to think and to organize themselves in certain directions because of that organizational scheme.

Summary

In this chapter an attempt has been made to illustrate the basic frame of reference for organizing a school curriculum around the separate-subjects approach and, in turn, to show the implications of this organization for the task of a teacher. This has been accomplished through a discussion of characteristics of individual subjects and the general subject organization. Some attention was directed to the historical development of subjects in the schools of this country, in order to demonstrate the impact this approach has had upon our elementary schools. The subjects were described in two general classifications; namely, the skills of communication and expression, and the areas of living. Finally, the basic assumptions behind the separate-subjects approach were indicated, followed by the inference of these for the organization of teaching materials.

Organization by separate subjects is still the predominant mode of curriculum construction. This indicates that most professional people accept the basic assumptions of this form of subject-matter structure. A teacher who is employed to teach in a school where this pattern of organization and this implied philosophy prevail, must create a teaching-learning environment in harmony therewith. Thus it is the teacher's responsibility to keep method in harmony with the rest of the pattern of school organization.

Ideas for discussion and activity

1. Make a comparison between the comments of this chapter about

the organization of school subjects and the organization of a set of children's textbooks for one subject such as reading, arithmetic, or science.

2. List what you consider to be the advantages and the disadvantages of organizing school subject matter by separate subjects. Keep this list to use when you finish the next chapter.

3. Discuss the significance of transfer of training for any organization of subject matter.

4. What is the relationship between an adopted series of school textbooks and the school's curriculum?

Suggested readings

Beck, Robert H., Walter W. Cook and Nolan C. Kearney, *Curriculum in the Modern Elementary School.* Englewood Cliffs, N. J.: Prentice-Hall, Inc., 1953, Chapter 12.

In this chapter the authors present an overview of curriculum structure. Various ways the curriculum has been organized are shown along with the rationale of the schemes.

Hurley, Beatrice Davis, *Curriculum for Elementary School Children.* New York: The Ronald Press Company, 1957, Chapter 5.

Conflicting points of view about curriculum organization and their basic assumptions are presented.

Klausmeier, Herbert J., Katharine Dresden, Helen C. Davis, and Walter Arno Wittich, *Teaching in the Elementary School.* New York: Harper & Brothers, 1956, Chapter 4.

This chapter is devoted to the same subject as the two references cited above, but the organization of curriculum is related to patterns of instruction in the school.

Krug, Edward A., *Curriculum Planning.* Revised edition. New York: Harper & Brothers, 1957, Chapter 4.

This is a discussion of the major purposes of the all-school program and their relation to the organization of classroom activities.

Smith, B. Othanel, William O. Stanley, and J. Harlan Shores, *Fundamentals of Curriculum Development.* Revised edition. Yonkers-on-Hudson, New York: World Book Company, 1957, Chapters 10 and 11.

These two chapters probably contain the best and most thorough discussion of the characteristics, problems, practices, and criticisms of the subject curriculum, that is available to us today.

CHAPTER 7

The Experience Approach

THE FACT THAT the last chapter was devoted to the separate-subjects approach to curriculum organization, implies that there is at least one other. To the question, "Is there an organizational pattern antithetical to the separate-subjects approach?," one would have to answer, "Yes." However, exactly which terms and words one would use to give an answer to the question are more difficult to choose. This is one area in which our writings on curriculum are quite confusing.

We must turn to some idea for organizing subject matter, other than that in the form of subjects themselves. Now if there is an extreme at the opposite end of some hypothetical continuum from the separate-subjects approach, it probably is the experience approach. To be properly cautious, it should also be said that not all writers in the field will agree with this interpretation. This is relatively unimportant so long as the reader understands that the selection of the experience approach as antithetical to the separate-subjects approach is somewhat arbitrary on the part of the writer.

ITS MEANING

To grasp the meaning of the experience approach, it is helpful to refer to the notion of the experience curriculum. The experience curriculum idea has as its principal point of departure the philosophic notion of experience in the sense expressed by

129

John Dewey. Through the use of his concept of experience Dewey tried to help us see that there is a greater function to education than the mere transmission of knowledge to children and youth. Furthermore, the simple fact of learning on the part of children would not satisfy the educational act. For an individual to have an experience, Dewey would insist that it would be necessary for the learner to engage himself in activities from which he can learn something that he has not learned before. In addition, through that activity he must recognize and foresee the consequences for his present and future behavior, because of what he has learned. This action establishes continuity within the life experience of the individual and gives meaning to his actions. Obviously the significant psychological process by which an individual thus acquires experience is critical or reflective thinking.

In order for an individual to have an experience in this sense then, the learner must see the utility and consequence of his learning in the broad perspective of life. In the broad perspective of life, problem elements are not identified or labeled in terms of our conventional school subjects. In life or life-like situations, problems are not identified as problems in arithmetic, problems in spelling, or problems in science. Problems are posed in a fused environment in which the elements of the various subjects lose their separate identities. It is up to the learner to extract from this kind of situation the necessary stimulus elements to be able to call forth from his repertoire of knowledge or experience those elements necessary to solve his problems. The principal assumption behind the experience approach to the organization of curriculum and teaching materials, is that the separate-subjects approach will not satisfy these criteria. It therefore becomes necessary to seek a means of organizing the learning environment of the school, in order to facilitate as much as possible the acquisition of experience by the school pupils.

Thus it can be noted that in the experience approach a great deal of emphasis is placed upon the learner as being the significant consideration in the organization of curriculum and teaching materials. It will be recalled that under the separate-subjects approach the principal emphasis was upon organization of the subjects, or the subject matter within each subject. The emphasis in the experience curriculum is upon organization of the subject matter so that the learner can organize himself better within the framework of the subject matter with which he is expected to deal. Emphasis is upon the interaction of the learner with his environment as he lives his daily life, because this is the best prerequisite for future learning and living. Frequently differences are characterized by stating that *the experience curriculum is organized psychologically*, whereas *the separate-subjects curriculum is organized logically*. The significance of this idea can be understood further if we examine some of the applications that have been made from the experience approach.

SOME APPLICATIONS

To understand the following illustrations of ways in which the experience approach has been applied to curriculum and curriculum organization, it must be recognized that the experience approach in itself is not a separate entity. Rather, it is more helpful to think of the experience approach as the philosophy of a movement away from the separate-subjects organization.

Movements away from separate subjects

In more specific terms and in actual practice, the movement away from the subject-centered approach came slowly and without dramatic change. Probably the first attempt was the correlation of topics among the various subjects. In this case the separate subjects were maintained, but teachers arranged to teach the same topics at the same time in the school year. In this manner, children's attentions were focused upon a major

area, with the various subjects contributing to a different enlightenment for each pupil over the entire area. For example,
when a history teacher was dealing with the New England
Colonies, the geography teacher would stress the geography of
New England; the art teacher might present Colonial art forms;
and the literature teacher could teach "The Courtship of Miles
Standish." To a present day reader this may not appear to
be much of a break away from the subject-centered idea, and
actually it is not. However, it did represent a departure that
led to new practices.

A second type of departure from the subject-centered approach
can be termed as attempts at fusion. Fusion is a practice of
merging two or more subjects together in such manner as to
produce one. There are two principal reasons for fusing separate
subjects together, and they are quite obvious. One is to help
children to see relationships among the content of the various
subjects as applied in learning activities. In a sense this simply
is an extension of the idea of correlation, except that the fused
product is taught by one teacher. The second reason is to reduce
the number of class periods in each day in order to provide
greater flexibility for planning and activity in the classroom. The
best illustration of fusion practices in most elementary schools
is what is now known as the social studies. Historical, geographical, political, and sociological concepts were amalgamated
to produce one subject. This type of action has been criticized
as an attempt to weaken reputable and independent disciplines.
However, it is not possible to teach all of the social disciplines
to the children in the elementary schools as separate subjects.
The best we can do, and probably what we should do, is to select
representative elements from the various social sciences that we
deem important to teach to elementary children, and bring them
together in some teachable form. In the light of our present
knowledge the most teachable form is the social studies. This
represents a distinct break from the subject-centered idea, and

it has caused more heated controversy than have attempts at correlation.

A third level of movement away from the subject-centered approach can be identified as attempts to construct a curriculum around the problems of living, rather than around the various separate subjects. In this type of organization the separate subjects tend to lose their identities completely. Pupils are presented with problems, or series of problems, that need to be solved. In order to solve these problems, pupils must bring various skills and knowledge to bear upon them. This is an extreme departure from separate subjects. In fact it represents a complete separation.

Illustrations in practice

To illustrate further the application of the experience approach in elementary schools, three specific interpretations can be cited. One of these applications is the concept of *Unifying Experiences.* Unifying experience is a concept demonstrated in *Missouri's Guide for Elementary Education.* To quote directly from that publication:

> The term "unifying experience," as used in this guide, signifies a way of organizing subject matter and activities within an experience in order to give a feeling of wholeness, relatedness and unity to a child to help him achieve integration within himself.[1]

In the Missouri guide the organization of unifying experiences is demonstrated in the social-studies–science program. The titles of unifying experiences are raised in the form of questions such as "How can we help others at school?," "What conditions help people work?," "What changes do we see at different seasons?" Under each unifying experience is listed in one column the unifying experience and in a parallel column ideas for teachers to try in working out the experience in the classroom. Figure 7 is an

[1] Missouri State Department of Education, A *Guide for Elementary Education* (Jefferson City, Mo.: The Department, 1955), p. 31.

illustration of an outline of a unifying experience taken directly from that publication.

OUR COMMUNITY

OUTLINE OF UNIFYING EXPERIENCE NUMBER FOUR

Content	Ideas to try
IV. What conditions help people work?	Make a mural showing how people in your community travel when they go to work.
*A. What are the many types of transportation and communication?	Take a trip on a bus or train.
1. What types of transportation do we have in our community?	Make a mural showing how people in your community communicate with each other.
a. Walking	Write letters. Mail at post office or corner mail box.
b. Horse-drawn vehicles	Visit a post office to see how mail is made ready to send.
c. Bicycles and scooters	Invite postman into classroom to answer questions.
d. Automobiles	
e. Taxis	Draw and cut out pictures of types of transportation and arrange on a bulletin or corkboard display.
f. Busses — school, local and cross country	Experiment with simple machines.
g. Trucks	Move a box by means of a lever.
h. Streetcars	Use a lever for play (seesaw).
i. Trains	List things that pulleys are used for.
j. Airplanes	Experiment with the force of steam. (Watch cover on pan of boiling water)
k. Boats and ships	
l. Elevated and subway trains	
m. Elevators and escalators	Experiment with air currents.
	Experiment with magnets.
2. What types of communication do we have in our community?	Collect pictures of machines that are used in transporting people and goods.
a. Conversation	Learn to recognize different kinds of airplanes or boats.

* Science, health and safety content.

Content	Ideas to try
b. Telephone	Experiment with paper, kites, and
c. Telegraph	toy windmills to show that wind
d. Radio	has power.
e. Television	Observe a grader or other heavy
f. Cablegram	equipment to see how it works.
g. Letter and card	Locate pictures, stories and poems
h. Newspaper	which tell about types of trans-
i. Magazine	portation and communication.
j. Handbill	
k. Siren and signal	
(light house)	

FIGURE 7. A *Unifying Experience. Adapted by permission from* A Guide for Elementary Education, op. cit., *p. 105.*

A highly specific and organized version of the problem-of-living approach has been termed by Stratemeyer and others as persistent life situations. Persistent life situations are arranged in major categories within each of those areas. The major areas within which persistent life situations are found are health, intellectual power, moral choices, aesthetic expression and appreciation, person-to-person relationships, group membership, inter-group relationships, natural phenomena, technological resources, and economic-social-political structures and forces.[2] Under each of these major areas are indicated typical life situations that children and youth must face. Persistent life situations are defined as, "those situations that recur in the life of the individual in many different ways as he grows from infancy to maturity." [3] Figure 8 illustrates a breakdown of one of the major areas into minor categories with the accompanying persistent life situations.

[2] Florence B. Stratemeyer, Hamden L. Forkner, Margaret G. McKim, and A. Harry Passow, *Developing A Curriculum for Modern Living*, 2nd Ed. (New York: Bureau of Publication, Teachers College, Columbia University, 1957).
[3] *Ibid.*, p. 115.

INTELLECTUAL POWER

MAKING IDEAS CLEAR

Using language to communicate ideas — Contributing to informal discussions and conversations

Making oral presentations

Expressing ideas in written form

Using media other than language to express ideas — Using graphic forms to express ideas

Using aesthetic forms to express ideas

FIGURE 8. *Examples of persistent life situations. Adapted by permission from Stratemeyer et. al., p. 157.*

In all probability the extreme application of the experience approach is the emergent curriculum. In the purest sense emergent curriculum is unplanned. It should emerge from the day-by-day activities and experiences of children in the classroom. In this case the content of the school curriculum cannot be determined until after the classroom activities have taken place. Theoretically there is no room for previous planning, but it places a burden upon the teacher to make sure that what is done or what emerges has some continuity with what has previously taken place. The needs of society are to be met through the developing needs of children as they and their teachers are able to identify problems to attack. In order to follow the emergent curriculum notion, it would be necessary for a teacher to be highly trained in the art of teacher-pupil planning and to be highly perceptive in maintaining continuity among emerging pupil activities. There is also the philosophical question of whether a school has a right, that is a social right, to conduct a school program on an emergent basis. Those who would argue against this point of view say that there is a group of social demands for certain kinds of educational experiences for children in schools, and that school personnel have not the right to ignore these demands. Therefore, they must plan for them in advance of the classroom situation.

It can be seen from these examples that they all have the common dimension of moving away from the separate-subjects organization in order to improve the transfer effect of learning in school classrooms to the solution of life-like problems. This improvement in transfer effect assumedly comes about because of the emphasis upon the organization of instructional materials to facilitate the psychological process of the learner.

The unit as a framework

As we moved away from the separate-subjects approach toward the experience notion, curriculum structure became a problem. Many advocates of the experience approach rejected planned structure, and in its place substituted the emergence of curriculum from teacher-pupil planning. Others sought some organizational scheme. Some of these have been described in the previous paragraphs. However, throughout virtually all of the efforts to organize plans for instruction, the unit scheme of organization seems to predominate. It will help the reader to acquire the spirit of the unit concept if several definitions are cited. One group of authors state:

> A unit, or a unit of work, can be defined as purposeful learning experience focused upon some socially significant understanding which will modify the behavior of the learner and enable him to adjust to a life situation more effectively.[4]

Adams defines the unit of work as follows: "The unit of work consists of a series of unified coordinated elements, each of which is a part of the functional whole. Each of these major elements is an organized aspect of the total unit." [5] Saylor and Alexander, after reviewing many meanings of the unit concept, prefer to

4 Lavone A. Hanna, Gladys L. Potter and Neva Hagaman, *Unit Teaching in the Elementary School* (New York: Rinehart & Company, Inc., 1955), p. 101.
5 Fay Adams, *Educating America's Children*, 2nd Ed. (New York: The Ronald Press Company, 1954), p. 140.

think of it as "a unitary organization of experiences." [6] Foshay describes the unit as follows: "Essentially, the unit of work involves a central theme or problem of some kind. This is used as an organizing principle for the selection and organization of school experience." [7] Likewise after reviewing definitions of the unit of work, Kyte comes to this conclusion:

> A unit of work is an educative series of purposeful and related activities that provide normal and natural learning experiences contributing to the sound development of the individual in a recognized and significant area of living.[8]

Thus it can be noted that the modern notion of the unit is a series of related experiences organized around some central theme, particularly a theme having to do with some area of living. The unit of work is organized on a psychological basis; that is, in order to further the learning of children in what is considered to be the most meaningful manner. Separate-subject boundary lines are disregarded more frequently than not. For this reason the unit is thought to be especially adaptable to the experience approach in organizing curriculum and instructional materials.

To observe more specifically the value of the unit of work in the experience approach, it will be helpful to note the features of the unit organization. A very fine statement of the essential elements of the unit is given by Adams as follows:

1. A *Major Objective*, the learning product to be attained; the ability, knowledge, understanding and appreciation, or combination of all these, which will help the child to adjust more adequately to his life environment

[6] J. Galen Saylor and William M. Alexander, *Curriculum Planning* (New York: Rinehart and Company, Inc., 1954), p. 397.

[7] Arthur W. Foshay, "Changing Interpretations of the Elementary Curriculum," *The American Elementary School*, Harold G. Shane, (ed.), Thirteenth Yearbook of The John Dewey Society (New York: Harper and Brothers, 1953), p. 118.

[8] George C. Kyte, *The Elementary School Teacher At Work* (New York: The Dryden Press, 1957), p. 194.

2. More *Specific Contributory or Functional Objectives*, which serve as the basis of activities
3. *The Approach or Introduction*, in which the teacher helps the children identify their own interests with the major objective of the unit
4. *The Planning and Purposing*, in which the children more completely accept the objective of the unit and discuss what they want to know and do about it
5. *The Selection and Pursuit of Activities*, which will result in the attainment of the desired objective or goal. At this stage there must be careful diagnosis of individual differences with modification of activities to provide for them
6. *Important Incidental Outcomes.* These are the ideals, understandings, appreciations, techniques, and attitudes, which result incidentally from the activities. While they are not pursued directly by the learners, they may be very important outcomes of any unit
7. *Culminating Activities*, which provide an opportunity to demonstrate and fix the major outcomes of the unit
8. *The Evaluation or Measurement of Unit Outcomes*, which determines the extent to which the major goal has been attained [9]

Other writers have similarly outlined what they consider to be the essential elements of the unit, but they do not markedly disagree from those offered by Adams. The reader will note from these essential elements that both teachers and learners necessarily proceed in a learning cycle from objectives to evaluation of activity. This emphasizes the continuity of the unit approach because it lends wholeness to the activity through this cyclical approach. The breadth of the unit is limited only by the scope of the topic. One also should note the absence of reference to the usual school subjects. The subject matter of the unit, or the unit topic, is only appropriate to the degree that it helps the learner to fulfill the major and specific objectives. This kind of organization is in harmony with the experience concept. It is designed to foster the interaction of the learner with his environment in such a way that the learner gains greater control over his environment. In itself the organization of the unit is psychological rather than logical. All of these factors are

[9] *Op. cit.*, pp. 140-141.

related to the philosophy of the experience approach to curriculum organization.

It must be added hastily, however, that the use of the unit has not been restricted to broad or fused subjects. Many persons recognize the principle of continuity for the learner as being good, and therefore, they accept unit organization of teaching materials. However, they do not in many cases accept a different approach to the organization of subject matter for the elementary school from the separate subjects themselves. Thus the philosophy of continuity for the learner was adapted to the subject unit or to separate topics within a separate subject. This dual use of the unit concept is well expressed by Burton:

> Extreme proponents of subject-matter curriculums and teaching tend to assume that, if essential knowledge is developed, personality traits will follow also. Extreme proponents of experience curriculums tend to assume if emphasis is upon development of personal-social-moral traits, the necessary knowledges will be achieved in the process. Each view has elements of truth and of error. Specific provisions for each type of outcome must be made in the planning for instruction. Subject-matter teachers must take pains to see that attitudes and personality traits are not neglected; teachers stressing personality development must see to it that the essential knowledges, generalizations, and meanings are achieved.[10]

Burton is here using the subject-matter curriculum in the same sense that this volume has been using the separate-subjects curriculum. In much of the writings such terms as subject-matter unit, experience unit, topic unit, problem unit, and others are used. All this illustrates that attempts to move away from separate-subjects organization have been accompanied by endeavors to maintain the separate-subjects framework modified by a philosophy of experience in education. We thus can note in various professional books, chapters devoted to a strict philosophy of the unit organization as being significantly different from

[10] William H. Burton, "Implications for Organization of Instruction and Instructional Adjuncts," *Learning and Instruction,* Forty-ninth Yearbook, Part I. National Society for the Study of Education, 1950, pp. 222-223.

separate-subjects organization; but in subsequent chapters they treat the use of the unit in arithmetic, social studies, science, and so forth, as though the unit were simply a way of organizing subjects for teaching. Hanna and others claim that such practice is in violation of the true spirit of the unit of work when they state:

> Because of the nature of unit teaching it would be impossible for teachers to have science units, social studies units, language arts units in process simultaneously. The unit of work rightly encompasses all of these, not simply the social studies.[11]

The important thing to note from all of this is that the use of the unit as a means of curriculum structure in applying an experience approach to teaching and learning seems to provide psychological organization, to de-emphasize homogeneity of subject-matter, to anticipate more direct transfer of learning, and to stress the role of the learner. On the other hand, the separate-subjects approach provides for logical organization, emphasizes homogeneity of subject matter, has faith in less direct transfer, and stresses the significance of the subject. We must, however, understand that throughout all of the attempts at ways of organizing school subject matter, people genuinely have been seeking better education for children. Some differences in viewpoint are discrete; others are vague. We have much yet to learn.

METHOD APPLICATIONS OF
UNIT ORGANIZATION

In earlier paragraphs of this chapter, several ways in which curriculum materials have been organized under the experience approach were identified. It will be recalled that in general the curriculum was organized around broad facets of life, in the form of problems of living, persistent life situations, or areas of living. There are varying degrees to which these problems of

11 *Op. cit.*, p. 105.

living and so forth might be specified in an instructional guide. In some cases they are briefly outlined by topic and sub-topic; in other cases they are rather clearly specified with objectives and suggested activities. In any case it becomes necessary for the teacher to make some transition between the curriculum materials however organized, and the actual classroom teaching situation. There are two ways in which the unit concept has been used in making this transition. One of these is the resource unit and the other is the teaching unit.

The resource unit

The resource unit is particularly useful when the curriculum materials are briefly outlined by topic only. The resource unit is a supplement to curriculum planning. It is a means whereby a teacher or a group of teachers collects the necessary information and instructional materials about a given topic or problem so that the stage can be set for teaching and learning. In some respects it is a summary of an area of study for the teacher. Wingo and Schorling suggest that the following materials will generally be contained in a resource unit:

1. An outline of the basic content involved in the unit
2. A list of authoritative sources which teachers may use to fill in details of content
3. Suggestions of appropriate activities for children, which might be included in the development of the unit
4. A list of reference materials for children to use
5. A list of films and other audio-visual aids which might be used
6. Suggestions for making or obtaining various teaching aids.[12]

From these it can be noted that a teacher must assemble and organize the content and instructional materials, as well as anticipate appropriate activities for the unit. It would be possible to construct an entire school curriculum or instructional guide around a compilation of resource units. The important thing to

[12] G. Max Wingo and Raleigh Schorling, *Elementary School Teaching*, 2nd Ed. (New York: McGraw-Hill Book Company Inc., 1955), p. 198.

note is that the resource unit is not the teaching unit because as yet the efforts of the teacher have not been directed toward anticipating the unique features of the classroom group.

The teaching unit

The unit outline previously indicated from Adams is as good an outline of the teaching unit as any available. Basically, the teacher here prepares materials from the resource unit in anticipation of the specific things that he thinks may be appropriate for the pupils. The teaching unit thus is a plan the teacher makes for use with a specific group of children, because of his knowledge of them.

It is the teaching unit that the teacher takes with him to the classroom in order to work with the children in the development of the unit itself. At this point teacher-pupil planning takes over, and the pupils, in cooperation with their teacher, plan the specific activities that they are going to execute, and ways and means to carry out those activities. The activities are performed under the motivation of the children and the teacher, and together they evaluate their efforts. It should be noted that this matter of planning, or involving the children in the planning, is not one of turning the complete responsibility over to them. This responsibility can never completely be relinquished by the teacher. In democratic societies we hope that all persons who are going to be affected by decisions can participate to some degree in making those decisions. We should transfer this principle to the school classroom to the maximum degree. An important point to remember is that planning in itself is educative, and people must learn to plan together. This we deem important in the democratic society.

Summary

The experience approach to the organization of curriculum and teaching materials is a distinctly different approach from that of separate-subjects, or subject-centered, approach. The principal difference is observable when one becomes aware of the logical assumptions of the subject-centered approach and the psychological assumptions of the experience approach.

In actual practice, attempts to organize curriculum and teaching materials can be described as movements *away* from separate subjects *toward* a somewhat idealistic experience concept. The unit seems to be our best means, or framework, for organizing materials as we move in this direction. Two uses stand out in unit application—the resource unit and the teaching unit. In Chapter 9 the use of these devices will be further exemplified in a discussion of planning procedures.

Ideas for discussion and activity

1. List what you consider to be the advantages of organizing subject matter for the elementary school on some basis other than separate-subjects.

2. Using the essential elements of a unit as outlined by Adams as a guide, write out a unit of work on a topic of your own choice.

3. Check your understanding of the following concepts:

> subject matter
> subject
> unit
> experience
> fusion

4. Analyze the similarities and differences between the unit and the unifying experience or the persistent life situation.

Suggested readings

Adams, Fay, *Educating America's Children.* Second edition. New York: The Ronald Press Company, 1954, Chapter 5.
 This particular chapter presents the unit as a general method of teaching. It is well illustrated with units. Subsequent chapters illustrate the use of units in the subject areas.
Burton, William H., "Implications for Organization of Instruction and Instructional Adjuncts," *Learning and Instruction,* Forty-ninth Yearbook, Part I. National Society for the Study of Education, 1950, pp. 217-255.
 Burton's chapter in this yearbook presents implications of learning

principles for the organization of instructional materials. Interesting comparisons of subject-matter units and experience units are made.

Hanna, Lavone A., Gladys L. Potter and Neva Hagaman, *Unit Teaching in the Elementary School*. New York: Rinehart & Company, Inc., 1955. The whole book is devoted to the use of the unit in elementary school teaching. Chapter 5 — "The Unit of Work" — is very appropriate in conjunction with the chapter you have just finished reading.

Preston, Ralph C., *Teaching Social Studies in the Elementary School*. New York: Rinehart & Company, Inc., 1950, Chapter 5.
This is a very good chapter on the unit method, but of course, it is pointed toward the use of the unit in teaching the social studies.

Strickland, Ruth G., *How to Build a Unit of Work*. Federal Security Agency, U. S. Office of Education, Bulletin 1946, No. 5.
This bulletin contains a very realistic presentation of techniques of unit construction and the use of units in the grades. Suggestions for topic and problem areas are included.

CHAPTER 8

Selecting
Instructional Materials

THERE ARE THREE important considerations about selecting instructional materials as a basic dimension of teaching. One of these is the rationale behind the use of instructional materials in an instructional program. Another is the simple problem of acquiring good materials. Sometimes this is related to economic barriers and the use of good judgment in spending limited funds. The third is a matter of intelligent use of the instructional materials. It is the purpose of this chapter to examine these considerations in a manner that will be helpful to aspirant or beginning teachers.

THE RATIONALE

The important purposes for selecting instructional materials lie in the communication of ideas and experiences. Instructional materials become a means whereby learners can come in contact with ideas, values, and concepts that have been expressed by others. In this sense they become tools of learning. The cone of experience as designed by Edgar Dale graphically describes the rationale of teaching materials. This cone is illustrated in Figure 9. It can be noted that the cone represents a hierarchy of experiences with the most direct and simple entered at the base and the most abstract and difficult at the apex. The relationship between entries in the cone of experience and the usual

146

sequence of instructional areas of the curriculum are very similar. The cone of experience begins with direct, contactual types of experience, immediately followed by contrived and dramatic participation. Most of our beginning activities for children in the elementary school fall within these categories. A large number of these experiences for children are not only desirable at the early levels but also very necessary as well. They are necessary

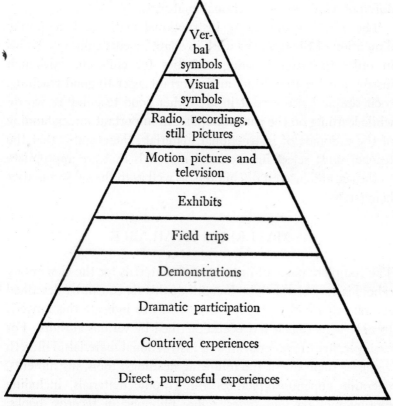

FIGURE 9. *The cone of experience. Adapted with permission from Edgar Dale, "Improved Teaching Materials Contribute to Better Learning,"* The American Elementary School, *Harold G. Shane, (ed.), Thirteenth Yearbook of The John Dewey Society (New York: Harper & Brothers, 1953), p. 239.*

because children cannot have vicarious experiences involving the reading process at the early ages, because they have not as yet been taught to read. They, therefore, must explore their environment in a manner that does not involve complicated communication skills like reading and writing. As the apex of the cone, visual symbols and verbal symbols become part of the learner's repertoire of experience, and because of this the school is able to provide other kinds of experience through the use of different kinds of instructional materials.

The selection and use of instructional materials is a specific dimension of the teacher's work in adapting curriculum materials in order to foster learning activities for children. Although instructional materials are an important asset to good teaching, their simple use does not insure either good teaching or worthwhile learning on the part of pupils. An important understanding of the rationale of instructional materials, therefore, is that the teacher must select instructional materials that are appropriate to the age and interest of children, as well as to the subject matter being taught.

MATERIALS AVAILABLE

The complete range of instructional materials for the elementary school is very broad. The breadth of this range can be described several ways, and probably the best way to indicate this range is to note ways that it has been described by various authors. For example, in a chapter devoted to instructional materials, Hildreth discusses them under the following headings: tools, instruments, scientific apparatus; pictures and graphic materials, including motion pictures and slides; radio; phonograph records; books; the school library; the expanded classroom; community resources; demonstration materials, and exhibits.[1]

[1] Gertrude Hildreth, *Child Growth Through Education* (New York: The Ronald Press Company, 1948), pp. 259-280.

Lee and Lee divide their discussion of instructional materials into two large categories. One of these is audio-visual resources and the other, reading resources. Under audio-visual resources they list objects, specimens and models, pictures, the motion picture, charts and graphs, maps and globes, duplicating devices, the radio, transcriptions and other auditory resources, and television. Under reading resources they list the textbook, supplementary books, and the library.[2] In reviewing research on instructional materials in education, Estvan divided the chapters of one issue of *The Review of Educational Research* into Printed Materials, Audio-visual, Community Resources, Free and Inexpensive Materials, and Resource Centers.[3]

A glance back to Figure 9 will indicate the areas of teaching materials that Dale thinks to be descriptive of the total range.

A convenient way of grouping the many kinds of instructional materials is as follows: 1. Those kinds of instructional materials found in the community. 2. The audio-visual aids. 3. Textbook materials. 4. The library. 5. A special grouping is often made of free and inexpensive materials.

Materials in the community

The school's community can be a very valuable source for instructional materials. Material sources can be found in the community for children in all age brackets in the elementary school. These materials or sources of instructional materials can be classed into four categories: people, institutions, objects, and natural resources.

PEOPLE. People can be classed as one of the most valuable instructional material resources in any community. People have been used as resources in education for many years. In all

[2] J. Murray Lee and Dorris May Lee, *The Child And His Curriculum*, 2nd Ed. (New York: Appleton-Century-Croft, Inc., 1950), pp. 273-290.

[3] Frank J. Estvan, Chairman, "Instructional Materials," *Review of Educational Research*, 26: 111-197 (April, 1956).

probability we have only begun to learn how to use them to the greatest advantage. Among the people in a community who can be used for the purposes of improving and augmenting the instructional program are the fireman, the postman, the storekeeper, the business executive, the engineer, the craftsman, the politician, the farmer, the physician, the dentist, and so forth. The fireman and the postman have been used as instructional sources in the early grades in the elementary school for many years and probably will continue to be so used for many more. The others are useable for resources throughout the elementary school years when various facets of community life are studied.

INSTITUTIONS. Like the people in a community, their institutions can become materials of instruction. The family, the church, government, industry, and the public library are illustrative of the kinds of institutions that are in nearly every community and that must be studied if many of our objectives of education are to be achieved. We consider it to be important that children in elementary schools become familiar with the operation of our basic institutions such as the church, the family and the state, because this knowledge will permit them to live better lives in our society. Where knowledge of our institutions can be approached or studied by direct, contactual experience, that experience is proportionately more meaningful for the learners. From a study of social, governmental and industrial institutions through direct and contactual types of experience, it is possible for the relatively immature mind to acquire rather complex concepts earlier than it would be able to do through less intimate contact.

OBJECTS. Every community contains physical objects that become focal points of the elementary school program. Such things as historical monuments, public buildings, a coal mine, a factory, the fire engine, the train, the airplane, and many others of this sort are illustrations of physical objects to be studied. Many of the objects are related to both institutions and people that have been previously mentioned, but they are repeated here because we have different purposes in approaching either people or institutions. For example, we may regard the airplane as the product of an industry involved in the transportation of people and commodities, as an object of man's invention having certain kinds of technical characteristics, or in terms of the man who flies airplanes. We can study the coal mine as a feat of man's creativity, somewhat different from the contribution of coal as a natural resource to our way of life or to coal mining as an industry.

NATURAL RESOURCES. Besides the objects in a community, a community boasts of natural resources that contribute to our way of life. When we study objects *per se*, not in relation to institutions and people, such things as oil, coal, iron, water, farm land, and forests would be illustrations of possible natural resources as features of our geographic environment. Here as in all kinds of instructional materials, direct, contactual experience is apt to contain greater meaning for the immature mind of the elementary school child than vicarious experience.

The usual audio-visual aids

Another kind or class of instructional material is composed of the usual audio-visual aids. These are numerous and varied. They range from very inexpensive to very expensive. The degree to which teachers capitalize upon the use of these materials is financially dependent upon the amount of money the local board of education makes available for teachers to spend on these kinds of materials. These audio-visual materials can be classed in several different categories that are descriptive of their make-up.

MOTION PICTURES. The motion picture has become a rather commonplace audio-visual aid in American public schools. The equipment necessary to use motion pictures is more expensive than that for other audio-visual aids. The most expensive feature, of course, is the projector itself. Projectors without sound equipment are less expensive than those with, but at the same time they eliminate the use of sound motion pictures. The procurement of film poses administrative, clerical, and financial problems. Few schools buy motion picture films in any appreciable quantity unless the school is in a large city system with enough money in its budget to build up a film library. In smaller schools and school systems it becomes necessary to rent films from various film centers. These must be scheduled and sometimes films fail to arrive at the time when the teacher needs them most. However, with careful planning much of this difficulty can be overcome.

STILL PICTURES. Many forms of still pictures and charts make a large group of audio-visual aids. Included in this group might be the conventional 3-by-4 slides and 35mm. slides, all kinds of pictures including photographs and prints, and maps, charts and graphs. Filmstrips should also be included here. The kinds of equipment that are necessary to use these materials effectively are the slide projector and the filmstrip projector for use with slides and filmstrips. The 35mm. projector and the filmstrip projector can be the same machine with two different attachments. A bulletin board is a useful device for displaying pictures, charts, and graphs. A map rack is a handy device for displaying and storing maps. A picture file is almost a neccesary part of any good elementary school teacher's equipment. The opaque projector is useful for casting upon a screen, pictures, maps, or charts that are either loose or in books.

MULTI-DIMENSIONAL OBJECTS. A very large group of audio-visual aids is composed of the many kinds of multi-dimensional objects that are used as materials of instruction in the elementary school. In the early years in the elementary school, such materials as blocks and toys become multi-dimensional objects from which children learn. Later on such things as globes, models, and real objects are either presented or constructed by children to foster their learning. In all kinds of science and demonstration teaching, specimens, apparatus, and tools become assets to the instructional process.

RECORDS AND RECORDINGS. The phonograph and the tape-recorder are particularly useful devices as auditory aids in teaching. They can be used to good advantage in music and speech activities. The use of the tape-recorder as a device for recording and evaluating discussions among groups in the classroom, is a rather new procedure and one that looks to be very promising.

RADIO AND TELEVISION. Radio has been an auditory device used in schools for many educational purposes. Television combines the advantages of the sound transmission of the radio and the transmission of visual images. We have only begun to explore the possibilities for the use of television in the elementary-school classroom.

Textbook materials

Much has been said, pro and con, about textbooks. The two probable extremes of argument about textbooks are, on the one hand, that they are virtually the sole basis for an educational program in an elementary school, and on the other hand, that textbooks are a restrictive evil to a good elementary school program. When the extreme arguments are reduced to their bare essentials, the argument tends to dissolve into one of proper versus improper use of textbooks. There can be little argument that the textbook is a very potent source of curriculum content. In many elementary schools where the textbooks are, for all practical purposes, the only books that children have at their command, they play a major role in determining the content of the school program. In those schools where there is an abundance of books, the textbook becomes a single reference or perhaps a guiding reference.

Regardless of one's attitude toward textbooks, they must be considered as instructional material. In most elementary schools they are a major instructional material. The supplementary textbook or the supplementary reference book also falls into this category of instructional material. They are aids to learning in the same sense that the motion picture, the specimen, and the record are.

The library

The library is a most valuable instructional material resource, and it is the richest source of instructional material for vicarious experiences for children.

Much depends upon the size of the elementary school and the size of its library, but the library usually contains basic reference materials, periodicals, and books of many categories, including literature, adventure, fiction, biography, and technical areas. The library far exceeds the textbook and the supplemental text materials because it goes far beyond them in scope. The library is a research center for both information and pleasure.

Free and inexpensive materials

A special category must be made for free and inexpensive materials even though they may be of a kind previously mentioned. A special category also is made of them because they are not standardized in any sense, nor are they universally accepted to the same degree that text materials, motion pictures, radio, and so forth are. In fact there is some controversy about many free and inexpensive materials being used in school classrooms.

The controversy about these materials centers around the possibility of propaganda and favoritism toward the businesses or industrial concerns that produce them. The fear of propaganda and favoritism stems from the fact that a large number of the free and inexpensive materials are published by private and industrial concerns. Because they are produced by privately owned organizations they usually are so labeled, by having either advertising information printed thereon or simply the name of the concern supplying the materials. The simple fact is that teachers have some fears of being accused of favoritism by using materials published by one business concern to the exclusion of others, plus the fear that some of the advertising materials might be resented by parents of the children. However, there are a large number of free and inexpensive materials that are highly desirable for instructional purposes, and teachers can enrich their programs by using them.

There are several sources from which these materials can be procured. *The Elementary Teachers Guide to Free and Inexpensive Material* is one of the largest inventories of free curriculum materials that is published for use by elementary school teachers.[4] Another is published by the George Peabody College for Teachers, Division of Surveys and Field Services.[5]

ACQUIRING GOOD MATERIALS

The problem of acquiring good instructional materials is one of the great and perennial problems of teachers. In part, this problem stems from the desire of teachers to find better ways for children to learn effectively and to learn more; and part of the problem stems from a felt need for instructional materials that will assist the teacher in solving problems of individual differences in the classroom. In both cases the motivation is good and highly professional.

The availability of materials in any given elementary school depends upon several factors. Obviously, the wealth of the school community has great influence. The size and composition of the community have influence upon instructional resources available. Another important factor is a willingness on the part

[4] Patricia A. Horkeimer (ed.), *Elementary Teachers Guide to Free and Inexpensive Materials*, 12th Ed. (Randolph, Wisconsin: Educators Progress Service, 1955).
[5] George Peabody College for Teachers, Division of Surveys and Field Services, *Free and Inexpensive Learning Materials*, 7th Ed. (Nashville, Tenn.: The Division, 1956).

of administrative personnel in the school system to exercise their leadership in procuring materials. The resourcefulness of teachers themselves is extremely important. These are but a few of the factors involved in the availability of materials to teachers.

Regardless of the existence or nonexistence of the aforementioned factors, the onus is still upon the individual classroom teacher to locate and use those materials. The following paragraphs will indicate some of the ways in which teachers can work to solve their problems of acquiring good instructional materials.

Working with the community

One way to reduce the problem of acquiring good instructional material is for the teacher to work with the community and within the community in such a way that the community is well-known to the teacher and the teacher is well-known to the community. However, it takes considerable effort on the part of the teacher to bring about this set of circumstances. In the first place, the teacher needs to study the natural resources, objects, and institutions that may have some bearing upon the curriculum of the school. The teacher should get to know community personnel who occupy a variety of positions in the community. It is well for the teacher to know those civic leaders of the community with whom it is possible for him to become acquainted. It is equally well for a teacher to become acquainted with various helpers in the community, such as postmen, storekeepers, policemen, firemen, the sanitary engineer, and many others who could be utilized as resource personnel to help children understand better their community and the way it operates. The teacher should become familiar with problems, issues, and means of dealing with problems and issues in the school community; in other words, how the community works.

It is impossible to outline in detail all the specific ways the individual teacher can accomplish these things, but it is possible to indicate some of the general ways or some of the general procedures that teachers might follow to become better acqainted with their communities. One is to read local publications. Nearly every community publishes a newspaper or a weekly journal of some sort that will indicate current happenings that may have significance upon the school program. The teacher should travel about the community in study, that is, in such a way as to become familiar with the objects, the sources, the institutions, and the industries that are in that community. A teacher may attend and participate in some civic affairs such as council meetings, political meetings, open forums, and general discussions, and thus become acquainted with vital aspects of community living. A teacher should make acquaintances and friends with persons outside the professional group.

If these things are done, the teacher is then equipped with information about the community in such a way that he can do two things. On the one hand, he is in a position to guide children's explorations of their community outside the school. On the other hand, he is in a position to be able to contact people in the community and expect that they will respond as resource persons for the pupils, both within and without the classroom. The important thing to note is that these states of affairs will not come about as if by magic; it takes effort on the part of the teacher.

Working with sources

In addition to working with the resources of the community the teacher must work with other sources of instructional materials. For example, he familiarizes himself with film guides and guides to free and inexpensive materials. The public and school libraries and their contents should be very familiar to the teacher. A teacher should know what textbooks and supplementary references are available and appropriate for his grade and subjects. And certainly the teacher should be familiar with the professional literature on the subject of instructional materials. The problem here is not a matter of knowing the contents of these various sources but, rather, one of knowing where to find instructional materials when they are needed. The accumulation of this knowledge on the part of a teacher is professional knowledge that constantly needs to be reinforced. This is a continuing study on the part of any good teacher who wishes to remain in contact with the availability of instructional materials.

Collecting materials

A good teacher will collect and maintain a file of instructional materials that is his personal property. This collection of materials can begin as soon as an individual decides upon teaching as a career. The student who is taking work in curriculum and method at the undergraduate level should begin to assemble his own personal file of familiar and useful instructional materials. This can be continued for as long as the individual remains in the profession. For example, a picture file is a valuable asset. Almost from the moment one begins teaching, flat pictures are used. They may be used for a bulletin board, as a demonstration device, or as a teaching model. They become a part of a teacher's teaching repertoire. Many teachers accumulate pictures in a well-organized file. They may be prints, paintings, or photographs; they may cover holidays, special events, social groups in action, buildings, animals, and so forth. Pictures may be related to specific subjects like the social studies or to units of work on such topics as the Indians or transportation. However, they should be properly mounted and filed according to some system.

Any teacher, through pre-service and in-service efforts, may construct a number of very good resource units that will be useful in teaching. A good resource unit can be adapted to almost any teaching situation and to almost any group of children on the age level for which the unit was originally planned.

Many student teachers are required to develop units as part of their work. Frequently student teachers have more time and facilities to work up good units than at any other time in their professional lives, and the units they develop are very worthwhile.

Professional magazines and books that have to do with materials, curriculum, and method are important elements in a teacher's collection. Too frequently undergraduate students make the mistake of selling the textbooks they use in pre-service education, and then they spend the rest of their professional lives wishing they had not done so. All kinds of teaching aids are described or implied in such volumes. In addition all types of self-made apparatus, models, recordings, or other kinds of materials that are created out of a teacher's pre-service and in-service experience can be included in the file.

Several precautions need to be stated about a teacher's collection of instructional material. A collection may become too large for a teacher to be able to keep. There may not be storage facilities sufficiently large either in the school or in the teacher's home to house a collection if it becomes overly bulky. A second danger is that the collection may contain items that are obsolete and hence useless. To offset this a teacher should periodically screen his materials file for obsolete materials. A good rule of thumb is to clean out materials that have not been used in two years. Two years may not make material obsolete, but just plain bulk makes such action necessary in a teacher's personal file. In the third place, there is some danger that once a file has been accumulated, a teacher may be motivated to continue to use such elements as pictures and resource units regardless of whether they directly fit the current teaching situation. This is what we sometimes call getting in a teaching rut. These precautions are good to observe, but they should not prevent an individual from assembling his own collection. A bit of intelligent caution coupled with a generous portion of creative intelligence will cause the materials file to become one of the most valuable teaching resources.

Working with other teachers

The teacher who seriously wishes to reduce the problem of acquiring good instructional materials will capitalize upon the knowledge and experience of other teachers. Other teachers may have material files of their own that are different, depending upon each teacher's experience and training. These can be shared for the mutual profit of all concerned. Others have varying interests and backgrounds, and because of these they are resource people that can be called upon for assistance. For example, one teacher may be very interested in rocks and minerals. That person may have a good deal of information and collections that could be used in the classroom. Another may be particularly interested in architecture and be similarly armed with instructional materials appropriate to the subject. Numerous other illustrations of this type could be given, but the point is that each teacher bears some special interest and knowledge that, when shared with others, tends to enrich the whole instructional program. In this connection it should be noted that no single teacher can solve the problems of instructional materials for an entire school. Furthermore, instructional material problems are not those of only one teacher. They belong to the entire staff. Therefore, it behooves the entire staff to pool its thinking and its resources to reduce its problems.

Working with supervisors and administrators

Just as a teacher must work with other teachers in regard to instructional materials, he must also work with his supervisors and administrators. Usually the administrator controls the expenditure of funds for instructional materials; therefore, he is an important person to be taken into account in acquiring materials. Because of his position the administrator must be responsible for the realistic expenditure of those funds. The supervisor or coordinator is responsible for the caliber of instruction. This individual, therefore, must be consulted and used as a resource in acquiring and using materials. In many cases where there are no supervisors or coordinators, the administrator also assumes these responsibilities. In the case of the elementary school, the principal often fulfills both of these responsibilities. The modern elementary school principal is responsible for the fiscal aspects of his school, such as the purchase of materials and the storing and maintenance of them, and he is the person who is primarily concerned with the improvement of instruction in that school. He thus becomes a person who is concerned with virtually all problems having to do with instructional materials. Administrators and supervisory personnel are also resource people because of their knowledge and experience. Frequently these people have been selected for these positions because of the breadth of their knowledge and experience in elementary education. The good teacher will respect this and use these persons as important resources.

Although we frequently emphasize the importance of administrative and supervisory personnel making decisions about such things as the procurement and use of instructional materials, it should be stated emphatically that not all leadership with respect to this procurement or use should come from persons in these positions. Classroom teachers have a personal and professional responsibility to study the probems of instructional materials and make recommendations to supervisory and administrative personnel. The classroom teachers themselves are the ones who are going to be most affected by whatever materials are procured; therefore, they need to assume responsibility for participating in decisions about them.

Working with resource centers

A good teacher works with resource centers whenever and wherever they are available. At one time resource centers were thought of mostly as depositories for materials. In recent times we have come to think of the resource center as a place for professional laboratory growth. The concept of a resource center is also larger than that of a materials bureau or an audio-visual laboratory. For example, Bristow and Simon, in the most recent *Review of Educational Research* on the subject of resource centers, discusses the curriculum laboratory, the museum, the audio-visual laboratory, and the library as resource centers.[6] Each of these centers has a particular type of contribution to make to the needs of teachers for instructional materials.

The existence of various resource centers has rather obvious implications for action on the part of teachers in satisfying their needs for instructional materials. One such implication is that the teacher should become familiar with the contents of the resource center in order to know the resources contained therein for the educational program in his classroom. This kind of study should be profitable in discovering new ideas for the instructional program. A teacher should foster the use of material centers by pupils to the greatest possible degree. Teaching children to use resource centers is one aspect of helping them to learn to use research procedures in the solution of their problems. Certainly where the resource centers have trained personnel in charge, these personnel can be helpful to both teachers and pupils. The spirit of such use of resource centers is well put by Bristow and Simon when they state:

> Various types of resource centers were originally thought of more as repositories of materials than as workshops and places of learning. Resource centers were also more concerned with materials for pupils than for teachers. The workshop movement has highlighted the importance of teachers using the resources of museums, libraries, and curriculum and audio-visual laboratories. Today, resource centers serve both pupils and teachers.[7]

[6] William H. Bristow and Leonard Simon, "Resource Centers," *Review of Educational Research*, 26: 184-196 (April, 1956).
[7] *Ibid*, p. 193.

INTELLIGENT USE OF MATERIALS

The location and acquistion of instructional materials is only one phase of the total problem for teachers. Intelligent use must be made of them once they are located and acquired. In this connection several general rules are helpful for teachers.

It is generally accepted that direct, contactual types of experience are preferred over vicarious experience for learning on the part of elementary school children. This is true for several reasons. The younger children in the elementary school have not had enough education in the use of the skills of communication and expression to explore their environment satisfactorily. Contactual experience gives the learner enough opportunity to relate firsthand the knowledge being acquired in school with his world outside of school. Furthermore, the implications of what he learns for use both within and without the school are more apparent. It is true that in practice direct, contactual types of experience are provided for children more frequently in the early elementary school years than in the later years. Part of this is attributable to the things mentioned above, and in part it is attributable to the nature and scope of the subject matter that the children study in the early elementary school years. Children in the early years usually are studying those aspects of their environment nearest to them. Because of this, it is more feasible to take children into the community to study community relationships firsthand. On the other hand, in the upper grades where they may be studying our national community, the opportunities for direct exploration of the national community are limited for obvious reasons. However, even at the upper level, teachers should search for more opportunities for direct, contactual types of experience than are usually offered. For example, let us use the illustration of an upper-grade group studying our national community; it is possible that a community may contain federal offices that are responsible for the administration of federal services in that area. This gives a teacher in such a community an opportunity to capitalize on direct, contactual experience, that is denied to those teachers and pupils who live in communities where such facilities are not available. The acceptance of this generalization should not mean to a teacher that effort should be made to reduce drastically or eliminate vicarious experiences for children in the elementary school. Much to the contrary. Direct experience and vicarious experience throughout the elementary school years need to supplement one another.

Some instructional materials substitute for direct experience. In many circumstances where direct types of experience are either impossible or unfeasible, some types of instructional materials can be substituted for the direct experience. For example, our books for elementary school children are full of illustrations that are placed there not only for eye appeal but also to give the reader a visual image of the environment under discussion to supplement the printed word. We can use maps and pictures to establish geographical relationships and to indicate the character of removed environments. The motion picture is particularly good as a substitute for direct experience, because it gives the viewer a sense of motion and a sense of identification with the motion, the objects, and people being viewed. Such substitutes for direct experience are most useful when children are studying peoples of other lands.

Many instructional materials have motivational value. Too frequently teachers overlook the motivational value of instructional materials. Many readers will have had the experience of walking into elementary school classrooms where boys and girls were arranged in seats in neat rows parallel with the windows. The teacher was deposited at the desk facing the children in the center of the front of the room. The walls were bare with the possible exception of pictures of George Washington and Abraham Lincoln. On the blackboard at the front of the room and in terse statements was written in the teacher's handwriting the assignments in the workbooks the children were doing. In all probability the teacher of that classroom either did not know, or chose to ignore, the motivational value of instructional materials.

One can contrast this illustration with a glimpse at another classroom. The children in this classroom are arranged in groups, thanks to moveable furniture. On the bulletin board near the door of the classroom is a group of pictures and clippings placed there by both the teacher and the pupils. It shows a center of interest about recent developments in guided missiles and their implications for world affairs. On the one side of the room is a mural picturing the children's interpretation of problems in world communication. In one corner of the classroom is a reading corner where some children are assembled reading materials of their own choice. The teacher moves among the groups offering her counsel and help where wanted and needed. Down the hall in a projection room a group of children from this classroom are previewing a motion picture to determine its usefulness for the class as a whole. The differences in attitude of the second teacher over the first toward the use of instructional materials both as motivational devices and as instructional aids are obvious. Teachers should never forget that a new "lesson" suddenly sprung upon children is apt to be a shock to them, and it may be expected that their reaction will be negative. The preparation for a new "lesson" through careful arrangement of bulletin board materials, pictures about the room, selection of books in the reading corner, or a well-reviewed motion picture can set the stage for acceptance of the new area of study on the part of boys and girls. Certainly, it can help them to become personally involved or identified with the subject, and this process results in self-motivation.

Instructional materials can be used for demonstrating purposes. The use of instructional materials for demonstration purposes is an old stock-in-trade of school teachers. A piece of wood or a piece of cardboard shaped like a pie and then cut into quarters, sixths, or eighths can be used to demonstrate the meaning and manipulation of fractions. Scientific apparatus has been used for demonstration purposes in science and should so be continued. The scale model in social studies is a useful instructional device. Of course all other forms of visual aid such as pictures, maps, and graphs can likewise be used.

Children should use instructional materials to explore ideas and gain insights. Entirely too frequently we think that the only person who should be concerned with the use of instructional materials is the teacher. Much to the contrary, children as well as teachers should use instructional materials for learning purposes. They can use books to explore and test ideas and gain new ones. The experimental apparatus can be used by children to gain insights they could not otherwise acquire. The field trip is useful for them to explore relationships. The actual construction of models and other devices such as charts, maps, and pictures is a highly educative activity. The use of appropriate instructional materials in general is an educational activity; therefore, children should be allowed to use them to the maximum degree. But it is most important to realize that they can initiate the use of them if teachers will only encourage them to do so. Pictures, objects, and books can be brought from homes. This is one way a teacher can tap the resources of a community. Although children should be encouraged to acquire and use instructional materials within and without school, they must be taught how to acquire them and then how to use them properly.

Teachers should screen instructional materials before using them with children. The most obvious application of this generalization lies in careful selection of textbooks and reference materials. These must be selected in terms of such considerations as their effectiveness for carrying out the school's curriculum, the up-to-dateness of the materials, the care with which the materials are organized, and their appropriateness for children of the ages for which they are intended. Another application is the act of previewing any films before they are shown to the children. This is a law that should never be violated. Any motion picture should be previewed by the teacher or someone whose judgment the teacher respects so that the teacher is assured of the appropriateness of the film for both the children and the subject to be taught. Of course all commercially prepared, free and inexpensive materials should be screened for unusual bias and for accuracy of content. This generalization is not offered solely for the purpose of protecting children from some of the practicalities of life, but rather to insure that the teaching-learning time is more efficiently used.

Instructional materials are a means of program enrichment. They can bring variety. They can be used to increase the range of efforts of children, and thus they help with the problem of individual differences. One of the great values of a good library, of art materials, of experimental apparatus, and so forth is that they allow children of different abilities and with different rates of educational growth to proceed in varying directions.

The effectiveness of the use of instructional materials should be evaluated. Whenever instructional materials are used, the obvious expectancy is that children will learn as a result of those efforts. If the activity is worthy of being launched in the first place, then it must be evaluated in terms of changes in behavior in children. With specific reference to the instructional materials, one question that needs to be answered is whether the materials did what they were intended to do. Another question is the problem of the reaction of the children to those materials. More will be said concerning specific techniques for carrying out some of these evaluation activities in the chapter on evaluation. The point to be emphasized here is that if a device is worthy of being used in the classroom, then its effectiveness must be evaluated.

Summary

The selection of instructional materials as a dimension of teaching has been indicated to have at least three purposes. One of these purposes is to provide a variety of experiences for children in schools. A second is to motivate children to impel themselves into worthwhile activity. And a third is to substitute instructional materials for direct, contactual types of experience where the latter are impossible or unfeasible.

The range of instructional materials for teaching is very broad. It runs from simple objects to complicated human beings, from free and inexpensive materials to costly equipment, from simple to complex materials as from pictures to books. The range encompasses resource people, resource institutions, tools, pictorial objects of all kinds, real objects, and books. The opportunities for selection are very great.

Problems of acquiring instructional materials center around three considerations. The community may be limited in wealth and resource persons and institutions. This would limit the opportunities for selection of materials. The degree of resourcefulness of teachers and administrators is a second possible problem in this task of teaching. A third is the degree of willingness of the individual teacher to work at the task.

Instructional materials should be selected and used so as to fulfill the needs or purposes for them. Haphazard use may do more harm than good; at least such use is apt to be non-productive educationally. They should be selected with care in order to get the maximum benefit from their use. Instructional materials should be used in varied ways both in the selection of different materials and in using the same materials differently. Finally, the use of instructional materials should be evaluated so that techniques and procedures in selection and use can be improved.

Ideas for discussion and activity

1. Prepare for your personal file a list of sources for instructional materials. The suggested readings will be helpful to you.

2. What are some good visual materials you have seen or read for teaching arithmetic? Are they primarily useful for developing understanding or for providing motivation?

3. The statement has been made: "I can tell how good a teacher is by just looking around her classroom." Analyze this statement.

4. Plan a display you might use in initiating a new unit (of your choice) to children.

5. Why is the motion picture considered to be a superior audio-visual aid to other forms like flat pictures, slides, and so forth?

6. What do you see to be the coming role of television in the elementary school?

Suggested readings

Dale, Edgar, *Audio-Visual Methods in Teaching*. Revised edition. New York: The Dryden Press, 1956.
This book is a revised edition of one of the first and best of its kind. The entire volume is devoted to the use of instructional materials. It contains many verbal and pictorial illustrations.

Department of Elementary School Principals, National Education Association, *Instructional Materials for Elementary Schools*. Thirty-fifth Yearbook. Washington, D. C.: The Department, 1956.
This yearbook contains many reports of firsthand experiences in the use of instructional materials. One can read any or all of the various sections. At least look at this one.

Estvan, Frank J., chairman, "Instructional Materials," *Review of Educational Research*, 26:111-197; April, 1956.
This is the first issue of the Review devoted entirely to instructional materials. Its coverage is thorough, and the bibliographies are most helpful.

National Citizens Commission for the Public Schools, *How Good Are Our Teaching Materials? A Guide to Understanding and Improvement*. Working Guide No. 8. New York: National Citizens Council for Better Schools, 1956.
This pamphlet was designed to help lay citizens understand instructional materials used in classrooms. Teachers should be familiar with it.

Wendt, Paul R., *Audio-Visual Instruction*. What Research Says to the Teacher Series, No. 14. Department of Classroom Teachers and the American Educational Research Association, National Education Association. Washington, D.C.: The Association, 1957.
Here is an interpretation of the findings of research in audio-visual instruction for the classroom teacher. The intent and the language of this entire series is focused upon teaching functions.

CHAPTER 9

Planning for Teaching

In many respects planning prior to teaching is as important, if not more important, for teaching success than the conduct of the teacher in the classroom. Planning is stressed in all educational literature. In some cases the teacher is expected to plan within the confines of an accepted curriculum, and in other situations he is expected to plan without reference to any preplanned structure. In the latter case many teachers are lost because of lack of direction. This is especially true in the case of beginning teachers. We need more guidance for teachers and prospective teachers in keeping the role of teacher planning in proper perspective. Naturally, the purpose of this chapter is to help readers formulate more clearly their thinking about the place of planning as an important dimension of method for teaching in the elementary school. In order to accomplish this purpose it will be necessary to discuss the various possible departure points for teachers' planning, variations in lesson planning, the organization of the daily program, the relationship between long- and short-range planning, the maintenance of planning records, and finally, the purposes and techniques of teacher-pupil planning.

DEPARTURE POINTS FOR PLANNING

In order for a teacher to do realistic planning for teaching, it is almost mandatory that an anchor point, a reference point, or a point of departure for planning be established. Although planning for teaching is but one dimension of teaching method, we can better see the logic of having a departure point for planning by reference to the total educational activity as discussed in Chapter 1. It will be recalled that there were indicated three levels of the complete educational activity. The first of these was the curriculum-planning level. This level established the objectives of the school program, the curriculum content, the organization of the content, and an evaluative schema. The second level, or the teaching-learning level, involved the planning and execution of classroom activity. The matter of planning for teaching is one aspect, then, of the teaching-learning level. However, the reference point or the departure point for planning must obviously be located at the curriculum level.

Now, it could be argued that the act of a teacher participating in curriculum planning at the curriculum-planning level could be interpreted as planning for teaching. No doubt this is true. The activity presently under discussion, however, takes place subsequent to the curriculum-planning level, but it is dependent upon the type of curriculum planning that has been accomplished at the curriculum-planning level. The teacher has several kinds of choices. In fact these choices are almost dictated by the kind of curriculum planning that has been done. The most obvious departure points for planning that we can discuss are the curriculum, an accumulation of resource materials, the emerging situation, and an adopted series of textbooks.

The curriculum

A curriculum as defined and described earlier is the best point of departure for planning for teaching. The very existence of planned curriculum indicates that the persons concerned with that elementary school have thought highly enough of the institution and of their professional task to consider seriously its entire educational operation and to create a design for that operation. When such cooperative care has been exercised over such a dynamic function as education, an individual teacher within that framework derives security and encouragement to do the best job of planning that he can do in order to make that design function most effectively. Furthermore, if teachers themselves have cooperatively participated in the creation of the curriculum, they have contributed toward making the curriculum a good point of departure for planning for teaching.

In general, planning for teaching involves at least three basic steps. The first of these is to establish objectives for the activity. The second is to indicate the subject matter of the activity and to select procedures to be utilized. The third is to evaluate what has been done in terms of the objectives established. Obviously the curriculum is a choice point of departure for actual planning because the general objectives are indicated from which specific objectives can be planned. Suggested over-all content is indicated from which content and activity can be selected, and finally, an evaluative schema is indicated which will give cues for evaluation procedures to be planned.

Resource materials

Another departure point for specific planning for teaching may be that from compiled resource materials. It is possible for these resource materials to be created in many forms. Some of them were mentioned in Chapter 7 where the experience approach to the organization of curriculum materials was discussed. The most common of these, of course, is the resource unit. In some schools it has been the practice for teachers, individually and collectively, to prepare an accumulation of resource units rather than to prepare a curriculum as it has herein been defined. Usually when these resource units are created, they are prepared with a specific grade, or grades, in mind and in one sense of the word this can be called curriculum planning.

When such materials have been organized, these become the

basic frame of reference for a teacher who is planning for teaching. These then must be adapted by a teacher to a specific group of children through the planning activities. The same problems of organization for teaching are here as in the case of the curriculum itself as a point of departure.

Emerging situations

In those situations where a school staff has accepted the philosophy of the emergent curriculum, the point of departure for planning is more difficult to identify and pin-point. If the curriculum is to emerge from the day-to-day activities of the children in the classroom, the act of planning prior to teaching is difficult to conceive. Theoretically, anyway, planning prior to teaching should be denied if one believes completely in the emergent curriculum.

This does not mean that no planning takes place. In fact a great deal of teacher-pupil planning takes place within the classroom. The emerging situation becomes a springboard for planning, but it is not planning for teaching on the part of the teacher. Rather, it is a matter of actual teacher-pupil planning immediately followed by the involvement of the children in activity resulting from that planning. All the teacher can do prior to the actual classroom situation is to plan for the planning.

Adopted series of textbooks

A very common departure point for planning is an adopted series of textbooks. There are many elementary schools in the country that do not have a planned curriculum nor an accumulation of resource units. Nearly all elementary schools, however, adopt textbooks in the various subjects. In these elementary schools the curriculum is dictated by the contents of the various textbooks.

Where this is true, the logical point of departure for planning for teaching is the textbook itself. In some situations where this set of circumstances holds, teachers will do a good deal of planning for their teaching. In other cases, teachers will do little planning and expect the textbook to do the teaching for them. Actually this divergence in practice is at the root of most of the argument about textbooks mentioned in Chapter 8. Teachers who take time to use the textbook as a point of departure for planning for teaching, tend to use the textbook in the most intelligent manner. On the other hand, those who use the textbook simply as a vehicle for making assignments and subsequently checking upon children's work, are at least in part responsible for many of the derogatory comments levied against textbooks. Only when teachers plan from them, can the materials from a textbook be adapted and modified to satisfy the differences among pupils in the classroom. This is why it is important to consider the textbook as a departure point of planning; thus used, the textbook is really a resource for learning.

All of the foregoing departure points are possibilities for teachers to use in their planning for teaching. Perhaps it should be said this way: these are the most likely possibilities for departure points for planning that a new teacher will be able to identify when he goes into a school system.

THE LESSON PLAN

The lesson plan is a result of the efforts of a teacher in pre-teaching planning. Although some teachers are able to carry their planning in their heads, the majority of those who do plan create a written plan. As in many things, there are different levels of lesson planning. These different levels are characterized mostly by the thoroughness of the plan. It is safe to say that the most thorough job of preparing lesson plans is done at the student-teaching level. Because of their inexperience and because of the supervision of their work, student teachers are forced to be careful and thorough in planning for their teaching. In most cases they never again have to plan so thoroughly. Great variations in planning are practiced by in-service teachers. Generally, too little planning for teaching is done because most elementary school teachers are in charge of children during the school day, and the time element inhibits planning to a certain extent. It is possible to identify at least three levels of lesson planning.

A list of assignments

Next to no plan at all, probably the lowest level of lesson plan is the simple list of assignments. Here the point of departure for planning is nearly always the textbook. The list of assignments will indicate the name of the subject and the pages or exercises that have been assigned, in the order in which they occur in the school day. For example, the first subject of the day may be arithmetic, and the first fifteen examples on page 176 are assigned. The second subject of the day might be language arts and the assignment might be for the children to write a story about how they spent their weekend, and so forth throughout the school day. This kind of planning gives the appearance of being very routine and, unless it is supported by some other kind of planning, cannot be considered effective for good learning. Burton criticizes this level of planning for teaching as follows:

> Despite fifty years of attack by competent critics armed with unlimited, valid evidence, there persists the wholly unexplained assignment aimed only at "covering the text." *It would be difficult to devise an educational practice so grossly ineffective, so certainly calculated to interfere with learning, as a page assignment to a single text followed by a formal verbal quiz.*[1]

The statement by Burton is especially pertinent to the type of planning that tries only to cover the text. If effective learning

[1] William H. Burton, "Implications for Organization of Instruction and Instructional Adjuncts," *Learning and Instruction*, Forty-ninth Yearbook, Part I, National Society for the Study of Education (Chicago: The University of Chicago Press, 1950), p. 227.

is to take place, something other than the lists of assignments must be the guide for teaching.

The general lesson plan

The usual mode of recording a plan for teaching has been called the lesson plan. The format of the lesson plan has varied from place to place in the history of teaching. All of them, however, have certain common characteristics. One of these is that a particular area of work is identified. Second, some tentative objectives are indicated. Third, some notations are made of the teacher's ideas for ways and means of getting the children involved in the work to be done. Fourth, a list is made of possible activities for the children to perform. Fifth, a list of materials of instruction is compiled; and sixth, some techniques and procedures for evaluating the area of work are indicated.

Of course there are variations within this general framework. Much depends upon the magnitude of the area of work to be undertaken with children. If, for example, a teacher is launching a study of early colonial life, that area of study could not be accomplished in a single day. Therefore, the over-all plan as indicated in the paragraph above would become an all-inclusive plan. Then the teacher would be placed in the position of needing daily planning in order to insure forward movement and continuity to the total project. In this case a day's work may be devoted only to the establishment of objectives, for example, and perhaps the selection of activities. Another day might be directed toward organizing children into groups to do the work involved. In those cases the daily plan of the teacher would be directed toward those aspects of the total area of work.

It should be cautioned that whenever an over-all plan is made, and then specific plans are made for daily operation, the teacher's responsibility for planning for the daily operations is equally important with the over-all plan, because carelessness at the operational level can defeat the best of over-all plans.

Occasionally, there are short lessons to be taught that are accomplished within a single day. In those cases all of the features are thoroughly planned. Objectives should be stated, activities planned, and evaluation procedures indicated. The total act of planning for teaching is not complete unless these considerations are weighed.

A few specific suggestions for the new or beginning teacher about the development of a lesson plan might be helpful. One of the most critical points in teaching is that point at which a teacher attempts to involve the children in the area of work. It may sound superfluous to suggest that a teacher actually write down leading questions or topics to discuss with pupils as a means of involving them in the discussion; but for many teachers this technique has been extremely helpful in their actual work with children. Until one has had a good deal of teaching experience, he may not be sensitive enough to the types of questions to be asked to keep a plan moving along. However, when these things are thought out ahead of time, the teacher has the security of knowing the direction in which he is going. Obviously a danger in this is that the teacher may not be sufficiently flexible to modify his discussion when things do not go as they were originally planned. To be able to change horses in the middle of the stream, so to speak, is a technique that one usually learns through experience. Occasionally it is desirable for a teacher to try to anticipate the reactions of the children to suggestions and questions. In these cases alternatives should be considered so that a teacher can say to himself, "If this does not work I will then do this."

One of the better ways to involve children in a learning activity is through the kinds of materials that are in the classroom. Reference here is to the kinds of suggestions that were made concerning motivational devices, such as a carefully displayed group of books and pictures that can be referred to in the discussion, or that may be expected to stimulate questions and interest on the part of children. The physiology of the environment can be a very important way of getting children involved in learning activities. A third suggestion is to think of many possible activities so that all children can find worthwhile projects or activities. This not only works in the direction of helping the children find activities, but it also works in the reverse direction so that a teacher is not surprised or dismayed at some of the suggestions that children may make for activity. The two important action questions that a teacher should constantly ask himself in planning are: (1) "What am I going to do?" and (2) "What am I going to ask the children to do?"

The teaching unit

The most popular form of teaching plan in modern elementary education is the teaching unit. We ordinarily think of the teaching unit as a means of organizing a series of studies or activities around some central theme or problem. In the thinking of the reader there may be some confusion between the teaching unit and what was referred to in Chapter 7 as the resource unit. The similarities between the two types of units are great. In fact, the elements are for all practical purposes the same, but the teaching unit is organized for a specific group of persons, with specific objectives to be achieved, and specific activities organized to achieve those objectives. On the other hand, the resource unit contains objectives and activities for groups of children in general.

The outline of the essential elements of a unit as organized by Adams and presented in Chapter 7 is as good as any. However, it will help the reader to understand more clearly interpretations of teaching units if reference is made to suggestions of others for unit organization. For example, Burton indicates the following for developing teaching units:

1. Objectives are stated.
2. An overview is given.

3. An approach is developed.
4. The working period is outlined.
5. Evaluation techniques are planned.
6. Adequate instructional equipment will be noted and its specific use within the unit indicated.[2]

Another group of authors list the following features for both a resource unit and a teaching unit and indicate that the teaching unit should contain the same features as a resource unit, except that it is particularly adapted as previously indicated:

1. Title and topic.
2. An introductory statement.
3. A statement of proposed objectives.
4. A content guide.
5. Suggested pupils' activities.
6. List of teaching aids.
7. Suggested evaluation procedures.[3]

In discussing the planning of the experience unit, Macomber indicates the following problems in pre-planning, and these problems form the basis for the unit:

1. Deciding upon aims.
2. Worthwhile learning experiences.
3. Obtaining adequate instructional materials.
4. Thinking of ways in which the unit might be developed.
5. Evaluating.[4]

In actual practice the teaching unit has been constructed by using an organized curriculum guide, courses of study, textbooks, and resource materials as points of departure. Because of the use of various departure points in unit construction, the unit idea has been associated with many forms of organization. In this sense the teaching unit is very flexible. The important

---

[2] Burton, *Op. cit.*, p. 242.

[3] Herbert J. Klausmeier, Katharine Dresden, Helen C. Davis, and Walter Arno Wittich, *Teaching in the Elementary School* (New York: Harper and Brothers, 1956), pp. 135-136.

[4] F. G. Macomber, *Principles of Teaching in the Elementary School* (New York: American Book Company, 1954), pp. 123-124.

consideration, and the thing that makes the teaching unit such a desirable method of organization for teaching, is its insistence that objectives be indicated, activities be selected, materials be planned for, and activities be evaluated in terms of the sought objectives. In this sense the teaching unit provides for a complete cycle in teaching activity, and this cycle is psychologically and educationally good.

Long- and short-range planning

All teachers must expect to do both long- and short-term planning. There are really two factors that indicate a distinction between long- and short-range planning. One of them is the interval of time to be covered by the area of study, and the other is the immediacy of action to be taken subsequent to the planning. With regard to the matter of time intervals, a teacher needs to think of the year as one interval for which planning is made. Another interval is a block of time encompassing days, weeks, or even months, which is dictated by the magnitude of the unit of work to be undertaken. A third interval is the school day and a fourth possible interval for planning is a period within a school day.

Long-range planning is usually characterized by the over-all plan for adapting the curriculum materials to a specific group of children. For example, Kyte indicates that the first two steps in initial planning by a teacher at the start of either a new school year or a new unit in the classroom, are to consult curriculum materials or courses of study in order to determine what the general range and framework of activities are to be, and secondly, to study all available data regarding the pupils to be taught, so that the teacher has a basis for making judgments about the adaptation of curriculum materials.[5] Kyte then states:

The third step in the teacher's initial planning is the development

[5] George C. Kyte, *The Elementary School Teacher at Work* (New York: The Dryden Press, Inc., 1957), pp. 410-412.

of an instructional program based upon the information obtained from the first two steps. This step is a complex one, taking into account six items: (1) the specific educational needs of the class and individual pupils, (2) the school time available for meeting these needs, (3) the learning activities that will provide the essential experiences, (4) the instructional aids necessary for implementing the program, (5) the preparation of the instructional environment, and (6) the procedure for cooperative planning with pupils. These six points must be considered separately first and then together in order that the tentative plan may take comprehensive form.[6]

Short-range planning, on the other hand, is characterized more by planning for specific functions within a day or two, or even within a portion of a day. In this case a teacher needs to plan for her own actions, the anticipated actions of children, and the interaction of teacher and the children. To illustrate, Wingo and Schorling indicate the following as being important parts of a good teaching plan:

1. Purpose of the work to be undertaken that day. State precisely as possible what your aims are. It is also a good idea to state the aims of the work as the pupils will see them.
2. Specific activities to be carried on.
3. Time budget. State the approximate time you expect to devote to each activity.
4. Materials needed for the work. This includes books, illustrations, other audio-visual materials, art and craft materials, or anything else you plan to use.
5. Plans for discussion with the class. Include a few good questions you may wish to use to get the discussion under way and keep it going.
6. Directions for work. Make them clear and specific.
7. Plans for evaluation and discussion of future activities which, of course, will involve the members of the class.[7]

Thus it can be noted that a great deal of common thinking goes into both long-range and short-range planning. The principal difference seems to lie in the specificity of the plan for immediate and impending action. There is one thing that has

[6] *Ibid.*, p. 412.
[7] G. Max Wingo and Raleigh Schorling, *Elementary School Student Teaching*, 2nd Ed. (McGraw-Hill Book Company, Inc., 1955), p. 193.

not as yet been mentioned that a teacher should expect. This is that short-range plans have a tendency to disrupt or to modify long-range plans. Because of this somewhat disruptive tendency of short-range planning, it becomes important for a teacher constantly to keep the long-range plan in mind as the school year unfolds.

TEACHER-PUPIL PLANNING

So far we have been considering almost exclusively the planning to be done by a classroom teacher prior to the assembly of pupils in the classroom with him. This kind of planning is the teacher's anticipation of the program to be worked out for the boys and girls, but it will be recalled that part of this pre-planning should contain ideas for teacher-pupil planning to take place when teacher and pupils are assembled together.

Its purposes

There are at least three concrete purposes for utilizing the process known as teacher-pupil planning. The first of these is that teacher-pupil planning is a matter of fulfillment of the democratic right of pupils to participate in making decisions that affect them. Certainly the activities to be performed in the classroom affect the lives of children. Certainly they should be considered to be citizens of our democratic society. Logically then they should participate in making decisions that affect them.

A second purpose of teaching-pupil planning is that the process is motivational because it serves to help children become identified psychologically with the classroom activities. Through the planning activity children contribute their ideas. They have opportunities to make choices. They have opportunities to react to the ideas and feelings of others. All of these things tend to create an intimate association between the pupil's self and the activities of the classroom. When these things happen, we are about as close to real, intrinsic motivation as we can come.

A third purpose for teacher-pupil planning is that planning itself is an educational process. In the process, one's ideas are submitted to others for criticism, acceptance, rejection, or modification. An individual has the opportunity to do the same for the ideas of fellow classmates. In the process one learns from the ideas of others, and he learns more about how to work with people, how to think with people, and how to plan with people. In our society we consider these skills important.

Planning activities

There are a number of planning activities and techniques that may be used in the process of teacher-pupil planning. Many of the activities are similar to the activities that the teacher went through alone in pre-planning, but in this case they become group activities and lead to a group result. Probably the first thing that must take place is some kind of discussion of the plans of the teacher and the relationship of those plans to the point of departure, whether it be the curriculum, the resource materials, or another. This can be done by group discussion with the teacher, followed by small group discussion by pupils or an informal discussion between the whole group of pupils and the teacher.

The discussion of the teacher's plans should point toward an acceptance or a choice of an area of study. This may be the actual topic originally suggested by the teacher or some modification of it acceptable both to the teacher and to the pupils.

Once the topic or area of study has been selected, the group can begin to find their reasons for choosing this particular area of study and what they expect to get out of it. These we call their objectives. They may be simple or complex depending upon the age level of the children doing the planning, and the topic selected. For example, if the first grade is planning a trip to the fire department, their objectives will be few, and to the adult at least, very simple. On the other hand, if a sixth- or seventh-grade group is planning to visit the city hall for the purpose of studying the various facets of the organization of the city government, the list of objectives can be quite long and complex.

The next activity is a matter of choosing the specific activities that the pupils will perform. Through discussion these must be related to the objectives in order to insure that adequate activities have been selected to fulfill the sought objectives. Activities may include such things as excursions, the bringing in of resource people, the use of audio-visual equipment, readings, reports both oral and written, and any dramatic or culminating activity. It is worthwhile to spend sufficient time in the planning session to choose carefully the things that children are going to do. This is the point at which the individual pupil can become most intimately involved in the project. This is especially true if he feels strongly about one of the activities to be performed. One of the precautions in this connection is that an eager child should not constantly choose the same kind of activity and thus slight the rounding-out of his education.

Afterward the group must organize itself to do the work. It is possible that some of the activities can be done individually. Others can be done more appropriately in groups or committees. Ways and means must be established for intercommunication among individuals and among groups. In this process there is opportunity for a great deal of pupil leadership if committee or group work is practiced. Throughout the school year the teacher should try to encourage the flow of leadership within the total pupil group, and try to avoid the situations where individuals with the strongest leadership potential always end up as the leaders.

Just as the final step in unit planning is planning for evaluation, a final aspect of teacher-pupil planning is planning for evaluation of the work that has been done. It frequently is recommended that evaluation be done periodically and frequently during the pursuit of a unit, particularly if the unit involves several days of time. Some teachers like to conclude the day with an evaluation of the kind of day it has been and the progress that has been made. Very frequently a unit of work gets bogged down, and the children do not seem to be able to make much headway. This should be a cue to the teacher that an evaluation session is needed.

In all of these activities the principal technique for planning is discussion. Discussion can be between the teacher and the entire classroom group, or it can be among smaller groups within the classroom. When the latter is the case, some means of communicating the results of those discussions with the whole group needs to be established. As a group formulates its plans through the discussion technique, it is wise to have a recorder make a record of the plans so that all can see it, either on a blackboard or chart. Furthermore, the recorder should keep a record of a more permanent nature on paper, of the plans made by the group.

The reader is undoubtedly familiar with the old saying that one can lead a horse to water, but he cannot make him drink. The same is true about the relationships between a teacher and pupils in reference to teacher-pupil planning. We can set the stage and invite pupils to plan with us, but there is no known means of making them plan with us. It is, therefore, necessary that the teacher have a flexible attitude about his own pre-planning and a willingness to try new ideas with children, whether his own have been enthusiastically received by children or not. In this connection it is a good idea for teachers to have alternatives from which children can choose. It is generally agreed that children should participate in planning for their activities in school, but not all planning needs to involve original selection by pupils. This has been made clear through the discussion on curriculum planning and pre-planning by the teacher.

The question for the new teacher of when and how much teacher-pupil planning should be practiced or encouraged frequently arises. One group of authors has indicated that at least four considerations should be taken into account when thinking about the degree to which pupils should share in planning their program. One of these has to do with the maturity level of the pupils. Another is a question of how much past experience the pupils have had in planning. A third consideration is what has gone on previously in that particular school with reference to teacher-pupil planning. The fourth consideration is the degree of conviction of the teacher himself about the desirability and need for pupil involvement in planning.[8] These are important considerations. A teacher needs to be enthusiastic about teacher-pupil planning in order to be successful with it. It takes time for pupils themselves to learn how to participate. The total school environment should be sympathetic.

ARRANGING THE SCHOOL DAY

An integral part of planning is the arrangement of a day's activities. This process is commonly called the construction of the daily program. There are certain physical and administrative reasons why the daily program must be arranged, and there are educational reasons for such planning.

Scheduling facilities

In spite of the fact that most elementary schools operate on a self-contained classroom basis, there are a number of reasons why each room cannot operate completely independent of the remainder of the school. It is extremely difficult to find an elementary school in which no personnel or facilities need to be shared by various teachers and classrooms. Many elementary schools are departmentalized for activities such as music, art, and physical education. Where this is the case, facilities for music, art, and physical education need to be shared, particularly in those schools where there is a music room, an art studio, and a gymnasium. In those places where music and art are taught in

---

[8] Wilbur A. Yauch, Martin H. Bartels, and Emmet Morris, *The Beginning Teacher* (New York: Henry Holt and Company, 1955), pp. 181-182.

the individual classroom by special teachers, there is the problem of sharing the special teacher's time.

There are certain other facilities that must be shared if they are a part of the elementary school building. One of these is the library; another is the auditorium. Other possibilities are the lunchroom, the cafeteria, the projection room, the playground, and so forth. In order for these facilities to be shared, teachers will have to plan for their use at different times of the day. This scheduling will be done usually with the help of the school's principal.

Educational needs

The educational needs for scheduling depend somewhat upon the type of program that is offered. Where the school program is based upon the separate-subjects form of curriculum organization, time must be allocated during the day for the separate subjects. It is probably true to state that a separate-subjects approach involves more periods during the course of the day than any other form of organization. Where the program is organized around broad units, however, the daily schedule can allow for larger and more flexible blocks of time. These are illustrated in Figures 10 and 11.

9:00 – 9:45	Arithmetic
9:45 – 10:15	Reading
10:15 – 10:45	Recess
10:45 – 11:30	Science
11:30 – 12:00	Music
12:00 – 1:00	Lunch hour
1:00 – 1:15	Spelling
1:15 – 1:30	Handwriting
1:30 – 2:00	Other language arts
2:00 – 2:30	Physical education
2:30 – 3:00	Social studies
3:00 – 3:30	Art

FIGURE 10. *A subject-oriented daily schedule for a middle grade.*

30 – 40 minutes	Planning the day's work
45 – 75 minutes	Group work
30 minutes	Recreation
45 – 75 minutes	Individual study
	Lunch period
45 – 60 minutes	Skill development period
30 minutes	Recreation
45 – 60 minutes	Group work
15 – 30 minutes	Evaluating the day's work

FIGURE 11. *A flexible type program for use with unit organization of subject matter.*

In either case, attention to the physical and psychological needs of children is important. The general need is for variability in the tasks posed for children in order to avoid fatigue or boredom. The daily program can help keep children in the best physical and psychological condition throughout the school day.

In some states school laws provide for a specific amount of time to be devoted each day, or each week, to certain activities. For example, in some states a certain amount of time must be devoted to physical education. In others a required amount of time must be devoted to health instruction. Whenever this kind of legal mandate is placed upon the schools by the state, it must be incorporated into the program.

Desirable features of daily programs

There are several ways of expressing the quality of daily programs. Kyte indicates that class schedules should provide for balance, variety, and flexibility to take into account the needs of all children enrolled in school.[9] Yauch and others state that desirable features of a daily program are an overview, rhythm, balance, timing, and evaluation.[10]

Three things should be noted here. One is that the program

[9] Kyte, *Op. cit.*, p. 432.
[10] Yauch, Bartels, and Morris, *Op. cit.*, pp. 183-184.

should help to provide for the psychological and educational needs of the individual children in the classroom. A second is that the program should combine many of the features of a good lesson plan or unit in terms of organization. A third is that a good program fosters the best kind of educational practice by allowing for planning, by providing time for attention to all facets of the curriculum, by applying good learning principles, and by providing for evaluation. A good daily program provides for opportunities for group study and interaction. It provides opportunity for individual study. It will allow every pupil to have some time during the day for reflective thinking or doing something he himself wants to do. A good program will provide large and flexible blocks of time for work that demands this kind of time scheduling. It will also provide opportunity for short-time intensive study such as spelling drill or drill in arithmetic skills. A good program provides opportunity for periods of rest and recreation in order to keep children physically and mentally alert. All of these things combined tend to give the day balance and rhythm.

PLANNING RECORDS

A subject that is not frequently discussed when talking about planning, either by the teacher alone or teacher-pupil planning, is the matter of what kind of planning record teachers shall maintain. Some teachers frankly feel that the kind of record they keep about their planning is their own private business. People who have had some administrative responsibility, on the other hand, even though they may respect the individual prerogatives of teachers, feel that some record of a teacher's intentions for classroom activities should be maintained. There is something to be said for this point of view.

A teacher who contracts to work with a group of boys and girls throughout a school year assumes responsibility for the continuity of the program for the children in that classroom. This responsibility remains with that person even in such emergencies as his illness. This does not mean that a teacher must forego the comfort of a sick bed, but he has some responsibility to the boys and girls whether he is there or not. This responsibility is usually expressed through some means he takes to make it easier for a substitute teacher to take his place. A substitute who is armed with some knowledge of what has been going on and what has been planned for the future, can do a better job of maintaining the continuity of the classroom program than one who does not have that kind of information.

The most simple kind of record that can be maintained for the purpose of preserving the continuity is the assignment list. This is simply a list of the assignments by unit, by subject, or by period, that the children are expected to have covered each day.

Another type of helpful record is a teaching log. The teaching log can be in outline form, in topical form, or simply notations of activities imposed upon the daily schedule or daily plan. This is an historical record that is helpful only for seeing what has gone on in the past.

Of course the most elaborate records are the actual plans that have been made. These may be the actual plans (either lesson plan or unit plans) made by the teacher. These may also be the actual plans kept by a pupil recorder of teacher-pupil planning. Both of these records would be extremely helpful to a substitute taking the place of the regular teacher.

Some schools provide teachers with a plan book. A plan book usually is ruled off into several possible periods during a school day for each day of the week. It is possible for a teacher to do a good deal of planning with such an instrument or to use it for the purpose of abstracting from larger plans for the benefit of a substitute. Occasionally the plan book is used as a means of supervising teaching. The supervisor will use the plan book as a means of helping teachers to locate their planning difficulties and thus improve their instruction.

Finally, a special notation of immediate plans can be made for substitutes in case of an emergency. This could be done in a few moments prior to leaving school at the close of each school day. This constitutes extra work, however, and teachers frequently avoid a persistent effort of this kind for the few number of occasions that substitutes are necessary. It should be remembered, however, that the process of noting plans causes a teacher to think more carefully about his teaching. In essence this is additional planning. Any additional planning tends to be productive of better teaching; therefore, if you are required to maintain some form of plan, you should be encouraged not to think of it as lost motion.

Summary

The conclusion has been drawn that careful planning is a significant dimension of method, and it is one that is critical to the success of a teacher. Planning is a continuous task if effective teaching is to be maintained.

A teacher may use any one of several departure points in planning for teaching. The four that have been discussed are the curriculum, resource materials, the emergent situation, and the adopted textbook. In all probability the organized curriculum should be considered as the best of these because the curriculum is designed to fulfill the purposes of that school.

The lesson plan represents the teacher's transitional thinking between the point of departure and the assemblage of pupils and teacher in the classroom. As such, a plan for teaching should reveal the over-all objectives to be sought, ideas for getting children involved in the activities, some probable activities, a tentative schedule of operations, and some ideas for evaluation. The form of the lesson plan is varied, but these elements should be there in some form.

Teacher-pupil planning provides the transition from the lesson plan of the teacher to the action plan for the group. The main difference between the plan of the teacher and the result of teacher-pupil planning is that in the latter case, specifications for action are decisively indicated.

Two physical considerations for planning are the arrangement of a daily program that will permit teaching plans to operate effectively, and the records that are to be made of planning efforts. These arrangements are likely to be peculiar to an individual school.

Ideas for discussion and activity

1. Why is a teaching unit different from a resource unit? Illustrate your points.

2. To what extent do you believe pupils should be permitted to help plan the school day? Why?

3. Formulate a list of criteria for building a good daily program. Illustrate them in a program for a grade of your choice.

4. What suggestions can you offer to provide continuity in the program for children when a substitute teacher is in the room?

5. Which of the departure points for planning listed in this chapter would you prefer to use? Why?

Suggested readings

Klausmeier, Herbert J., Katharine Dresden, Helen C. Davis, and Walter Arno Wittich, *Teaching in the Elementary School.* New York: Harper & Brothers, 1956, Chapter 5.

The chapter contains a discussion of unit planning (both resource and teaching), daily planning, and planning for evaluation.

Kyte, George C., *The Elementary School Teacher at Work.* New York: The Dryden Press, 1957, Chapters 13 and 14.

Here are two excellent chapters — one on planning and the other on programming.

Theman, Viola, *A Good Day at School.* New York: Bureau of Publications, Teachers College, Columbia University, 1950.

This is a practical and helpful booklet pointed at making a good school day through providing rhythm and balance in activities for children. Illustrations are included.

Thomas, R. Murray, *Ways of Teaching.* New York: Longmans, Green and Company, 1955, Chapter 7.

The author compares old and new methods of planning. A good section on lesson planning is included.

Wiggins, Sam P., *The Student Teacher in Action*. Boston: Allyn and Bacon, Inc., 1957, Chapter 6.
   Descriptive accounts are made of two student teachers and their lesson plans.
Wingo, G. Max and Raleigh Schorling, *Elementary-School Student Teaching*. Second edition. New York: McGraw-Hill Book Company, Inc., 1955, Chapter 7.
   Here is a fine presentation of the importance of teachers and pupils planning their work together, along with practical suggestions for doing so.
Yauch, Wilbur A., Martin H. Bartels, and Emmet Morris, *The Beginning Teacher*. New York: Henry Holt and Company, 1955, Chapter 10.
   This chapter contains suggestions for the new teacher in planning the first few days of school.

PART **IV** Dimensions of Method
in the
Teaching-Learning Process

I<small>N</small> PART IV our attention will be directed to the dimensions of method in the teaching-learning process. These are the areas of method for which teacher techniques are most famous. The pedagogical literature written upon these subjects is voluminous. The dimensions that will be discussed are (1) organizing pupils for work, (2) fostering communication and investigation, (3) intelligently using drill and routine procedures, (4) guiding and pacing learners, and (5) discipline.

Although these dimensions are to be discussed in separate chapters, it is important to remember that in the teaching-learning process, all of them may be at work simultaneously. Their separation for this discussion is solely for purposes of clarity and organization. The act of keeping these dimensions in proper perspective is one of the things that makes teaching such a difficult and complex process.

There might be added to this section a review chapter on the purposes and techniques of studying children, but most of these were covered in Part II. It is suggested that the reader refresh his thinking from Part II before proceeding into the subsequent chapters, because the interaction of teachers with children is so vital in a teacher's work. We study children so that we can work with them more effectively. The same principles behind a teacher's task in studying children can be applied to the dimensions of teaching to be discussed in the following pages.

CHAPTER 10

Organizing Pupils for Work

THE ACT OF ORGANIZING pupils for work is an important dimension of method for teaching in the elementary school. The usual configuration of pupils for work organization is referred to as the group. Grouping has been attempted many ways in elementary schools and for many purposes. In this chapter we will examine some of the ways grouping has been tried both for administrative and for teaching purposes. We will aso examine the purposes of grouping, some techniques of grouping, and group processes and roles that children may assume and play. In all cases particular emphasis will be placed upon the significance for teaching.

ADMINISTRATIVE GROUPING PLANS

There are a number of attempts that have been made to group children for purposes of instruction in elementary schools. Some of these have been more successful than others, and some plans have created issues in education about which people debate at considerable length. From an administrative point of view attempts have been made to facilitate the instructional process by administrative organization of the entire school. The general hope behind administrative grouping plans was, and still is, to reduce the problem of individual differences for teachers by reducing the wide range of ability—the fewer the individual differences, the better the learning environment.

Homogeneous grouping

One administrative grouping plan is called homogeneous grouping. When children are assembled into homogeneous groups, some criteria are established to produce homogeneity within the groups. Usually this had been some index of ability. The most common criterion that has been used is the intelligence quotient. Children have been placed into groups according to their abilities as indicated by their intelligence quotients. Another usable criterion is the results of achievement of testing. The results of standardized achievement tests can be used to establish grade level equivalents, and the grade level equivalents then become the criteria for assembling children into homogeneous groups in accordance with their academic achievement. There have been a few attempts made to group children in accordance with social maturity. The principal barrier to this process is the lack of trustworthy criteria or instruments by which criteria can be established.

It has not been definitely established that efforts at homogeneous groupings on administrative bases have been outstandingly successful in producing better results. Experience with homogeneous grouping has indicated that whenever children in the elementary school are grouped by one criterion, they tend to become as different or more different in other characteristics. For example, frequently when they are grouped in terms of intelligence quotients, problems arise because of increased differences in social maturity. In the early grades the intelligence quotient may have little to do with the time at which a child may begin to read. Thus those who have attempted homogeneous grouping have found that not all of their problems of curriculum and instruction were solved by this grouping process. In some cases even more problems were created.

Heterogeneous grouping

Heterogeneous grouping simply means that no attempt is made to assemble children in classrooms for instruction by any particular criterion. Ever since we have had the grading system, of course, children have been assembled in classrooms by grades, but when they are simply assembled by grade without any other criterion imposed, we say that they are grouped heterogeneously. In small schools where there is only one section to each grade in the elementary school, the children must be grouped heterogeneously.

Teachers who have worked under circumstances of heterogeneous grouping have had to accept the philosophy that theirs was the responsibility to provide for the entire range of abilities in that classroom and to enrich the program for all children to the maximum. Actually heterogeneous grouping represents no attempt at administrative solution to the problem of individual differences and all of its ramifications at the administrative level. Administrators who accept this notion believe that these problems must be solved in the classroom by the teacher.

Age-grade grouping

The most common form of modern organization pattern for children is called age-grade grouping. In some respects it is a compromise between purely homogeneous grouping and purely heterogeneous grouping. Children are grouped heterogeneously by age and grade on the one hand. On the other hand, it could be said that by assembling them by age in a grade, age becomes a factor in establishing homogeneity, or it could be considered a criterion for homogeneous grouping. Arguing in this way back and forth is like perpetuating the old argument as to which came first, the chicken or the egg. The practice is simply one of assembling children into grades in accordance with their chronological age. To a certain extent this follows from compulsory school attendance laws. Where schools must accept children into the first grade at the age of six because the law says that children must come to school at age six, it logically follows that those children would go into the first grade. Most children are promoted from grade to grade annually, and by accident of practice we find that seven-year-olds are in the second grade, the eight-year-olds are in the third grade, and so forth throughout the elementary school. (The problem of retention of pupils and the disturbing of this sequence by such action will be discussed in a later chapter.) This arrangement seems to have worked as well as any other arrangement, as far as administrative grouping of children for the purpose of instruction is concerned.

There is one interesting variation upon age-grade grouping that some school systems have found to be reasonably successful. That is one of assembling children by grade and by section within a grade in accordance with age. In those cases where children come to school as five-year-olds in kindergarten and there are enough children to make three sections of kindergarten, the younger of the five-year-olds would be placed in one section, the middle of the five-year-olds in a second section, and the five-year-olds approaching six in the third section. Those sections would then be maintained throughout the grades on the basis of chronological age. In a certain sense this is a very logical approach. For many reasons we are somewhat forced into the age-grade grouping concept, and chronological age appears to be a useful and social criterion. By establishing sections within grades by age modification, we are consistent in the organization of classrooms.

Another modification that has been used of the age-grade grouping concept is to establish levels within the elementary school, such as the ungraded primary or the ungraded intermediate. The ungraded primary is usually a flexible organizational pattern for the kindergarten and first and second grades. It is possible that a child would spend anywhere from two to four years in an ungraded primary, depending upon his ability to progress satisfactorily with school matters. Even under this type of organization a child spends an entire year with a teacher and in some cases two, depending upon the philosophy of the school with regard to the assignment of teachers to children. Some people rather naïvely hoped that the ungraded primary and ungraded intermediate might be a system of administrative organization that would eliminate problems and decisions that must be made with regard to the retention of pupils in elementary school grades for failure to progress satisfactorily in their school subjects. Actually, children are not fooled a bit about spending four years in an ungraded primary when they see many of their classmates only spend three years there. The point is that the problem is not at all solved by administrative organization. Nevertheless, let it be hastily added that persons who have utilized such organization at the ungraded primary tend to think more flexibly about schools, about children, and about the problems of teaching and learning than do those who use a more rigid interpretation of organization.

GROUPING FOR TEACHING

There is some similarity between administrative grouping as previously discussed and grouping for the purpose of teaching. This similarity centers about the dedication of both tasks to the improvement of instruction through attempts to make teaching efforts more efficient, as well as to satisfy better the educational needs inherent in the wide range of individual differences among children. Administrative grouping usually applies to an entire elementary school and tends to persist through the entire school year. Grouping established for the purpose of teaching tends to be more flexible and less permanent than this.

Purposes of classroom grouping

One of the important purposes of classroom grouping is to make the acts of teaching and learning more feasible. In the process of applying our many democratic ideals to the elementary school, one of the things we have said is that each child who attends the elementary school is entitled to the maximum benefit possible from that institutional experience. When this principle is carried over into the classroom and interpreted in terms of the function of the classroom teacher, it places a demand upon the classroom teacher to so divide his time and attention that each pupil receives his proportionate amount of guidance from the teacher. We frequently speak of this as individualized teaching. In most elementary school classrooms it would be impossible from the viewpoint of time for a teacher to provide only individualized instruction. Each pupil would receive a very small amount of help from the teacher in a classroom where thirty or more pupils were assembled. Instruction becomes much more feasible when a teacher can work with sub-groups instead of individuals. If a teacher has five groups in a room, then one fifth of his time can be spent with each of those groups, assuming a proportionate division of time, of course. Furthermore, sub-grouping permits greater opportunity for pupils to learn from one another, and this is an important aspect of the total learning environment in the classroom. This is what Elsbree and McNally call "educational osmosis." [1] A second and very important purpose of classroom grouping is to involve children psychologically in the classroom activities. This is one way of coping with problems of interest and need. Children with similar interests and need patterns can be grouped together to share their interests and knowledge. The opportunity to explore common interests stimulates the psychological involvement of each personality with the activity. Grouping the total classroom into sub-groups gives greater opportunity for the ideas of individuals to be expressed, considered, and challenged by others. All of this gives the individual a feeling of greater oneness with and membership in the group, and the feeling that he has made some contribution to the group. Through grouping

[1] Willard S. Elsbree and Harold J. McNally, *Elementary School Administration and Supervision* (New York: American Book Company, 1951), p. 123.

there is greater opportunity for motivation. Within the smaller group the individual tends to be more willing to release his energies in the direction of profitable activity. Within the small group there is greater opportunity for success. The success may not be at a very high level, but it is success nevertheless, and is more likely to be recognized in the smaller group than in the larger group. These things and others contribute to a greater feeling of oneness with the classroom environment, the other pupils, and the activities carried on there. This gives the individual person a greater opportunity to identify himself with that environment, and through the process of identification we have some reason to expect better and greater learning.

Closely related to the two foregoing purposes is a third. Grouping is one means of solving some of the problems of individual differences. This is especially true when groups are formed on the basis of differences in ability. However, this does not mean that groups formed by criteria other than ability do not also contribute to the solution of problems of individual differences. In a group organized on the basis of interest, there is still great opportunity to allow variation in performance by the more gifted pupil as well as the less gifted pupil. They can also learn from each another. It is somewhat true that the grouping of children within a classroom attracts attention to individual differences, but greater purposes are served by the process of grouping.

Forming groups

There is one basic principle about forming groups to which a teacher should adhere. That is one of flexibility. One should guard against the idea of permanent organization of classroom groups. Children during the elementary school years are in such rapid process of change that to place them in permanent groups may be an act that denies the recognition that those changes are taking place. The interest patterns of children throughout the elementary school years change dramatically. Elementary school children are constantly making new patterns of social choices as to playmates, workmates, and friends. These things lead us to the conclusion that classroom groups must be organized on a flexible basis.

Experience in recent years has shown us that more classroom grouping and more flexible classroom grouping is practiced in the early elementary school grades than in the upper elementary school grades. Exactly why this state of affairs does exist and has existed is difficult to explain. It should not be that teachers who teach in the upper grades are less flexible than teachers who teach in the lower grades. It should not be that children in upper grades are more homogeneous than children in the lower grades. In fact they should be more heterogeneous. The author strongly suspects that the principal reason for this state of affairs is the greater proliferation of subjects in the upper grades than in the lower grades. The subjects themselves are more complex and more abstract than they were in the early years. The larger number of subjects to be taught during the school day tends to divide the school day for the teacher into a larger number of units, and this no doubt causes teachers to feel that they must spend that limited time with the whole group. Whatever the actual circumstance may be, we have much to learn about flexibility in grouping upper-grade children.

Various kinds of groups will be formed for different purposes. One of the most familiar of the classroom groups is the reading group. First- and second-grade teachers in particular have been grouping children in accordance with their reading levels for the purpose of instruction in reading. It has been a common practice to have three reading groups. One of these would be the fast group, another the middle group, and a third the slow group. Sometimes these are identified by the name of a group leader like "Jane's Group" and "Tom's Group" and "Susan's Group." In other cases the name of an insect or animal is appended to the groups such as the Butterflies, the Bluebirds, the

Turtles. Everyone in the room knows the Turtles are the slow group. There is no objection to grouping children in skill subjects like reading in accordance with their ability level or their performance level, whichever the case may be, so long as children are able to recognize that they have the opportunity to move from group to group. In fact it would be a very good teaching practice to overhaul the groups periodically, whether to show recognition of the individuals' progress or just to indicate that it is not the teacher's attitude that once children have been placed in a group they must stay there. Psychologically it is futile to attempt to cover up the nature of the grouping by some clever act such as naming of the group. Children are completely aware of their status within the group with respect to their skill performance, even in the first grade, and attempts to fool them as to their status usually are very unsuccessful. Conversely, no attempt should be made to overemphasize the fact that children are in one group instead of another group. The reading group is only one example of grouping according to ability within a skill subject. The application of the same grouping procedure and technique could be made to the other skill subjects such as arithmetic, spelling, and so forth.

Another type of grouping is that of organizing pupils to carry out activities in connection with a large unit of work. By way of illustration, the author recalls a fourth-grade group that examined man's use of the six simple machines and explored its local environment for applications of those machines. The group divided itself into six sub-groups, one for each of the six simple machines. Each group studied literature to become familiar with the origin, development, and application of its machine. It then explored its local community to observe this application. The school in which these pupils were working happened to be in a coal mining area so the children had many opportunities to explore the use of the machines in a number of circumstances. Each group, and individuals within each group, prepared oral and written reports to communicate the information to members of other groups. Models were constructed to illustrate the nature of each machine and some application. This was a vivid illustration of the fact that not everybody in a complex unit must necessarily work on all aspects of the unit. Children can learn from the experiences of one another if channels of communciation are provided among them.

Another method of organizing children into groups is in accordance with their particular interests. For example, groups may be formed for studying literature. Some may be interested in biography; others may be interested in adventure; others may be interested in reading in some field of knowledge such as history. In any case, this can form a basis upon which groups can study or explore some phase of literature purely from the point of view of interest. Similarly, a complex unit in social studies, such as the study of an oriental society, can be the over-all framework within which interest groups might be formed for the purpose of work. One group might be interested in studying the art of the society, another the government, another the sports, another the music, and so forth. Through any of these approaches desirable insights can be acquired as to the relationships between the oriental society and their own. Furthermore, if communication is established among the groups, they learn from the efforts of each other. This illustration, however, suggests a precaution. Often when children are grouped recurrently by interest, some individual will attempt to explore the same interest over and over again. Now this is not always bad, but it may not be the most fruitful approach for that individual. For example, a pupil could elect in a series of similar units in social studies of different societies, to study always the art of each society. The student might profit more by studying the art of one society, the government in another, the sports in a third, and so forth. This type of shift of interest should have a broadening effect upon the individual's educational background.

Organizing groups

In keeping with the principle of flexibility, every group is formed for some purpose. The purpose should be a functional or operational task. Or it should be a specific task that has recognizable limits; that is, identifiable beginning and ending points.

The group must organize itself according to its established purpose. Organization in this case is not simply that by someone else, since the group can perform its task more thoroughly and efficiently through its own organization. The members of a group thus learn through practice the basic principles and techniques of group organization. In our kind of society this knowledge and skill is valuable information as a part of the training for citizenship.

Every group that is formed must have leadership. In this case we can think of leadership as a process whereby individuals and groups of individuals are aided in goal-seeking behavior. Goal-seeking behavior involves the establishment of goals, as well as the formulation of means of attaining them. Any individual who contributes to these ends is exerting leadership. In classroom groups, leadership can stem from an individual within the group or from persons very experienced in the group activity, or the group as a whole can establish its own leadership.

Several problems are posed for leadership personnel. They must help other individuals in their group to develop the willingness to participate and to continue participation in the activities of the group. Individual members of groups must be helped to define their own individual goals within whatever the activity of the group may be, and they must also be helped to find ways and means of achieving those goals. Obviously a good deal of leadership for group personnel must come from the classroom teacher. However, pupils accepting leadership roles within the groups can be a tremendous aid to the teacher in these functions. This is not said for the purpose of minimizing the responsibility of the teacher as leader of the entire group, but rather, it is stated because teachers need the help of leadership on the part of pupils within fairly large classroom groups, and the practice of leadership on the part of pupils is an educational opportunity for them. In the initial stages of organization, at least, one of the better ways in which leadership and organized groups can be established is to have the members of the group select their own chairman or leader, whichever term they choose to use. Ultimately some guidance in this function will be helpful or necessary on the part of the teacher. Too frequently pupils persistently select the same persons as group chairmen or leaders. Somehow this job should reach more persons. Sometimes this can be accounted for by regrouping techniques.

A group organized to carry out a specific function generally should make some record of its doings and progress. In all probability this will not be true for a group organized for the purpose of instruction because of different abilities in skill subjects. Such groups are really organized almost entirely for the purpose of efficiency in instruction. They need leadership, but to ask them to maintain a record of their doings and progress might be classified as busy work that has little educational value. However, for other groups that are organized to carry out a specific terminal type of activity such as a project or some phase of a unit of work, a record of the doings and progress of the group is an important thing for two principal reasons. One is that it records for future reference the step-by-step activities in which the pupils engaged, and the other is that the maintenance of a record helps the pupils to keep a forward momentum in their work.

One thing that can be done to maintain this record is to have the group select a recorder. It is the function of the recorder at the command of the group to keep records of its deliberations, its actions, and the results of its actions. When the group is discussing its activities and progress, the recorder can use a chart or a blackboard for the purpose of making notations, and thus free the group chairman or leader so he can concentrate his attention upon leading the discussion. When the discussion is concluded, the recorder can copy the record from the chart or blackboard on paper as a more permanent record of the proceedings.

Other kinds of records that can be made are the writings of the pupils in the group compiled as a result of their individual investigations. These can be of several kinds. The individuals may use such writings for reports to members of their group and to the class as a whole, or in many cases the written record can be used as reading materials for other people. In connection with this latter point it might be parenthetically stated that we frequently get the notion that pupils should read only materials in books or periodical literature. Pupils can learn a good deal from reading the writings of one another. It is the author's opinion that too little of this is practiced in elementary schools. Such practice would encourage more and better writing on the part of pupils, and it would encourage cross fertilization of ideas among pupils to a greater extent than when they all read the same materials.

The group may wish to make a record of its proceedings and activities through some kind of culminating activity such as a summary report or project that has been constructed, such as a mural, a model, or a map. Whichever may be done can still be interpreted as a record of the activities of the members of the group.

Sometimes it is helpful for a group to have a person occupy a position within the group that is slightly different from that of either the chairman or the group recorder. This individual can be called an evaluator or monitor. A person occupying this position has the responsibility to be checking constantly on the forward progress of the group, either in work or in discussion. He should check progress in terms of the goals that the group originally established as its ends. When a group is small, this is a task that can be assumed by all members of the group. However, until children become sophisticated in group action, they are not sensitive to forward progress once the heat of discussion becomes aroused. Furthermore, when individuals are not skilled in group action, it is possible for an individual member of the group to virtually sabotage the discussion or progress of the group, either because he has a vested interest of some kind that he wishes to exploit or for the psychological reason that he considers it his role to be a group disturber. It takes a good deal of patience and continual pressure by other members of a group to keep such a person in line with the progress of the group. This must not be interpreted to mean that pupils should not be allowed to have a dissenting voice in classroom procedures. In the democratic spirit we must foster the dissenting voice, but at the same time teach that person the role of the dissenter in a democratic group.

The members of a group must be organized, or preferably, must organize themselves to do the work or to share in the work imposed by its function. Again, the way this may be done depends somewhat upon the purpose for which the group is organized. In the case of the reading group, the arithmetic group, or the spelling group that is organized for the purpose of developing skill, the work effort is principally an individual matter. But for a group organized in connection with a broad unit in social studies studying some phase of communication in the United States, for example, it would be more profitable educationally for it to survey its total task, identify the various aspects of the total task, and divide itself in some way to share the various tasks. This is one place where some of the problems of individual differences can be resolved.

One must remember that children are quite aware of the capacities and interests of their fellow pupils. It is good a practice for a teacher to encourage pupils to accept responsibility for the division of labor in group activities. Rarely will children ask an individual with inferior capacity to do things that he cannot do. On the other hand, they will often encourage him to make better efforts. Encouragement from the peer group frequently produces better results than encouragement from the teacher. Each pupil must contribute to the group activities in accordance with his interest and capacity. This is the place where every individual is given the opportunity to make some worthwhile contribution, small though it may be, to the forward momentum of his group. Furthermore, this is the place where he can receive the highest recognition for his efforts.

When the work of groups is done they should be disbanded so that new ones can be constituted for new tasks. Again this is the principle of flexibility in operation. In the case of special-ability groups such as those for reading or arithmetic, member-ship may change frequently, but such changes are dictated by changes in the performance of individuals. Other kinds of groups will have totally completed their activities and can be disbanded in behalf of an entirely new operation.

Summary

In this chapter we have approached the organization of pupils in the classroom for work, as a dimension of method. Attention has been directed to the fact that two kinds of grouping have been practiced in elementary schools, namely administrative grouping and grouping for teaching. Attempts at administrative grouping have been made for the purpose of trying to solve at the adminis-tative level, some of the problems of individual differences by grouping persons according to some criterion established on the entire school level. Administrative grouping is characterized by long-term status.

Grouping for teaching has been the principal concern of this chapter. It is the grouping that is accomplished by teachers and pupils in individual classrooms for the purpose of fostering the teaching-learning process. It may be both long-term and short-term in duration. It has many objectives in common with administrative grouping, but it has the difference of specificity in function.

The purpose of classroom grouping was identified first as a means of dividing teachers' time among individuals in the classroom. Second, the grouping was described as a means of psychologically involving children in the classroom processes. Third, classroom grouping was identified as a means of solving problems of individual differences.

The principle of flexibility was identified as a basis for practice in the formation of groups. Groups may be organized for several purposes, including the division of persons according to ability for practice in skill subjects, the division of labor in the broad units of work, and interest.

Attention was directed to several problems in the organization of groups. In general, groups should be formed for a specific purpose and disbanded when that purpose has been achieved. In the case of ability groups, individuals should move in and out of those groups in accordance with changes in their abilities. Every group needs a leader and most groups should institute some means of recording its progress. Under some circumstances a monitor is desirable. Group members must organize themselves to share their work.

Ideas for discussion and activity

1. Distinguish homogeneous grouping from heterogeneous grouping, homogeneous grouping from ability grouping, heterogeneous grouping from age-grade grouping, and all of these from grouping for instruction within a classroom.

2. How might the sociogram (see Figure 3, p. 85), the reading readiness test, and the achievement test be used in grouping pupils for teaching?

3. Discuss various ways that classroom grouping can help the teacher with problems of individual differences.

4. Why would flexible classroom grouping be easier under the unit scheme of organization of subject-matter than under the separate subjects organization?

Suggested readings

Dougherty, James Henry, Frank Hermon Gorman, and Claude Anderson Phillips, *Elementary School Organization and Management.* Revised edition. New York: The Macmillan Company, 1950, Chapter 6.

Here is a good chapter on grouping. Arguments are given for and against various grouping proposals.

Hamilton, Warren and Walter Rehwoldt, "By Their Differences They Learn," *The National Elementary Principal*, 37:27-29; December, 1957. As a result of a controlled experiment in grouping, the authors recommend grouping practices based upon differences rather than similarities among children.

Johnson, Charles E., "Grouping Children for Arithmetic Instruction," *Arithmetic Teacher*, 1:16-20; February, 1954. The author discusses the problems and methods related to within-class grouping of children in arithmetic to provide for individual differences.

Lane, Howard and Mary Beauchamp, *Human Relations in Teaching.* Englewood Cliffs, N. J.: Prentice-Hall, Inc., 1955, Chapters 12, 16, 19, and 20. These chapters particularly deal with groups and group membership. Group life is related to the dynamics of learning. Read as much of this as you can find time to read.

Shane, Harold G. and Wilbur A. Yauch, *Creative School Administration in Elementary and Junior High Schools.* New York: Henry Holt and Company, 1954, Chapter 10. This chapter presents descriptions of various grouping schemes. Although the book was written principally for students of school administration, this chapter is pertinent for all professional persons.

Thompson, Ethel, "The Ungraded Plan," *N.E.A. Journal*, 47:16-18; January, 1958. For those who are unfamiliar with the rationale of ungraded plans this will be informative reading.

Wrightstone, J. Wayne, *Class Organization for Instruction.* What Research Says to the Teacher Series, No. 13. Department of Classroom Teachers and the American Educational Research Association, National Education Association, Washington, D.C.: The Association, 1957. The pamphlet contains an analysis of the findings of research on class organization for classroom practices. Every teacher should read this material.

CHAPTER 11

Fostering Communication

and Investigation

THE MOST IMPORTANT dimension of teaching consists of those activities on the part of the teacher that attempt to foster communication and investigation. Schools are established and organized so that pupils may investigate their heritage and their environment. Communication is an important process in both the act of investigation and the process of transmitting to others the results of investigation. It is toward this end that all previous planning in the form of curriculum planning, teacher planning, and administrative organization has been directed. In very direct terms, this is the focal point of the process called institutional education.

The obvious purpose of this chapter is to explore this dimension of teaching as it relates to the tasks of a teacher in the interactive processes between teacher and pupils. In the following discussion attention is directed toward the principal tasks of a teacher in directing discussion, directing various pupil activities, and conducting in-process evaluation.

DIRECTING DISCUSSION

One of the very important tasks of an elementary school teacher is to direct discussion. Discussion, as an educational technique, is a means of sharing ideas and acquiring knowledge. All through our history of education, discussion in one form or another has permeated the educational process. Throughout our history of education, liberal use of the discussion technique has been most widely practiced under those social circumstances that fostered liberal social and political thought. It is a particularly appropriate technique for sharing ideas and formulating opinion in a democratic society. In the following paragraphs the various uses of the discussion technique in the elementary school will be discussed. This will be followed by an identification of the basic elements of good group discussion and the roles that persons may play in the process of group discussion.

Uses of discussion

By way of an over-all illustration of the magnitude of various uses of discussion in elementary school classrooms, a study by Willard can be cited.[1] Willard sought to identify the most common and least common classroom experiences. A checklist was created from various curriculum guides and submitted to fifty-three teachers in fifty-three different classrooms, each teacher's principal, his supervisor, and a trained observer. All of these individuals were asked to indicate what they thought to be the most common and least common learning experiences present in those fifty-three classrooms. The five most common experiences that were identified in the study were: (1) individuals were encouraged to participate in classroom activities, (2) children were encouraged to work in groups, (3) pupils were encouraged to show respect for the ideas of others, (4) opportunities were provided for assuming responsibility, and (5) opportunities were provided for social experiences.[2] Obviously discussion at some point or another would have to enter into all of these identified common experiences.

There are more specific ways of indicating various uses of

[1] Ruth A. Willard, "The Most Common and Least Common Learning Experiences Reported Present in Fifty-three Classrooms," *Educational Administration and Supervision*, 42: 72-77 (February, 1956).
[2] *Ibid.*, p. 75.

discussion. In the following paragraphs several of these will be identified.

TEACHER-PUPIL PLANNING. The significance of teacher-pupil planning has already been indicated. Discussion of some kind is the only technique that can be utilized in this activity. It makes no difference whether teacher-pupil planning is done in small groups or with the classroom group as a whole. It is only through the use of discussion that the group can reach a plan of action that realistically belongs to the group.

SHARING IDEAS. The act of sharing ideas is an educative act in itself. Whenever one person sets forth an idea for consideration on the part of others, it becomes subjected to the scrutiny of other persons. Others may accept the idea; they may reject the idea, or they may modify the idea. In the process all persons are affected by the exchange. There are many ways in which ideas can be shared. Individuals may report the results of their investigations, and those results may be compared with the results of the investigations of other pupils. Small groups in the form of panels may discuss topics in order to explore their significance and value to those groups. Ideas are shared in the teacher-pupil planning process. They are shared in the evaluation process. In fact the sharing of ideas should permeate most any classroom activity that has discussion as its base of operation.

THE RECITATION. In many educational circles the recitation as a classroom procedure has fallen into disrepute. The principal reason for the demise of the recitation is the connotations associated with it. In the latter part of the previous century and in the early part of the present century the recitation was an extremely formalized, rigid affair. School pupils were given assignments to read and then were required to recite from those reading assignments. In more cases than not the recitation consisted of recital by rote of the passages read, and no attention was directed to interpretation or criticism of the ideas contained in those passages. No doubt there are still some schools in America where the recitation is formally and rigidly utilized, but they are in a minority. Because of this reputation of the recitation as an educational technique, teachers now must guard against doing something that is similar to throwing the baby out with the bath. In modern education the recitation has some role, but it must be intelligently used. For example, Saucier indicates that the recitation has three purposes. One of these is to give a teacher an opportunity to explore the degree to which pupils have acquired specific facts and skills. A second is to use the recitation as a drill procedure, and a third, that the recitation should become a means of teaching pupils to think.[3] To look at it another way, whenever we ask a pupil to make a report on something that he has read or studied, in a sense we are asking him to recite. To use the recitation intelligently, it must be varied with other activities and much of the meaningless memorization by rote eliminated.

ROLE PLAYING. Role playing is an activity that is often used in elementary school classrooms for the purpose of helping children gain insight into solutions to social problems. For example, a story may be read to partial completion and then individuals may act out a conclusion to the story. In other cases a social scene may set the stage for a controversy between a child and his parents about eating breakfast. Children might be asked to play the roles of parents and child in such a way as to come to what they consider to be a desirable solution to the dilemma. These and other techniques become ways in which children can gain insights into solutions of social and personal problems. Obviously discussion is at the root of the activity.

EVALUATION. Evaluation when defined as a process of determining whether or not desired goals have been achieved is another circumstance in which discussion can be used as a technique. This is mostly true when groups are at work in evaluating their activities.

[3] W. A. Saucier, *Theory and Practice in the Elementary School*, Rev. Ed. (New York: The Macmillan Company, 1951), p. 182.

REPORTING PROCEDURES. Another technique by which discussion becomes useful will be discussed in detail in the section of the book devoted to evaluation with respect to reporting procedures. Discussion can become a fundamental basis whereby teachers and parents may communicate about the progress in the school. It is particularly important because it gives both parents and teachers an opportunity to interact in the process of exchanging ideas rather than having a one-way communication process, as in the case of the written report card or letter.

Good group discussion

Several considerations distinguish good group discussion from haphazard conversation. It must be remembered that group discussion becomes a function of the group and not of the separate individuals.

One characteristic of a good group discussion is that all the members of a group become involved in it. To accomplish this, it is necessary that two circumstances prevail. The group must be sufficiently small in size so that all members of the group *can* become involved in the discussion. All members of the group *must* become involved in the discussion or else the discussion cannot represent the entire group.

Through discussion the group establishes its purpose for holding the discussion. This is the thing that sets a good group discussion off from haphazard conversation. The identification of and dedication to purpose should emerge early in the discussion.

Another basic element of good group discussion is that the discussion focuses its attack upon the problem or topic. In most discussions there is a great tendency to deviate from the topic because of temporary and side interests of group members. Occasionally irrelevant data are introduced into the discussion. These must be weeded out and set aside. The group must constantly keep its attention focused upon its task or role as identified in the organization of the group and in the establishment of its purpose.

Another basic element of good group discussion is the tendency for the group to move forward constantly as the discussion progresses. In loosely controlled discussion there is a tendency to stay with some element of the major topic until the discussion becomes aimless. A good group discussion is characterized by forward momentum, with all members of the group concentrating upon forward motion toward the accepted goal.

In a good group discussion the attitude of the members is one of serious contemplation, and one in which all members offer their ideas for the consideration of others. Anger must not prevail, for as soon as anger enters group discussion emotions tend to flare and proper consideration cannot be given to the ideas being proffered. Again this should not be interpreted to mean that differences of opinion or conflicting ideas should be eliminated from the discussion. In fact the discussion can become fruitful when varying and conflicting ideas are presented for the consideration of all.

In a good group discussion the intellectual level of the topic and the degree to which the foregoing elements can be imposed are dependent upon the age and the experience of the group holding the discussion. It would be completely unrealistic to expect the kindergarten or first-grade child to be as sophisticated in discussion technique as the sixth-grade child. Furthermore, the kinds of topics that children of different ages might attack and the degree to which these might be explored are also dictated by the age and experience of the members of the group. A good discussion can be defeated in the early grades by expecting children to discuss problems too difficult for them. To allow a discussion among older children that is too immature for them is to deny them their right for maximum educational opportunities.

There may be elements of group discussion other than those mentioned above. However, the latter do seem to be basic to any good discussion, and they can be used as guides in the teaching process.

Discussion roles

The basic elements of good group discussion indicated in the paragraphs above are one way of describing the discussion activity. Another way is to describe the activity in terms of the roles that members of the group either should or do assume.

There are the usual roles, which have already been stated in connection with the organization of groups, that certain individuals must play as they occupy positions within the group. The person occupying the position of group leader must demonstrate a leadership role even though others in the group may, in the course of the discussion, temporarily assume leadership roles. The recorder and the monitor of the group assume roles in connection with record keeping and monitoring the discussion. Other members of the group may also assume monitoring or recording roles but not consistently identify themselves with those roles.

The foregoing roles are ones that are not only acceptable in a discussion group, but also must prevail. On the other hand, there are some roles that are played by persons in discussion groups that may be called character roles or roles that may actually be disruptive of the discussion process. For example, there is the discussion *dominator*. We have all seen the dominator at work in a discussion. He is the figure who must stand out above all others as a matter of ego satisfaction or perhaps as a matter of deliberate attempt to control the group with malice aforethought. This is different from the role of the *voice*. The voice role is simply one of noise making. This individual simply likes to hear his own voice but does not have particular malice in so doing. Another role that a group member may play is *quiet cooperator*. This individual is apt to be a strong silent person. He is cooperating with the group, and he is participating with the group except that all of his participation is done without oral exercise. Unless the group is very small, this individual is difficult to bring into the discussion. Then there is the *quiet saboteur*. The quiet saboteur is the individual who says little or nothing that is addressed to the group. However, at an informal break in the group meeting, this is the individual who usually through the medium of the whisper attempts to negate everything that is constructively built up in the discussion. He actually is destructive, through whispering or reducing the argument in a ridiculous fashion. Then there is apt to be the *fact person* in the group. This is the individual who consistently recites circumstances and insists that only facts are worthy of being considered and any opinion other than fact is unworthy of consideration. There may also be in a group the *compromiser*. The compromiser is the individual in the group who cannot stand controversy. He enters into the discussion when two or more ideas have been brought out in the open and are in conflict with one another. The compromiser wishes to eliminate the conflict as quickly as possible whether or not the ideas inherent in the conflict have been clarified.

A good group discussion may be destroyed by some of these character roles. Persons assuming these roles may dominate a group discussion, and not because they are offering ideas of real worth. Individuals must be taught that such roles are destructive of good group discussion, and that there are appropriate roles to play that would satisfy their individual goals as well as those of the group. Actually many of these character roles, if played by individuals at appropriate times, may make excellent contributions to a discussion. It is a matter of recognizing that the persistent playing of a role by a single individual is destructive to the process.

DIRECTING INVESTIGATION ACTIVITIES

A word of explanation is necessary here with regard to the use of the term activity in connection with pupil investigation. Activities in this sense refer to the things that pupils may decide to do or a teacher may cause pupils to do by one means or another. Discussion as a pupil activity has already been presented, and it may permeate any of the investigation activities. Activity is used here as being other than drill or routine. More specifically, pupil investigation activities refer to the activities in which teachers and pupils may engage to establish an assignment of work, in connection with making excursions or field trips, in organizing and maintaining group study, in individual study activities, in connection with improving study habits, and in connection with sharing results of investigation.

It should be noted that the act of choosing activities for and with children is an aspect of method just as are teachers' actions in impelling pupils into those activities. Thus those investigative activities that are to be chosen or utilized must be considered in relation to the content or subject matter to be investigated, the objectives of the investigation, and/or the process that is to be utilized in the investigation.

The assignment

An older interpretation of the assignment was a rather rigid concept. A teacher decided upon the activity or activities that he wished the pupils in his classroom to accomplish and then proceeded to *direct* the pupils toward that accomplishment. More frequently than not his assignment was a general one for all pupils in the room. At one time method books spent considerable space carefully instructing teachers how to make this kind of assignment with great clarity so that no pupil would misunderstand the tasks he was to perform. Because of the problems of individual differences this procedure was basically unsuccessful. It was unsuccessful with those for whom the assignment was inadequate at both extremes of ability. The next evolutionary stage in pedagogical thought was the individual assignment in which each pupil was allowed to proceed in accordance with his own individual rate. In some cases individual contracts were agreed upon by both pupil and teacher so that the assignment per pupil was still a clear mandate.

A modern interpretation of the assignment is to consider it a cooperative endeavor which includes the objectives, the action to be taken, and the organization for action. It is cooperative in the sense that it is decided upon by both teachers and pupils. Thus the modern interpretation is one of teacher-pupil decision-making as opposed to teacher domination in an earlier interpretation. Again this is the result of cooperative teacher-pupil planning that is encouraged because of the educational benefits for pupils in that activity. As one author puts it, *"Shared authority and shared responsibility go hand in hand."* [4]

It should be noted that the assignment as a pupil activity was placed before other activities in this chapter. This was done because subsequent actions are a result of the cooperative endeavor that may be classified as assignment.

The excursion or field trip

The excursion or the field trip is one class of investigation activity in which pupils may engage. There are many illustrations that could be offered, such as a trip to the local foundry, an excursion to the zoo, or a visit to the state capitol. The excursion or field trip is a direct type of experience, for it permits the individual to come into personal contact with some dimension of life that he is currently studying. This kind of experience helps to develop insight into relationships and applications, and interpretation, to saying nothing of understanding. It may lead to other kinds of activities when children return to the classroom, such as creative expression or construction.

In the Willard study, the previously cited reference to the most common learning experiences reported in classrooms, it is interesting to note that this type of activity falls among the least

[4] Kimball Wiles, *Teaching for Better Schools* (Englewood Cliffs, N.J.: Prentice Hall, Inc., 1952), p. 121.

common occurrences. Willard reported that trips and field studies, use of community resources, use of actual life situations, use of continuous evaluation, and use of firsthand experiences were the five least common experiences found in her study.[5] It is possible, of course, that if Willard's study were repeated in other communities and other schools, the results might vary. However, to the extent that the findings of Willard's study are accurate for other school situations, this kind of investigative activity could be more profitably used.

Several things need to be done when teachers and pupils prepare for field trips or excursions. In the first place, most schools require children to bring to school written consent from their parents to go on the trip. This practice insures school personnel that the home is informed of the fact that children will not be on school premises during those hours, and that the parents are willing that their children leave the school for those reasons and under those circumstances.

Unless the teacher and pupils are to walk to their place of visit, transportation must be arranged. Here again the policy of the local board of education becomes important. Some boards of education have established the policy that children are not to be transported in privately owned vehicles. In other words, they must be transported in those communities by agencies that have licenses and appropriate insurance for public transportation. Obviously this is a safety device.

Plans must be made with the place of visitation so that the pupils may have the opportunity to see the elements necessary to fulfill their objectives, and also that the place of visitation will not be disturbed. This will help insure that future groups of school pupils will be welcome. There is no reason, under most circumstances, why pupils may not participate in planning with the personnel of the place of visitation. In fact it is highly desirable for them to do so because it teaches the children re-

[5] *Op. cit.*, p. 75.

sponsibility in connection with this type of behavior, that they cannot experience elsewhere. It is particularly important that time of arrival and time of departure be indicated and that points of contact and personnel to be interviewed be specified.

Closely related to plans with the place of visitation are plans of the pupils for their own actions during the excursion. These present an opportunity to teach elements of visitor courtesy, some of the social graces, ways of asking questions to seek desired information, and to point up the things to look for during the visit. Behavior plans should be directed toward making sure not only that the children "behave themselves" while they are on the excursion, but also that they may behave themselves in such a way that their learning will be most profitable.

Organizing and maintaining group study

The matter of organizing groups for study purposes was discussed in earlier pages under the techniques of the formulation of groups. It must be recalled that with respect to study, groups are organized for two main reasons. Individuals are organized to work in groups so that they might learn the various techniques and attitudes that are desirable for group action, and they are often organized to do a piece of work that can be done better by a group than by an individual.

One type of study that would fall under the category of group study is that of group research. Groups of individuals are organized within the classroom to investigate certain areas of knowledge. They have three tasks in so doing. In the first place they must seek out the necessary data to accomplish their investigation. Second, they must assemble the data or information in a useable form. Third, they must interpret these data in the light of their original objectives for the research. It is recognized that the use of the term research here is broadly and generally interpreted. However, the use of basic research techniques for seeking out information can begin at a very early age. This kind of study can be done even at the kindergarten level, but in problems or areas of investigation that are commensurate with the age group.

Construction activities are another type of study functions in which pupils may engage as groups. In a very real sense, construction activities are a mode of group study because children in the process of construction are constantly reappraising their information and applying it to a different set of circumstances. Furthermore, when a group is engaged in construction, the members of the group work with one another continually to find the best procedure in the activity. Some examples would be the familiar painted mural, the construction of relief maps, or scientific models such as the wiring of a door bell or a demonstration of the effect of air pressure.

A third type of group study can be classified as creative expression, including such things as dramatics or role playing. Children must work together on a cooperative basis in order to produce the desired results, whichever the case may be. Again these activities are performed for specific purposes that lend direction to the activities for both the pupils and the teacher.

The teacher's role in organizing and maintaining these kinds of group study are mainly twofold. The teacher must serve in a guidance capacity in the organization and selection of the activity. Once the activity is organized and selected it becomes a teacher's role to keep it moving along toward the established objectives. Secondly, a teacher is a constant resource person in the group. Perhaps this is the most important function of a teacher in directing group study. If pupils have been conscientiously working at discussion techniques and establishing and identifying group roles, they should learn to organize and maintain their own activity. However, the teacher is always needed by the group as a resource person. In fact it is safe to say that the classroom teacher is the principal resource for all learning activity for the boys and girls in his classroom.

Supervising individual study

Another role that the teacher must play in directing pupil investigation activities is to supervise individual study. There are several circumstances under which individual study may occur in elementary school classrooms. A major circumstance of this kind is the individual project or problem that an individual pupil has to solve. This can be a problem or project of his own selection, or it may be a specific assignment given him by the teacher. An individual may elect, for instance, to study conservation problems caused by strip-coal mining. Another example might be an individual with a set of arithmetic problems to be solved as a result of a specific assignment made by the teacher. Another circumstance may be a group project, but one in which individuals have specific assignments that they are undertaking alone, made by their own group. Other pupils might be engaged in a kind of reflection of a personal nature. For most pupils the school day is a busy affair, and for children of elementary school age the day is reasonably long. During each school day it is wise to provide some opportunity for every pupil to engage in reflective thought or to engage in some activity purely of his own choice so long as it is not detrimental to the remainder of the group.

In supervising individual study the teacher may play several roles. He must help pupils to develop an attitude toward learning that is constructive and healthy. Individual study cannot be of the most profitable nature unless a proper mental attitude toward learning is developed. A great deal of the development of this attitude should take place through the various planning activities or through the manner in which the assignments to activity are made.

The teacher is a resource person in the same sense in individual study as he is a resource person for groups at study. At one time he may be a source of ideas for pupils. Another time he may check on the procedure of a pupil. A third time he may be helping an individual in problem-solving techniques.

The teacher must be a quiet defender of the right to reflect. Children will only use periods of reflection to the extent that teachers permit and make provision for such action. Since a teacher defends the right of individual pupils to reflection about their own problems, he must also help other pupils to respect the same right.

A teacher guides habit formation. One of the teacher's primary responsibilities is to improve the study habits of his pupils. There are innumerable little tasks that may be done in fulfilling this responsibility. Helping children to think more critically about the materials they read is to aid them in their study habits. Study habits may be improved through helping pupils to develop better research procedures by becoming more skilled at locating information. Helping pupils to develop habits of persistence and speed are other examples by which teachers may improve study habits. Pupils' study habits do not improve accidentally because they remain in classrooms over a protracted period of time. A teacher must concentrate on the many tasks that he may perform to push this kind of growth.

Sharing results

An integral part of communication and investigation in an elementary school classroom is the act of sharing results of investigation. The actual techniques that might be used in sharing results have already been mentioned. For certain kinds of result-sharing, the recitation is appropriate. Whenever persons have been asked to study the same materials, it can be educationally profitable for them to share their reactions and interpretations of the materials studied.

The report is another means of sharing results. This may be an individual or group report, and it may be oral or written. It makes no difference whether the report is oral or written; a report should be shared with others. It is most unfortunate when reports, particularly written reports, are prepared by pupils and then presented only to the teacher for his consideration. Many informative things lie in those reports, and they should be shared by other pupils in the classroom.

The panel discussion is another excellent technique for sharing results of study and investigation. This is possible by having members of committees who have engaged in specific projects sit down before their class and discuss among themselves the results of their investigations. Another way that a panel discussion can be organized is to have one member from each of several committees or groups form one. In this case the individuals bring to the entire class the highlights out of each group's investigation. It should be remembered that whenever a panel discussion is presented, other members of the classroom should be given the opportunity to interact with members of the panel.

A culminating activity such as a model, a mural, or a dramatic skit can be other means of sharing results of study. These are most appropriate for the purpose of sharing results when the final interaction need not be particularly detailed, or when only highlights need to be illustrated.

Generally the selection of these activities for purposes of sharing results is decided upon at the time of teacher-pupil planning activities. However, this should not preclude the possibility of interim and spot reports being made to the entire class by individuals or members of the group whenever an occasion presents itself. Frequently an individually prepared report can be inserted simply because an individual has found something about which he is enthusiastic, and it seems worthy of the group's attention. The main function of the teacher in the process of sharing results, is one of helping to schedule the activity during the day and to encourage pupils to participate in it.

IN-PROCESS EVALUATION

In-process evaluation is an important dimension of teaching

and one that is used altogether too little in elementary school classrooms. In-process evaluation should be distinguished from curriculum evaluation for the purpose of clarity of discussion.

It will be recalled that curriculum evaluation was discussed as a process designed to determine whether or not goals were achieved, whether content and method were appropriate, and whether both of these were worthy of the endeavor. To complete curriculum evaluation, in-process evaluation must also go on. The point of distinction is that in-process evaluation is used for the purposes of moving the instructional program along and determining the quality of specific elements of the classroom program. Thus in-process evaluation is concerned with specific objectives in connection with precise activities and the methods used to achieve those activities in that particular classroom. Evaluation applied to the objectives, activities, and methods used in a fifth-grade transportation unit is different from evaluation applied to the entire fifth-grade program or the curriculum of the school.

Several specific things can be done by both teachers and pupils as they carry out this type of evaluation.

Diagnostic testing

A teacher may periodically wish to carry on some diagnostic testing in order to determine the momentum of his pupils. For example, if one wishes to check upon the progress of a fourth-grade group in addition, subtraction, multiplication, and division in arithmetic, a diagnostic test either of a standardized nature or one constructed by the teacher may be used. The results of the test will show the teacher the areas of strength and weakness in those processes. These help the teacher check upon the progress being made, and help him select and organize teaching materials to correct weaknesses and move the pupils along in arithmetic. The same technique can be used in other subjects.

Maintaining anecdotal records

The anecdotal record consistently maintained by a teacher can be used as an evaluative device. The anecdotal record is one important means of being able to observe actual changes in social behavior of pupils as they act and react with their fellow classmates. But in order for this to show up, the record must be kept with care and persistency. A change in choice of reading materials by a sixth-grade boy could go unnoticed if some comparative record were not observed. The anecdotal record is such a device.

Personal evaluation

Another technique of in-process evaluation is individual and personal evaluation by a pupil. It is a good technique to subject individuals periodically to a personal evaluation of themselves. This may be done either in writing or in consultation. This is one of the better ways that pupils can be helped to accept increasing responsibility in directing their own affairs. Furthermore, there is no reason why a school pupil should not engage in self-examination. One person may keep and periodically analyze a diary of his activities. Others might make records of their errors and use them for remedial work, as in the case of individual spelling lists. Personal evaluation is simply another means of helping pupils to help themselves and thus become more independent.

Group evaluation

No doubt the most useful technique of in-process evaluation, from the viewpoint of frequency of use, is group evaluation. Group evaluation can be accomplished two ways at least. First, a group may decide to formulate some culminating activity that represents the value of what they have done. A report, chart, dramatic skit, or model may be used to represent the significance of the learning acquired. A second means, and one that is very desirable, is to evaluate through group discussion. Pointed questions such as, "What did we do?," "How well did we do?," "What could we have done better?," and "What did we learn?" lead to evaluative conclusions. One of the interesting things about children of elementary school age is their ability and willingness to look honestly at what they have done. They should be encouraged in this activity.

Summary

In this chapter we have been concerned with the fostering of communication and investigation as an important dimension of teaching. A teacher's functions in directing discussion, directing pupil investigation, and in-process evaluation were indicated to be the principal categories of action in this dimension of teaching.

The chief teacher-and-pupil activity that runs throughout this dimension is that of discussion. It appears to be of cardinal importance that pupils in elementary schools learn discussion techniques and develop an attitude of willingness to participate in such activities. When discussion as a classroom procedure is seen to apply to specific activities of children, such as study, excursion, evaluation, and so forth, its significance becomes even more important. It becomes the basis for interaction among individuals and groups and the basis for communication as a mode of learning.

Throughout this presentation there has been indicated the responsibility of the teacher for the individual development of every pupil in his classroom in an upward direction. Techniques of communication and investigation and the results of those activities are the most important products that elementary schools have to offer children. They warrant the most serious consideration of all classroom teachers.

Ideas for discussion and activity

1. Show how use of the discussion technique can be supported with principles of learning.
2. What kinds of subject matter, or subject-matter organization, are most fitting for group work? For individual work?
3. Note several ways in which research procedures can be used in teaching elementary school children.

4. Visit a class in which a discussion is being held and try to identify some of the role characters described in this chapter. Try it in your own group.

5. How must one relate his interpretation of teacher-pupil planning, grouping of children, and techniques of directing communication and investigation in order to develop his own philosophy of teaching?

Suggested readings

Association for Childhood Education International, *Continuous Learning*. Bulletin No. 87. Washington, D.C.: The Association, 1951.
This bulletin focuses the reader's attention upon the need for continuity in learning as children cope with their school activities.

Macomber, Freeman Glenn. *Principles of Teaching in the Elementary School*. New York: American Book Company, 1954, Chapter 6.
In this chapter the author discusses several kinds of activity that a teacher may direct as children carry out their units of work.

Saucier, W. A., *Theory and Practice in the Elementary School*. Revised edition. New York: The Macmillan Company, 1951. Chapter 6.
Saucier interprets teaching procedure as consisting of three steps: assignment, working period, and recitation.

Shane, Harold G., "Sweep of Change in Classroom Practice," *Phi Delta Kappan*, 37:184-188; January, 1956.
In this article Shane notes the sweep of change in classroom practices over the last fifty years. Note particularly the influence of the progressive movement.

Wiles, Kimball, *Teaching for Better Schools*. Englewood Cliffs, N. J.: Prentice-Hall, Inc., 1952, Chapters 5 and 6.
Emphasis is placed upon teaching skill in organizing groups for work.

Willard, Ruth A., "The Most Common and Least Common Learning Experiences Reported Present in Fifty-three Classrooms," *Educational Administration and Supervision*, 43:72-77; February, 1956.
A report is presented of a study of classroom practices with reference to the most and the least common learning experiences provided for children. The results are most interesting.

CHAPTER 12

Intelligent Use of Drill
and Routine

THE USE OF DRILL and routine procedures is a dimension of teaching that sometimes reaches disproportionate magnitudes even though these procedures are the more mechanical aspects of teaching. The routines have to do with those activities in which teachers and pupils must engage, that are associated with the teaching-learning process but do not have a direct bearing upon the process. They are things that must be done but are considered to be of less significance.

The meaning and interpretation of drill is approached in different ways. For example, one publication makes a distinction between drill and practice. Practice is indicated to be a matter of purposeful self-direction, whereas drill is simply the continuous repetition of some activity without variation.[1] Other authors are not particular about this distinction. In fact more persons are prone to think of practice as a more appropriate term for modern education than drill.

In this chapter illustrations will be presented of the circumstances under which drill and routine procedures should be established. In the case of both drill and routine, some suggestions to teachers for handling them in a realistic manner will be included.

DRILL OR PRACTICE

In recent years the concept of drill and its use in the elementary

[1] Association for Supervision and Curriculum Development, National Education Association, *The Three R's in the Elementary School* (Washington, D.C.: The Association, 1952), pp. 128-129.

school fell into disrepute in the minds of many educators. For the most part this was because drill practices had been used that were indefensible. Morton gives us an interesting illustration:

> Not many years ago, at an educational convention, a city superintendent of schools cornered the writer and said: "I want to tell you what I think of these fancy ideas about making arithmetic meaningful and interesting. School kids have to learn the basic facts of arithmetic. For example, they have to learn that 8 and 5 are 13. I say, tell 'em that 8 and 5 are 13 and then drill 'em until they know it." A few utterances of that kind, and no wonder that drill is in bad repute! Fortunately, only a few superintendents still hold such a point of view.[2]

Such interpretations as this indicate a denial of most everything that psychology of learning has attempted to teach us about the use of repetitive procedures as a means of improving learning.

The crux of the argument about drill and its use very bluntly is the degree to which meaning must precede drill. In many cases classroom teachers become impatient or feel that they do not have sufficient time to wait for children to acquire meaning and significance before they launch drill procedures. Somehow it is mystically hoped that if drill is begun without meaning preceding it, somehow children will acquire meaning later.

From time to time teachers are accused of using too little drill. Usually when this accusation is made, those who make it assume that because most of the school day does not involve drill procedures with children, children's education is being neglected. The author is sometimes prone to think that adults are somewhat sadistic in this respect. Why we should expect small children to live in a dull, routinized day engaged in meaningless drill activities is difficult to understand. Few adults would want to do so.

[2] R. L. Morton, *Teaching Arithmetic.* What Research Says To the Teacher Series, No. 2, Department of Classroom Teachers and the American Educational Research Association, National Education Association (Washington, D.C.: The Association, 1953), p. 20.

Necessity for drill

The foregoing remarks should not be interpreted to mean that there is no excuse for engaging children in the elementary school in drill procedures. Quite the contrary is true. There are many circumstances in the elementary school in which drill or practice become a vital necessity. In general, drill becomes necessary whenever some function is expected to be used by children with great precision. One psychologist tells us that there are two principal reasons for practice. One of these is to repeat an activity for the purpose of stimulating retention, and the other is a matter of fostering repetition for improvement in some function.[3] For example, we may repeat number combinations in arithmetic again and again for the purpose of retention. An individual may practice scales on the piano for the purpose of improving his technique.

In his discussion about drill, Morton indicates that no research is available which would indicate that in the teaching of arithmetic, drill or practice with arithmetic functions can be eliminated.[4] In reviewing research on the teaching of spelling, Horn reports that it is more efficient to study words in lists than in context.[5] This would indicate that repetition or drill functions are desirable in the teaching of spelling.

Similarly, in reviewing research on the teaching of handwriting, Freeman indicates a preference for systematic practice as opposed to incidental learning. By systematic practice he refers to practice in aspects of writing that have been observed to cause

[3] William Clark Trow, *The Learning Process.* What Research Says to the Teacher Series, No. 6, Department of Classroom Teachers and the American Educational Research Association, National Education Association (Washington, D.C.: The Association, 1954), pp. 22-23.

[4] *Op. cit.,* p. 20.

[5] Ernest Horn, *Teaching Spelling.* What Research Says to the Teacher Series, No. 3, Department of Classroom Teachers and the American Research Association, National Education Association (Washington, D.C.: The Association, 1954), p. 16.

difficulty, even though the difficulties may be discovered through general writing.[6]

These reviews of research on the teaching of some of our important tool subjects in the elementary schools indicate that we dare not be careless in the utilization of drill procedures, and that furthermore, these should be used in connection with certain functions that must be taught to children. The main point of the arguments throughout research in this area has to do with the intelligent use of drill procedures in the classroom, and most of the arguments concerning this use center about the relationship between meaning and drill.

Meaning and drill

Most everyone agrees that *meaning* prior to practice or drill is essential. However, it is important to recognize that meaning with respect to practice and drill in the elementary school has two inherent dimensions. One of these has to do with the meaning involved in what is being learned, and the other has to do with meaning in relationship to the psychological attitude of the learner as he engages in the practice.

From the point of view of efficiency in learning, the meaning involved in concepts being learned is most important. Over and over again psychological experiments have demonstrated that less practice is required in those cases where a learner understands what he is asked to practice. This is especially important in arithmetic. Before we can ask children to combine numbers, in any of the fundamental processes, their understanding of the relationship between groups of different magnitudes is essential. Before we can expect that they can profit from systematic practice in addition, substraction, multiplication, and division, they must understand the meaning behind those processes. These

[6] Frank N. Freeman, Teaching Handwriting. What Research Says to the Teachers Series, No. 4, Department of Classroom Teachers and the American Research Association, National Education Association (Washington, D.C.: The Association, 1954), p. 10.

things are essential for gaining insight into the basic functioning of our number system.

It is also psychologically important that pupils understand the reason for practice or drill. Basic to the development of this insight on the part of pupils is their understanding of the use of the knowledge they are acquiring. Behind this question, of course, lies the total justification for the existence of many of our subjects in school. However, it should not be any great trick for a teacher to demonstrate to pupils the necessity for mathematical accuracy to members of our society. Furthermore, it should not be difficult to demonstrate the desirability of being able to read and write our language properly. With this groundwork of understanding, the next step is to help the individual become aware of errors or other kinds of poor habits such as carelessness in handwriting as justification for engaging in practice and drill.

A philosophy of drill

There are several good guides for teachers that might serve as a sort of philosophy of drill. Sometimes a teacher derives a good deal of security from periodically taking stock of what he is doing and why, in relationship to some criteria. Perhaps some of the following suggestions will be helpful.

It is good for a teacher to remember that there are certain kinds of functions in the elementary school that demand drill. No apologies should be made for engaging pupils in drill activities in these functions. That is, no apology should be made for engaging children in these functions so long as good psychological rules are followed. Before engaging pupils in drill, one should be sure that they understand what it is that they are to drill and the reason for engaging in that practice. Here many teachers need to learn patience. Not all pupils are going to acquire meaning at the same time nor to the same degree, and this means that they cannot engage in practice at the same time. Related to this is the matter of diagnosing the need for drill. Some children, particularly those who are most able, will need little or no drill. This is simply a function of individual differences.

Because of these considerations drill should be individualized. To engage an entire class in the same drill for the same period of time undoubtedly would waste the time of a good number of pupils. Individualizing drill does not necessarily have to be done in the absolute. Children can work at drill in groups of two or three, and they can actually drill one another in small groups. Not all children will drill for the same length of time. Each learner should be allowed to keep track of his practice and his improvement as a result of practice. This helps the pupil gain insight into his progress, and he is encouraged by that insight.

A teacher should help pupils who are engaging in drill to keep their drill activities related to the context in which they come. This means that teachers and pupils need constantly to relate their drill to what they were doing that lead them into the drill activity. If, for example, continuous errors had kept appearing with certain words or kinds of words in the written materials of pupils, and drill had been launched upon those words for the purpose of improving spelling efficiency, the idea of the relation between that drill and the act of writing as a means of communicating ideas needs to be maintained. The need for drill upon arithmetic skills constantly must be related to accuracy in solving the kinds of problems that appear in our social life.

One rule from the learning laboratory should be followed. This comes from experiments in which data have been collected to produce what we call the learning curve. This rule essentially is that drill periods should diminish in length, and the length of intervals between them should be increased as children's efficiency increases. A corollary to this rule is periodically to review well-learned skills throughout the elementary school years.

ROUTINE

It is difficult to lay down any particular rules or procedures for routines in elementary school because these things differ so much from school to school and community to community. However, we can identify some of the kinds of routines that face most elementary school teachers and identify responsibilities and some techniques for carrying them out.

Kinds of routines

The number of routine tasks and the degree of enforcement of practice in these routine tasks varies from school to school. Therefore, any listing of them in a book of this kind must be accepted as being general, and must involve the hazards of including some that are not practiced as well as leaving some out that may be.

TAKING ATTENDANCE. Of all the routine tasks that might be identified, the act of taking attendance is no doubt the most universal task of elementary school teachers. At least three good reasons exist for this task's being imposed upon personnel of the elementary school. One of them is because the law says that children shall be in school, and the taking of attendance is a facet of the enforcement of that law. Another is that in many communities state aid is granted upon the basis of pupil attendance in school, and these records are essential for procurement of that aid. A third is a more social reason. We want to know whether all children who are suppose to be in school are in school. When parents send their children off to school in the morning, they expect that they will be there until school is dismissed. In some school communities this kind of social pressure is felt so much that school personnel even contact the home when children are not in attendance. They do this to verify the accuracy of the record and to find out the reason why a child is absent. Frequently this poll-taking presents school officials and the communities with evidence having to do with health, such as knowledge of epidemics of colds and influenza. But most important is the security check as to the presence of the child in the home.

DISTRIBUTING SUPPLIES. Most school supplies are distributed to children at the beginning of each year or semester. In those communities where schools furnish books to children, they are distributed once a year, or more frequently if a series of books is used. In this circumstance, distribution is a one-time operation, and it causes no continual routine problem for the classroom teacher. Each school or school district establishes some system of accounting for books and supplies so distributed, but once this has been done at the beginning of the year the only further disturbance comes at the end of the year or in the case of transfer pupils. Within each classroom, however, there frequently are circumstances where other supplies are distributed. For example, in a number of classrooms elementary school teachers will collect crayon boxes and keep them in a common storage place until they are needed. This then presents a distribution problem unless they are stored on an open shelf and children are allowed access to them. There are innumerable other circumstances in which distribution of such things as paper, song books, paint supplies, test booklets and so forth, presents situations in which some kind of routine organization is necessary.

MOVEMENT OF CHILDREN. In practically all schools the movement of pupils about the school building presents routine problems. There is the problem of moving them in and out of the room to toilets and fountains, to special classes, and at dismissal time. We have all been in classrooms where this problem has been handled in different ways. Some teachers solve this problem by lining children up in single file as they go to their lockers, to the lavatory, or the fountain. Others allow them to go in small groups under their own guidance. Still others allow them to proceed independently. The author has a special bias against seeing children lined up in single or double file for purposes of moving from one classroom to another or going to the front door to be dismissed from school. This is a highly militant procedure, and one is prone to think of it as something like moving prisoners from their cellblocks to the dining room and back again. Some place we must learn that *we can only teach children to become independent with respect to their own behavior, when we allow them to practice independence in the control of their own behavior.*

CONTROLLING HEAT, LIGHT, AND VENTILATION. It is the responsibility of a teacher to maintain a healthful environment in his classroom, with respect to heat, light, and ventilation. Problems in connection with these physical aspects of a classroom have been reduced in modern buildings because of improved techniques of heating, lighting, and ventilation. However, modern devices still have not been able to control completely these conditions. If a teacher is not careful the atmosphere of the classroom in the late hours of the morning and in the late hours of the afternoon session of the school day can become quite unpleasant. A person who walks into classrooms from the outdoors frequently is immediately aware of some of these conditions. In some schools heat and ventilation can be somewhat controlled by use of the thermostat and by opening and closing windows. With regard to opening windows, care must be taken that children are not placed in drafts. In schools where a forced-air system is used, a teacher who opens a window is apt to get in trouble with the heating engineer or the custodian, whichever the case may be. Matters like this must be cleared with the school administration and with the custodian. In most cases teachers will find that custodians are very reasonable persons who will cooperate with them in the control of heat and ventilation. Lighting in modern schools is not a serious problem.

ROUTINIZED EMERGENCIES. There are a number of emergencies in the school program for which plans can be made. Reference here is to what to do in case of fire or accident. In most communities fire drill is periodically required by law. Whether fire drill is required by law or not, every school should have fire drill procedures. Sometimes teachers are prone to become complacent about such things as fire drill because they naïvely assume that fire cannot happen in modern buildings. A talk with any municipal fire chief would furnish one with much information to the contrary. Teachers should encourage their children to participate seriously in all aspects of fire drill. Drill procedure should become so routinized that the children can carry them out with or without the direction of the classroom teacher. What to do about other emergencies is a problem that must be settled at each individual school level. Such questions as what to do with injuries on the playground or in the school building, when and how to get the help of a physician, when and how to procure ambulance service, when and how to contact parents of children in case of illness, when and how children are to be sent home from school because of accident or illness, and so forth, all are problems of an emergency nature which have solutions peculiar to every school community. Policies should be established in schools to take care of these matters, and if such policies do not exist teachers should seek their establishment through the school principal.

MAKING OUT REPORTS AND RECORDS. For many teachers the task of making records and reports is the most tedious thing they do. In many cases they cannot see any sense to the reports that they are required to make, and fail to feel a sense of responsibility for their preparation. For example, in many schools teachers are required to make out attendance reports either by the week or by the month, and more often than not, they are required to do this in circumstances where no clerical help is available in the school. In schools where clerical help is available these reports can be made out by clerks just as efficiently as they can by teachers, but teachers must report the data to the clerical personnel. In some small schools this burden is placed upon the principal of the school. Actually this is an imposition upon the person who is placed in the position of principal, and teachers should be willing to share that burden with him until other arrangements can be made. Pupil personnel records are another source of contention for teachers. The matter of keeping track of and tabulating pupil personnel data seems to some teachers to be an unreasonable demand upon their time. These records are very directly related to a teacher's primary function, and therefore teachers must constantly work with them. The matter of making out report cards or other forms of progress reports to parents is a task about which teachers have groaned ever since those devices were invented. It is true that some reports are more worthwhile than others. It is also true that making reports is a difficult task; but we must never forget that it is one of our basic responsibilities to report to the parents of elementary school children their progress in school. Parents are entitled to at least that much information from the schools. Actually they are entitled to much more, but certainly they are entitled to that much. We should attempt to do the best possible job in this function.

HOUSEKEEPING. Every teacher does a number of little housekeeping details in the course of the school day. A bookshelf may be dusted; a blackboard may be cleanly erased; some paper may be picked up from the floor; or spilled paint wiped up from the floor. In some schools there has been continual controversy between teachers and custodians of the school because custodians do not feel that teachers keep their rooms neat enough, and those teachers in turn think that the custodians are just lazy and do not want to do the work for which they are hired. This is a problem of human relations that can be solved only by those people who get themselves into such a controversy. Probably teachers began with housekeeping details at that point in our history when they were paid a stipend in addition to their salary, for sweeping the floor and keeping the school clean. When the first custodian was hired, the stage was set for the first problem in human relations between teachers and custodians. No real problem exists here. Any problems that may be created because of this kind of conflict can be eliminated by sensible human interaction. Whenever one assembles a group of people, particularly children, in one room of a building there are hundreds of possible housekeeping tasks to be performed. There seems to be no way by which teachers can dodge some of them.

Responsibility for routine

Since both teachers and pupils are affected by routine practices, the question can well be raised as to which tasks a teacher must do alone, which tasks pupils may do alone, and which tasks may be done cooperatively. There are certain things that a teacher must do alone, that is, alone or in conjunction with other teachers. However, of those indicated in the paragraphs above there are only a few that fall in this category. For example, making report cards is a task that only a teacher can do. This is the teacher's responsibility, and the teacher in the only person who has the necessary knowledge to do the job. Certain kinds of record-keeping such as anecdotal records and records of educational achievement are functions of the teacher. A teacher is basically responsible for the health aspects of the room with respect to heat, light and ventilation, although the assistance of engineering and custodial personnel should be solicited. Planning for the routine movement of pupils is a function of the teacher, but it may be done in cooperation with other teachers, pupils, and the school administration. School regulations with reference to the movement of children as they come into the school building and as they leave at the end of the school day would fall into this category, and so would any other school regulations pertaining to the movement of children throughout the school building during the school day.

The remainder of the routine can be done by both teachers and pupils or just the pupils themselves under the guidance of a teacher. For example, pupils can assist in taking attendance. They can distribute supplies; they can help with housekeeping routines. They can help in making decisions that affect them as to their movements throughout the building. Children can aid with reports such as attendance reports, or with collecting money for school lunches or midday snacks. It should be remembered that routine is established for the purpose of making a better school day for children within the limitations that must be imposed by institutional organization. Children must be taught that part of the responsibility for making routine as pleasant and effective as possible is theirs as school citizens. Teachers would do well to engage children in accepting as much responsibility for routine behavior and care of their classrooms as pupils are ready to accept.

Summary

In this chapter we have been concerned with the intelligent application of drill and routine procedures as a basic dimension of teaching. Regardless of our attitude toward these particular procedures, it must be remembered that they are necessary functions in the teaching-learning process and in the process of keeping a school going. For these two vital reasons teachers should recognize the significance of these procedures and utilize the best of man's knowledge in their practice.

Drill or practice, whichever term one prefers to use, was indicated to be an essential process for learning in which efficiency is desired. There are two principal reasons for utilizing drill or practice procedures. One of these is to develop greater retention on the part of pupils, and the other is to improve some performance because it is desirable to do so. The two critical facets of drill have to do with meaning and application. Drill must be preceded by meaning if drill is to be launched efficiently and for favorable results. For a great number of children drill is a monotonous task. The monotony of this task can be considerably reduced if pupils are taught reasons and justifications for engaging in that practice. Furthermore, when children understand the reason for becoming involved in drill, they are much more apt to be motivated to practice and to involve themselves psychologically in the activity to a greater extent.

Attention was directed toward the kinds of routine that most teachers will face, along with some of the problems involved. It was noted that certain routine practices would have to be done by teachers alone. Others can be done by pupils under the guidance of teachers. The principal reason for this suggestion is that children are closely affected by the decisions that are made with respect to routine affairs, and for this reason, they should participate in making many of those decisions.

An important aspect of both drill and routine seems to be that of the meaningful involvement of children in both activities. Here again we see the application of two things. First, the application of good psychological principles of learning and motivation. Second, the application of a basic principle of democratic living; that is, the principle that those who are to be affected by decisions should participate in the making of those decisions.

Ideas for discussion and activity

1. Make a list of five or ten circumstances in the elementary school in which drill might be needed. How should children be prepared for each? Which of these is done primarily for retention-building and which primarily for efficiency or improvement?

2. Read one pamphlet from the "What Research Says to the Teacher" series listed in the suggested readings and report the viewpoint of its author on the subject of drill or practice.

3. On what basis might a class be broken up into smaller groups for drill?

4. Look up the legal requirements for taking attendance in your state or community.

5. Formulate three or four guiding principles to govern your behavior as a teacher in dealing with routines.

Suggested readings

Association for Supervision and Curriculum Development, National Education Association, *The Three R's in the Elementary School.* Washington, D.C.: The Association, 1952.
This volume was dedicated to the task of showing how the "Three R's" can be developed functionally. Since these subjects usually are thought of as the skill subjects, the role of drill or practice in teaching them is of great significance.

Department of Classroom Teachers and the American Educational Re-
search Association, National Education Association. What Research
Says to the Teacher Series. Washington, D.C.: The Association.
No. 1. Arthur I. Gates, *Teaching Reading*. 1953.
No. 2. R. L. Morton, *Teaching Arithmetic*. 1953.
No. 3. Ernest Horn, *Teaching Spelling*. 1954.
No. 4. Frank N. Freeman, *Teaching Handwriting*. 1954.
No. 6. William Clark Trow, *The Learning Process*. 1954.
  All of the above issues in the series are devoted to subjects related to
  the topics of this chapter. Try to read at least one of them.

Dougherty, James Henry, Frank Hermon Gorman, and Claude Anderson
Phillips, *Elementary School Organization and Management*. Revised
edition. New York: The MacMillan Company, 1950, Chapter 4.
  Problems of routine are related to good classroom atmosphere.

Shane, Harold G., *Research Helps in Teaching the Language Arts*.
Association for Supervision and Curriculum Development, National
Education Association. Washington, D.C.: The Association, 1955.
  This pamphlet is essentially a review of research in the teaching of
  the language arts. It interprets in simple language the results of
  research for the teaching situation.

Wingo, G. Max and Raleigh Schorling, *Elementary-School Student
Teaching*. Second edition. New York: McGraw-Hill Book Company,
Inc., 1955, Chapter 11.
  This chapter contains a fine section on the use of drill in the elementary
  classroom.

CHAPTER 13

Guiding and Pacing Learners

I T MAY APPEAR odd to the reader that a chapter on guiding and pacing learners should be included as a dimension of method in the teaching-learning process rather than as a phase of studying school pupils. The purpose for making this distinction is to emphasize the point that the problems and techniques of studying children to provide information is one dimension of the total teaching act, whereas the application of those techniques in the classroom in order to produce better learning on the part of children more rightfully belongs here with different emphasis.

In our professional literature there is some confusion resulting from the use of terminology, particularly the two terms *guidance* and *teaching*. This state of affairs is another cause for some attention to be given to this topic. Some of the confusion is unavoidable, but it can be reduced.

In this chapter our attention will be focused upon the relationship between the guiding and teaching functions of the classroom teacher. Special attention is directed to pacing as a particular technique in adjusting learning activities of elementary school pupils in a more profitable manner. Many of the techniques frequently discussed under guidance are appropriate in connection with pacing.

GUIDANCE AND TEACHING

It is impossible to make a straight delineation between guidance and teaching. The best we can do is to examine a generalized meaning of each of these functions and their inter-locking roles.

General meaning of guidance

Guidance is a term that few attempt to define specifically. The term is used generally to describe activities related to the adjustment, that is the personality adjustment, of an individual. The principal work of the guidance person is to provide an environment for good personality development. In Chapter 3, it was indicated that one purpose of studying and diagnosing children in the elementary school is to acquire knowledge that can be used by a teacher in pupil guidance activities, and that by pupil guidance activities is meant methods of helping a pupil fulfill his potential to the greatest degree possible in the classroom. In modern education, guidance becomes such a broad concept that it has many applications. For example, there are persons employed in the guidance field who are primarily concerned with helping persons in their choice and pursuit of vocation. This we think of as vocational guidance. Other persons are employed in what is called educational guidance. The term is self-explanatory. Others are involved in what may be called personal guidance or adjustment counseling. These persons are mostly concerned with the stability of the individual personality and its adjustment to its environment. The modern tendency is to think of all of these ramifications when using the term guidance, but vocational guidance is not the concern of the elementary school teacher.

General meaning of teaching

The objectives of teaching are twofold. One is to satisfy the social demand for institutionalized education, and the other is to help individual pupils to expand their potentials within the school structure. In order to fulfill these objectives a teacher must perform at least three general tasks. First, he must engage in curriculum planning. Second, he must manipulate the class-room environment by organizing subject matter and arranging pupils for interaction with that subject matter, so that the objectives of the curriculum can be fulfilled. Finally, he must participate in evaluating the curriculum and the teaching-learning situation.

Interlocking roles

From the brief comments above it is obvious that persons occupying positions of guidance and teaching must play interlocking roles. If a teacher is interested in those activities designed to implement curriculum experience, certainly he will be confronted by problems of personality differences of children in his classroom. These differences will cause the teacher to engage in activities that are related to better personality adjustment in order that the educational program can go on. On the other hand, the guidance person, in order to work with problems of adjustment in a school, must also be concerned with the kinds of curriculum experiences that are provided. Many of the activities related to testing and test interpretation are guidance functions even though in other circumstances they may be teaching functions. Perhaps the most discreet way to make a distinction is through the purpose for which each activity is launched. When one is principally concerned with the personality adjustment of a child, this is more specifically a guidance role. On the other hand, one may do many of the same things in connection with a child's personality adjustment or personality growth, but here he is concerned with applying the results in such a way as to produce a better educational environment for the child.

The guidance specialist

In recent years new specialists have been introduced to the staff organizations of a number of elementary schools in this country. These persons are called guidance specialists. The specific role that the specialist has to play in the elementary school has yet to be carefully defined. This is especially true when we think of the possibility that there might be employed in a school or a school system such a person as a psychometrician or a clinical psychologist. Either of these persons could perform some guidance functions. In many schools, persons classified as guidance specialists are performing these functions. It is no doubt safe to say that the hope of many school teachers in welcoming the guidance specialists to the elementary school is that they will get some help from these individuals in coping with serious personality disorders in the school. In some cases the guidance person is used mostly as a psychometrician; that is, one who is concerned with the administration and interpretation of tests. This is a narrow interpretation of the role of a guidance person. Regardless of what specific role the guidance specialists have played in the elementary school, they have generally been welcome persons to the teachers in those schools. But our original generalization that this is a position yet to be carefully defined, still holds true.

GUIDANCE FUNCTIONS OF THE TEACHER

To argue about which functions belong to whom, the guidance specialist or the classroom teacher, is a useless argument in the elementary school particularly. The argument becomes more ridiculous when people attempt to discuss which function is at a higher level in the educational echelon, guidance or teaching. The important thing to take into account is that guidance services need to be performed for children in the best possible manner. The question concerning which guidance services are to be performed and by whom, follows from this conclusion.

Essential services

There are a number of ways that guidance services in the elementary school can be indicated. Let us first look at one or two specific proposals. Here are what Arthur E. Traxler calls the ten essentials of guidance services in the elementary school:

1. Formulated purposes
2. A well-placed and carefully executed testing program
3. A well-organized cumulative record
4. Application of techniques for appraisal of personal qualities
5. A program that is adapted to the school
6. Developed procedures for parent contact
7. Cooperation with teachers in correction of pupils
8. A continuous plan for teacher education about guidance
9. Knowledge about referral to outside agencies
10. A program of follow-up of pupils.[1]

Raymond Hatch insists upon very much the same services, except that he groups them under three more general headings: (1) pupil inventory services, (2) the information service, and (3) the counseling service.[2] Both Traxler and Hatch write from a guidance frame of reference. A group of authors approaching the subject from the point of view of classroom teaching in the elementary school, discuss the following special guidance services: testing services, health services, recreational services, welfare services, special education services, mental health and psychiatric services, cumulative record services.[3]

These three references indicate to us the scope of possible guidance services in the elementary school. When these are all boiled down into the very plain language of elementary school operation, they mean that elementary schools must perform the following functions in order that teachers may better guide learners in their classrooms:

1. Schools need good pupil personnel records

[1] Arthur E. Traxler, "Essentials of Guidance Services in Elementary Schools," *Elementary School Journal*, 53:207-210 (December, 1952).
[2] Raymond N. Hatch, *Guidance Services in the Elementary School* (Dubuque, Iowa: William C. Brown Company, 1951).
[3] Herbert J. Klausemier, Katharine Dresden, Helen C. Davis, and Walter Arno Wittich, *Teaching in the Elementary School* (New York: Harper and Brothers, 1956), pp. 537-568.

2. Schools need a program of pupil diagnosis and instruction

3. School pupils need to be humanely treated

4. Schools need to maintain contacts with homes, including reporting procedures

5. Schools must know how to cope with problems of individual, social-emotional disturbances.

Implications for teachers

Now let us examine these school functions in terms of some of the specific tasks that teachers must perform in order to do a better job of guiding and pacing their learners, whether they be classified as guidance or teaching functions.

MAINTAINING RECORDS. Every teacher must contribute toward the maintenance of pupil personnel records. Data to be included briefly would be historical information, information having to do with pupil capacity, information having to do with educational achievement, and information having to do with personality adjustment. Certain of these types of information can be furnished to the pupil personnel record file by guidance specialists. This is particularly true of results of intelligent testing or any projective techniques that may be used. In some cases the guidance person may be instrumental in the procurement of information having to do with educational achievement, but more often this belongs to the teacher's responsibility. Most of the historical information and behavior information must be procured by the teacher. In the case of behavior information, the anecdotal record is likely the most important device.

DIAGNOSIS AND INSTRUCTION. A program of diagnosis and instruction for the elementary school must be centered around classroom activity. In fact, to say that the program of diagnosis and instruction belongs to the guidance program takes some stretch of the imagination. The function of studying and diagnosing pupils for the purpose of instruction has always been a task of cardinal importance for the classroom teacher. Our objectives should be to solicit the help of trained guidance people in the diagnosis of pupils, in order to effect a better instructional program for those pupils.

HUMANE TREATMENT OF PUPILS. Humane treatment of pupils in the elementary school classroom is as much a matter of teacher *attitude* as it is a matter of specific things that teachers should do. That children have the basic psychological needs of security, belongingness, success, and recognition, just as do adults, is most important. To insure that these basic psychological needs of children are met, more must be done than simply the administration and interpretation of test data or the manipulation of subject matter itself. Some kind of personal contact must be made between teacher and pupil. Every elementary school teacher who is aware of these pupil needs gears his school day so that he can spend some time in individual and personal counseling with pupils. This does not mean that each time a counseling interview is held with an elementary school pupil that the teacher and pupil need to go off into a separate room by themselves. Nor does it mean that a separate period of time during the day needs to be set aside for these interviews. The casual contact with the individual pupil is just as significant in this respect as is a planned interview. As a teacher stops beside a pupil while he is at work for the purpose of discussing with him what he is doing, why he is doing it, and what his particular interest is in performing that task, that teacher is engaged in pupil counseling. A conflict situation between two pupils may be a springboard to interviews with those pupils as to their general hopes and aspirations in school life, as well as to cause and effect relationships of the specific situation.

The most important thing for a teacher to remember in conducting any kind of counseling interview with elementary school pupils is that he must maintain faith in the integrity of the pupil as to both his accuracy of statement and his stipulated motivation. It is also important that the teacher who counsels a pupil constantly reflects an attitude of interest in each pupil's problems no matter how simple they may be, and always demonstrates courteousness and friendliness. For many pupils the most important result of teacher counseling is encouragement in attacking problems. The individual who is lacking in assurance needs considerable encouragement and praise. The individual who is overconfident also needs encouragement, but perhaps in the direction of humility. In any case a teacher must be forthright and honest with his pupils. In no circumstance should the teacher ever attempt to deceive a child.

HOME CONTACT. Sometimes it is impossible to gain a broad picture of an elementary school pupil's outlook upon life by observing him only in the school. Most writers will agree that home contact by elementary school teachers is a desirable feature of a total school program; and it is true that a teacher can acquire many insights into behavior of his pupils by some personal contact with the home. In many of our school communities, particularly in large urban areas, the problem of making visits to the home is very great. Large numbers of pupils and frequently long distances for teachers to travel from work make home visitation a difficult task. In some of the larger school systems home-contact teachers are available, but these persons are used only in serious cases. Nevertheless, the desirability of having teachers make home contacts is still something to be cherished. Every teacher who has had the opportunity to contact homes of pupils realizes he understands those pupils a little better because he sees firsthand the kinds of environment in which the children live. Of course, there is always the reporting procedure as a means of home contact, but in those cases where report cards are used this contact is very impersonal.

SOCIAL-EMOTIONAL DISTURBANCES. Obviously if an elementary school teacher has a child in his classroom who is for any configuration of reasons what is frequently called socially or emotionally disturbed, a functional problem is posed. Generally teachers must continue to have that child in the classroom, and because of this they must do everything in their power to make the school experience a profitable one for that individual.

One of the problems is the identification of individuals who may not be secure in the school environment. The teacher has initial contact with the school pupil; therefore, he must obtain initial information to identify this type of child. Here again reference must be made to the suggestions of Axline (see p. 86) with reference to caution in labeling pupils who are somewhat at variance with other children in their behaviors. Nevertheless, it is possible for a teacher to begin to identify some behavioral characteristics that indicate that the school pupil is not comfortable in his school environment. Frequently this can be done without any standardized device. For example, a child who constantly exhibits aggressive behavior toward his fellow pupils is for some reason or another at variance with his human environment. The pupil who constantly withdraws from group activities in the classroom and on the playground is somewhat out of step with his social environment. Probably the best way in which this kind of identification can be noted is through the behavior journal or other forms of the anecdotal record. It would be impossible to cover the entire range of possibilities for disturbances, but it is safe to conclude that many identifications of simple deviant behaviors can be noted by the classroom teacher. Serious cases are another matter.

Referral of special cases

The referral of special cases for guidance depends upon the services that are available to classroom teachers. A new teacher going into a school should quickly acquaint himself with the availability of these special services. The school may have a school psychologist who is trained in clinical techniques for diagnosing social and emotional disturbances and who can assist in therapy. Some school systems have a psychiatrist available for diagnosis and treatment. Other schools have social workers available who are trained in making home contacts and in diagnosing effects of the home environment upon child behavior. Then, of course, there is the school that has none of these facilities, and anything a teacher may do in the matter of referral must be through some outside agency like the welfare bureau, city or county health authorities, or privately procured help through the individual family. The avenues for referral should be reasonably clear and teachers should consult their administrators for this information.

It is dangerous to attempt to specify a critical point at which a referral case is distinguished from a non-referral case. Most of the smaller problems can be handled by intelligent application of knowledge acquired by most elementary school teachers, but whenever doubt exists in the mind of a teacher, he should consult someone else. If no specialized help is available for consultation, a teacher should go to the principal of the school to obtain his advice concerning further action. However, no teacher should go to a principal, to a school psychologist, or to a guidance specialist without information to direct the discussion. The best information a teacher can acquire that will be helpful to those with whom he confers is the anecdotal record. In most cases where the teacher is ignorant about children who behave in an unusual manner, a problem arises because he has not sought information. In this respect it is appropriate to say that all behavior is caused; we simply need to seek the cause. Knowing the cause provides the first step in remediation.

THE TEACHER AS A PACER

Ever since the first time children were assembled together for the purpose of instruction, teachers have been plagued with problems of providing for unique differences among those pupils. Whether we classify these attempts as guidance or use some other term is relatively unimportant. One classification of attempts to solve some of these problems was described under the subject of grouping techniques in the previous chapter. Another has been those attempts at individualization of instruction through different organizations of instructional materials. To the author, the notion that has the greatest value in meeting the complexity of individualization is *pacing*. Pacing simply refers to activities on the part of a teacher to adjust both the curriculum content and his rate of expectancy for pupils, to the capacity of pupils to learn. The role of the teacher is one of acting as the pacer. A comparison can be made with a technique that is sometimes employed in athletics, particularly in racing activities. In distance running a coach sometimes will put into a race an individual other than the person or persons expected to win the race. It is the function of this individual to time his running very carefully in accordance with a previously arranged schedule. The star or stars in the race can then adjust their pace to this individual who has been put there for the specific purpose of timing the event. They can thereby conserve their energies until they need them in the final sprint of the race. This individual can be called a pacer. The teacher acts much in this same capacity. He is the one who is responsible for adjusting the learning environment in accordance with the predetermined interests and capacities of pupils.

Individual differences and pacing

It has been indicated that in the course of the elementary school years the range of individual abilities, or differences, fans out increasingly as children mature. In the first place this expansion is a function of natural growth. It is difficult to disturb this function because of the established fact that children of greater capacity increase their total capacity at an accelerated rate over those of lesser capacity. Therefore time is an essential element in producing a wider range of individual differences as children proceed through the elementary school.

One of the lessons taught us by the study of individual

differences is that there is no systematic way of effectively reducing the range of individual differences in elementary schools by homogeneous grouping. It also is a cardinal principle of modern education that, since all children are different, they therefore need to be treated differently in the classroom. If education is what it purports to be, then the activities that children perform in the elementary school years should accentuate or increase ranges in individual differences rather than decrease them. Obviously then, attempts to group children so that they can perform alike or attempts to arrange individual assignments so that all children will do the same thing at the same time and to the same degree, actually are a denial of what we know about individual differences. In fact it is safe to say that the very great problem of elementary method of modern times is one of adjusting an instructional program to this range of individual differences.

The most fruitful concept for dealing with the problem of individual differences appears to be this one of pacing. It simply refers to all of the operations that contribute to the arrangement of learning experiences for children; in operation this concept does two things. First, it arranges learning activities in terms of difficulty, scope, and sequential organization, so each child will be able to perform with some sense of security and success in the classroom. Second, it allows an arrangement of learning experiences in terms of difficulty, scope, and sequence, that will challenge the ability of every individual pupil.

Teacher expectancy and pacing

Most important for the application of the concept of pacing to elementary school instruction is the matter of teacher attitude; that is, the attitude that a teacher holds with reference to what pupils shall do. This is a matter of what expectancy a teacher may have for pupils. As in any other field of human endeavor that has a range or degrees of operation, teacher expectancy likewise has two poles. On the one hand there is the danger that teachers will expect children to do too much, and on the other hand, that their expectations for children will be too low to challenge them in the classroom.

A most important aspect of this matter of teacher expectancy is the one of willingness on the part of the classroom teacher to face up to the problem of individual differences in the same light in which it is discussed here. There is a certain amount of educational lag in teaching method and practice. This lag is indicated here by the fact that thousands of elementary school classrooms all over the country are still organized as though children assembled in the same classroom were actually alike. They are expected to do the same things and at the same time and are graded on report cards under the same philosophy. They get high grades if they do what they are expected to do; they get low grades if they do not. In light of this kind of practice, teacher attitude is a most important feature in the application of the pacing concept.

At the risk of repetition it may said that in addition to proper attitude, knowledge on the part of teachers is an important prerequisite for sound pacing. Teachers must acquire a great deal of knowledge about the individual children in their classrooms before their attitudes can properly be adjusted and before they can be expected to engage in pacing activities. This is more difficult in schools where poor pupil personnel records are available, than in schools that have adequate records.

In addition to teacher attitude and to knowledge of pupils on the part of teachers, the organization of curriculum or teaching materials is important. It has previously been indicated that it is desirable that curriculum and instructional materials be flexibly organized so that teachers can adjust the educational program to individual differences. Realistic acceptance of the role of flexibility in the organization of curriculum materials is most helpful for teachers as a prerequisite for pacing.

Some techniques

Many of the generalized techniques by which a teacher acts as
a pacer have already been discussed. One of these was the matter
of organizing materials in a flexible manner and encompassing
a broad range so that every pupil has an opportunity to select
from the curriculum experiences, things in which he can succeed.
A second group centered around the organization of pupils
within the classroom according to their interests or some other
criteria for the purpose of carrying out planned activities.

It should be noted, however, that grouping alone will not
take care of all problems of pacing. In fact Millard indicates
that pacing should be used rather than grouping.[4] Millard here,
however, is referring mostly to the act of grouping at the administrative level according to some criteria, in the hope that more
homogeneous groups will be established and therefore reduce
the problem of individual differences. In this sense pacing is a
different concept from grouping. On the other hand, if one
thinks of grouping as a technique within a classroom for the
purpose of organizing pupils individually and collectively to
carry out a wide range of activities, then grouping becomes a
means of pacing. In this sense grouping is an acceptable pacing
technique.

More specifically, we might mention several things that teachers may do in the act of pacing individual pupils. In their
work *teachers should apply the principle of selectivity;* that is,
selectivity on the part of pupils for the activities in which they
will engage. To do this teachers must plan a wide range of
activities for children so that the desired learning can be attained
at whatever level pupils are capable of reaching. We must
remember that there is no *one* way by which children can obtain
a skill or bit of knowledge. There are many ways. For example,

[4] Cecil V. Millard, *Child Growth and Development in the Elementary School
Years* (Boston: D.C. Heath and Company, 1951), p. 141.

take the concept of gravity with its meaning and application. This kind of information can be acquired in innumerable ways and to different degrees. There is a vast range between the simple observation that objects that have weight fall to the ground, and the ability to apply the laws of gravity to the solution of problems in physics. Just as this wide range exists on the level of conceptualization and application, there is a wide range in the abilities of pupils to conceptualize and apply. In the application of the principle of selectivity teachers must be willing to accept the entire range.

Teachers should sponsor individual and group planning. This has been emphasized before, but it cannot be stressed too much when one takes into account the fact that every learner must somehow personally and psychologically involve himself in his learning activities. Through the planning activity he has an opportunity to select and to organize himself in relation to the activities he is to perform. There is always the problem of judging capacity and interest. One of the great outcomes of realistic planning, in addition to self-involvement, is that an opportunity is presented for others to help the teacher in the act of pacing. Youngsters in a classroom know each other well, and under the stimulation of good planning sessions they tend to pace one another. We have all seen situations in which one pupil has said to another, "You can do this if you try," or "We know you can do better and we will help you." Add to this the fact that people working in groups can and do learn from one another.

Pupils should be helped to relate their activities to their purposes. So frequently we do not take time to help pupils delineate their purposes or goals in their educational activities. By neglecting to do so we fail to insure that children establish a direction for themselves. Without this sense of direction many pupils become lost because they are incapable of establishing that direction for themselves. The fundamental process here is evaluation. Evaluation is one of the neglected dimensions of method in all education. We constantly make reference to the establishment of goals. We plan activities in light of those goals and, too frequently, we stop at the conclusion of those activities. To fail to relate the results of those activities to the originally established goals is to fail to complete the total educational act. Through evaluation children have greater opportunity to develop a sense of worth from what they have done and usually a sense of success. So frequently with children of elementary school age a sense of success at one level of activity is a prerequisite to the next. Teachers who fail to provide this prerequisite are missing one of the most important motivational devices available to them.

Summary

The teacher performs many functions of a guidance nature. Many of these have to do with school services such as record-keeping, testing, and reporting. Others have to do with inter-personal activities between pupil and teacher, including counseling. All of these are part of that dimension of method concerned with guiding learners in the classroom, which is different from those dimensions of method in the organization of instructional materials and studying pupils. Here we are concerned with focusing our attention upon the manipulation of children with their learning environments so that the learners can profit most from this inter-action.

Pacing has been identified as a most significant concept for this purpose. Pacing refers to a process of presentation and organization of learning experiences for individual children, according to difficulty, magnitude, and sequence. In addition to background information such as pupil capacity, educational growth, and social and emotional stability, teacher expectancy is a most important prerequisite for good pacing. The attitude of a teacher here is important in two respects. One is a matter of understanding pupils sufficiently so that his expectations can be realistically geared to their abilities. The other is a plain willingness to be realistic.

Ideas for discussion and activity

1. After reading this chapter, what do you think is the responsibility of the school for the personality development of children?

2. Check your understanding of the following concepts:
   guidance
   motivation
   pacing

3. How can the concept *pacing* be related to intelligent application of drill?

4. In your estimation, how can a classroom teacher best use the services of a guidance specialist?

5. Identify five guidance functions that a classroom teacher may perform.

Suggested readings

Gordon, Ira J., *The Teacher as a Guidance Worker*. New York: Harper & Brothers, 1956.
    Parts I and II are appropriate for the present discussion. The chapters in Part I deal with the nature of guidance, and those in Part II focus upon the teacher's specific roles.

Hatch, Raymond N., *Guidance Services in the Elementary School*. Dubuque: William C. Brown Company, 1951.
    Here is a pamphlet describing the guidance services of the elementary school. Three principal classes of service are discussed.

McCandless, Boyd, "Unreasonable Expectations," *Guiding Children in School and Out*. Washington, D. C.: The Association for Childhood Education International, Reprint Service Bulletin No. 25, pp. 15-18.
    This is a very challenging article on the expectations of teachers for the behaviors of children.

National Society for the Study of Education, *Mental Health in Modern Education*. Fifty-fourth Yearbook, Part II. Chicago: The University of Chicago Press, 1955.
    The entire volume is devoted to the mental health of school people. Select a chapter that appeals to you and read it. The chapters in Section III are most closely related to the subject under discussion in the foregoing chapter.

Ojemann, Ralph H., *Personality Adjustment of Individual Children.* What Research Says to the Teacher Series, No. 5. Department of Classroom Teachers and the American Educational Research Association, National Education Association. Washington, D.C.: The Association, 1954.
  The implications of research for teachers in the area of personality adjustment are summarized. Some very specific suggestions for teachers are included.
Traxler, Arthur E., "Essentials of Guidance Services in Elementary Schools," *Elementary School Journal,* 50:207-210; December, 1952.
  This is an article in which ten essentials of a guidance program for the elementary school are described.

CHAPTER 14

Discipline

DISCIPLINE, or the act of maintaining discipline, is a very important dimension of teaching. It is crucial to both the success and the happiness of a teacher in the profession. At one midwestern University it was the custom for a number of years to invite those recent graduates who were in their first year of teaching to meet with persons with whom they had worked while they were on campus. Consistently these returning teachers reported that their outstanding problem was discipline and that they felt they still needed help with problems of control. In a book addressed to the beginning teacher, a group of authors reported that inability to handle the conduct of children in an effective manner was a greater cause of failure on the part of teachers during their first year than any other cause.[1] In a study of the reactions of two hundred teachers to certain aspects of problem behavior in schools, it was noted that discipline and problem behavior cases in schools were the causes of some teachers to leave the profession, and that beginning teachers have had more trouble with problem behavior than have experienced teachers. The report further indicated that teachers need help from many sources in the solution of this kind of problem.[2]

[1] Wilbur A. Yauch, Martin H. Bartels, and Emmet Morris, *The Beginning Teacher* (New York: Henry Holt and Company, 1955), p. 184.
[2] Merrill T. Eaton, Garret Weathers, and Beeman N. Phillips, "Some Reactions of Classroom Teachers to Problem Behavior in School," *Educational Administration and Supervision*, 43:129-139 (March, 1957).

These observations indicate the significance of discipline as a dimension of teaching, as it is generally interpreted and discussed by teachers.

To different people discipline means different things. The number of interpretations that are made of discipline need to be clarified for the purpose of communication, and a teacher must become a student of discipline to be aware of the various interpretations of the concept.

INTERPRETATIONS OF DISCIPLINE

Two basic approaches have been made to the interpretation of the concept of discipline. One of these is through attempts at defining discipline, and the other is through the application of the concept in practice.

Discipline defined

In the *Dictionary of Education* discipline is defined as:

> ... (1) the process or result of directing or subordinating immediate wishes, impulses, desires, or interests for the sake of an ideal or for the purpose of gaining more effective, dependable action; (2) persistent, active, and self-directed pursuit of some selected course of action, even in the face of obstacles or distractions; (3) direct authoritative control of pupil behavior through punishments and/or rewards; (4) negatively, any restraint of impulses, frequently through distasteful or painful means." [3]

Sheviakov and Redl, in one of the most thorough and modern treatments of discipline, indicate that there are three prevailing meanings of discipline. The first of these has to do with the degree of order that is established in a group. The second meaning is attached to a trick or tricks by which order is established, and the third meaning is that of punishment. [4]

---

[3] Carter V. Good (ed.), *Dictionary of Education* (New York: McGraw-Hill Book Company, Inc., 1945), p. 184.
[4] George V. Sheviakov and Fritz Redl, *Discipline for Today's Children and Youth.* New Rev. by Sybil K. Richardson (Washington, D.C.: Association for Supervision and Curriculum Development, National Education Association, 1956), pp. 3-4.

In directing their comments toward elementary-school student teachers, Wingo and Schorling indicate that "... discipline in the social sense means the establishment of orderly social processes in a group." [5] In a discussion of interest and discipline Dewey states:

> A person who is trained to consider his actions, to undertake them deliberately, is in so far forth disciplined. Add to this ability a power to endure in an intelligently chosen course in face of distraction, confusion, and difficulty, and you have the essence of discipline. [6]

And further he adds:

> Discipline is positive. To cow the spirit, to subdue inclination, to compel obedience, to mortify the flesh, to make a subordinate perform an incongenial task — these things are or are not disciplinary according as they do or do not tend to the development of power to recognize what one is about and to persistence in accomplishment. [7]

Many of the similarities in these definitions are obvious, but at the same time differences in emphasis or application of the concept are also apparent. These will become more apparent as our attention is directed to applications of the concept.

Discipline applied

Interpretations of discipline are very greatly dependent upon the application that one associates with the meaning of the term. In addition to the specific applications that cause various connotations of discipline, the historical use of the concept has some bearing.

One can think of the application of discipline at levels and these levels can have extremes. No doubt the lowest and oldest level of the concept and application of discipline is that of corporal punishment. In spite of the fact that most of us would consider corporal punishment as the lowest level of discipline,

[5] G. Max Wingo and Raleigh Schorling, *Elementary School Student Teaching*, 2nd Ed. (New York: McGraw-Hill Book Company, Inc., 1955), p. 302.
[6] John Dewey, *Democracy and Education* (New York: The MacMillan Company, 1916), p. 151.
[7] *Ibid.*, pp. 151-152.

this is the most useful meaning of the word for many persons. This is particularly true when discipline is discussed in relationship to children. In the minds of many persons the disciplining of children is a matter of punishing them for their wrong doings.

A second level of application is in the notion of mental discipline. This notion stems from the era during which psychologists believed in formal discipline and faculty psychology. To put it briefly and bluntly, the psychologists of that time thought of the mind much in the same respect that we think of a muscle— as an organ of the body that could be developed through exercise. In applying this notion to education, certain of the school subjects such as Latin, Greek, and mathematics were thought to be the best subjects for purposes of administering exercise to the muscle. Therefore, those subjects were vigorously applied to school pupils under the assumption that the rigors of that exercise would discipline the mind. Most psychologists and educators have given up this notion. However, there are still a few people who expect us to apply some of the basic principles of formal discipline in modern elementary schools.

A third level of application of the concept refers to the disciplined mind. This level sounds suspiciously like the one mentioned immediately above. However, this is more in the spirit of the definition given by Dewey in the preceding section where he speaks of a person who is able to consider his actions and deliberately undertake them. This interpretation refers to an ability to pursue a course of action persistently toward a sought goal. Discipline in this sense involves learning, interest, and habit. The disciplined mind is possessed by the individual who can select an aim or a goal worthy of his attention, devise a scheme for achieving that goal, and persistently pursue that course of action. The disciplined mind in this sense is achieved not through any particular type of exercise nor by any special kind of subject matter. It is something that develops over a period of time as a result of consistently using intelligent action in the solution of problems.

The fourth and highest level of the application of the concept of discipline is what may be called the self-directional level. The self-directional interpretation is very close in meaning to that of the disciplined mind. Essentially they are two different expressions for much the same phenomenon. Some persons object to using the term disciplined mind because of the implications of faculty psychology and formal discipline, and therefore they prefer the notion of self-direction or self-control as being the highest level of discipline. In this notion, emphasis is placed upon control from within the individual himself. In a very practical sense this means that teachers constantly must manipulate the environment, pupils, and subject matter in such a way that youngsters assume greater control over their own behaviors. In a sense, this is opposed to the idea of imposing control upon them from without. As Marie Rasey rather humorously put it, "One does not pull a stalk of corn to hasten its growth. One fertilizes the soil." [8] It is toward this self-directional level that the vast majority of effort in modern elementary education is pointed. More of this will become apparent as the subsequent discussion unfolds.

THE PSYCHOLOGY OF CONTROL

From the foregoing discussion, it is apparent that there are two aspects of the application of discipline to human development. One of these is the matter of development of self-control, and the other is consideration of control established over the behavior of people. This dual aspect is thoroughly examined in an article by Wegener. Wegener's thesis is that human control is a result of proportionate influences of two poles. One of these poles is characterized by external and necessary forces. The other pole is characterized by internal and liberal factors. The first pole is

[8] Marie I. Rasey, "Discipline—What Is it?" *Discipline*, Bulletin 99, Association for Childhood Education International (Washington D.C.: The Association, 1957), p. 7.

more characteristic of childhood, particularly early childhood, and the other pole more characteristic of the adolescent and the adult. According to Wegener's argument, human development proceeds from the first pole toward the second pole, with the life of the immature more governed by the external factors and the life of the more mature by internal factors. The point is that never does one of these two groups of polar forces in one's life completely control human action. Until an individual is sufficiently mature to govern his actions primarily by internal control, external control must be applied.[9]

If Wegener's theory of control can be accepted, it will help to remove much of the confusion in thinking about the control of school pupils in our elementary school classrooms. We sometimes are prone to think that we somehow can mystically establish self-control on the part of pupils quite early in life and expect it to persist throughout the remaining school years. Under this kind of hallucination teachers are frustrated when they are forced to place external controls upon school pupils in order to keep school in session. Perhaps it will help if we realize that control for the young must be externally applied until an individual is able to control his behavior internally in a socially acceptable manner.

Problems posed in classrooms

Many problems are posed for teachers by virtue of the fact that pupils of elementary school age are assembled in classrooms. In the first place, pupils assembled in any given classroom have many individual interests and motives. The existence of these individual interests and motives causes them to want to behave in different ways and carry on different kinds of activities. As soon as the school situation requires an individual, especially an immature individual, to perform some activity that is contrary to his immediate interest, a possibility exists for a discipline or

[9] Frank C. Wegener, "The Organic Theory of Control," *Educational Theory,* 43: 170-176 (July, 1956).

control situation. In most elementary school classrooms this can happen at any moment of the day.

In adddition to differences in interest and motivation, children assembled in classrooms have variant abilities. Some can engage in learning activity and proceed very rapidly. Others proceed very slowly. The matter of timing here is very important. The individual who finishes school tasks early becomes bored if he does not have another task. The individual who is slow becomes frustrated if time does not permit him to finish. Each of these situations can create control problems.

The facilities within which we place children in schools limit the kinds of behavior that pupils may exhibit. Most elementary school classrooms are not conducive to the throwing of objects, the playing of games involving violent movement, or the yelling of exuberant voices. Most of these activities belong outdoors where space and Mother Nature can help avoid the disastrous effects they would have within the confines of a classroom. These activities must be restrained so children can work at the kinds of tasks planned for classrooms.

Finally, another problem posed by the assemblage of pupils in classrooms stems from the fact that group behavior is a skill to be learned. It takes a long time for this skill to develop to a high degree of efficiency. We must expect that external controls will have to be inflicted upon elementary school children to varying degrees throughout the elementary school years. As the children become older and proceed into the upper grades, we should expect, if our job has been done well, that many of the acceptable skills in group behavior will have been learned and will be in practice. A great deal depends upon the degree of consistency and persistency with which teachers in an elementary school building all work toward the teaching of these skills.

Choices for teachers

A teacher is in a very interesting position with regard to the control of children in his classroom. Because of a dedication to the task of helping our young citizens become more mature in a manner that is educationally accepted, the teacher must work in the direction of relinquishing control over children's behavior. On the other hand, because children are required to be in school and because society issues a mandate to teachers to perform a certain educational task, they must control children so that this task may be accomplished.

In describing possible actions on the part of teachers in carrying out this dual responsibility, Yauch indicates that a teacher has at his command four levels of appeal to children: the level of self-satisfaction, the level of reward, the level of fear and threat, and the level of punishment.[10] It should be noted that these are listed in descending order of "goodness." They indicate both the aspirational aspect of the teacher's task as well as the aspect of external control.

A special word might be said about reward and punishment. One of the things that modern psychology and education stress is that there should be some relationship among goals, actions, and consequences. They should not only be externally related, but they should be related internally or psychologically as far as the learner is concerned. For example, there is a real difference between pasting a gold star on a chart along side a pupil's name for doing well on an arithmetic assignment, and helping the individual become aware of the fact that he has acquired a new power, that it is useful to him, and that he has done well in the process. Conversely, it is most apt to be ineffective to punish a learner for failure to perform to an expected degree with some form of punishment completely unrelated to the act. For example, the author has often speculated how many times in his elementary school years he was forced to stay after school and write the expression, "I will not whisper" one hundred or more times depending upon the degree to which he had

10 Wilbur A. Yauch, *How Good Is Your School?* (Harper and Brothers, 1951), pp. 140-143.

irritated the teacher. It had absolutely nothing to do with stopping the whispering in the classroom. That has never stopped; he is still whispering in groups. About all it did was to teach him techniques of holding two and three pencils in his hand at one time so that he could write "I will not whisper" three times with one movement of the hand across the page. A physical whipping for failure to perform in spelling is more apt to produce a withdrawal attitude toward spelling than a healthy one. What is good punishment? The only thing that can be classified as a good punishment is the realization by a learner that he has perpetrated an injustice upon himself.

DISCIPLINARY FORCES

There are many disciplinary forces in the lives of children. Sometimes these various forces are in harmony with one another, and sometimes they are in conflict. Our major concern here will be those forces exerted by the home, the community-at-large, and the school.

Discipline in the home

The home is the source of the first, and probably the principal, disciplinary force in the life of a child. Here are transmitted the moral and ethical values that boys and girls will hold during their entire lives. In the home the tone of most behavior patterns is set, and it is set before children go to school.

The influence of the home upon the general behavior of children is exceptionally great because of the basically different roles that parents must play in relationship to their children. On the one hand, parents in our society are almost the sole source of real love and affection for their children. At the same time the parent is the major source of punishment for the same children. This causes children to perceive at a very early age, a discrepancy in the relationship between themselves and their parents. It is pure speculation to say so, but it may be that the principal reason why parents can be more effective than any one else in punishing children is because they also are the persons from whom children receive their love and affection. Perhaps this is the reason why corporal punishment is so frequently ineffective and harmful when inflicted by persons other than parents.

Obviously any strength or weakness in the moral and ethical behavior of children because of home practices is reflected in other social institutions, especially the school. These kinds of behavior patterns are well established before children are sent to school; and the school is the recipient of as many different behavior patterns as there are different homes from which children come.

The community-at-large

The community-at-large provides various kinds of disciplinary forces for children. They come from various sources, of course, and tend to have different kinds of effect. Usually the forces in the community-at-large, however, do not have the permanent, disciplinary effect upon children as do those of the home.

THE FRIENDLY ADULT. The friendly adult in the community helps children with their behavior problems. Frequently neighbors assume both guardian and teaching roles by helping in a friendly manner to see that children playing about the neighborhood get along well together and that they are protected from dangers such as automobiles in the street. The storekeeper, the mailman, and the delivery man all may have contact with children, which, if nothing else, gives them an opportunity to imitate adult behavior.

THE LAW. The law of a community is an obvious controlling influence over the behavior of the young. It has little effect upon the small child because he has little contact with law-enforcement agencies. However, the child who is sufficiently mature to move about the community at will, begins to learn that there are certain civic restrictions placed upon him because of adult-made laws. This is the child's first real contact with the fact that the adult world imposes pressure upon him that is different from that imposed upon him by his parents. In many cases the policeman is a good teacher of this controlling force.

THE PEER GROUP. The child's peer group is a strong disciplinary agency. The children in the intermediate grades and in the junior high school grades learn to belong to a conforming group called their peer group. This peer group is a conforming group, but it conforms only to itself unless it is forced to do otherwise. In many respects the peer group is formed psychologically as a mechanism to resist domination by the adult world. Forgetting for a moment the relationship between the peer and the adult group, it is important to note that the peer group tolerates no deviancy within itself. A person who becomes an acceptable member of his peer group does so with the expectation that he will behave as do the others. If he does not, he is excommunicated from the group. For example, with pre-adolescent boys it is common for them to remain completely aloof from members of the opposite sex. They play with boys and they work with boys but they rarely if ever have much to do with girls. This is part of the disciplining of that group. Later this changes and the peer group recognizes and demands communication and interaction with members of the opposite sex.

THE CHURCH. The church or the synagogue is another agency in the community-at-large that exerts disciplinary force upon children. The church, in cooperation with the home, attempts to lay the groundwork for acceptable moral values and behavior. There are some differences among churches and religions as to what some of these values are. However, with our Judeo-Christian culture the common denominators are sufficiently large so that these differences do not present a significant problem for the school.

THE SCHOOL. The school is a major disciplinary force in the

lives of children for two principal reasons. One of these is that children remain in school for a large portion of their childhood and therefore are subject to long-term pressure about their behavior patterns. Secondly, the school among other things is an agency of cultural transmission. The acceptance and use of this culture, in an educational sense, is a disciplinary force that can promote the individuals' ability to account for themselves, for their environment, and for their own behavior in that environment.

ULTIMATE GOALS IN TEACHING

The ultimate goals in teaching, as far as discipline is concerned, are fairly obvious in the foregoing statements. However, they are sufficiently important to warrant clear restatement. It should be remembered as we think of our goals in teaching with respect to discipline, that we are concerned with two things. First, there is the matter of maintaining control over pupils and the total classroom environment in order that the educational program may go on. Second, we must help children to develop better inner control. As Wegener helped us to see, these two acts are not mutually exclusive. They are both operative in the life of the human being at all times.

Dewey states one of our goals in teaching as a problem of instruction:

> The problem of instruction is thus that of finding material which will engage a person in specific activities having an aim or purpose of moment or interest to him, and dealing with things not as gymnastic appliances but as conditions for the attainment of ends.[11]

Thus one of our goals for teaching must be that of finding and arranging materials of instruction so that an individual can organize in his thinking an aim and a mode for fulfilling that aim as prerequisites for carrying out an activity.

[11] John Dewey, *op. cit.*, p. 155.

Through education we hope to teach school pupils enough knowledge of their environment, sufficient cultural skills, and enough ability to think, so that they will be equipped to pursue persistently, acceptable and successful courses of action toward socially desirable goals. We cannot expect an individual to organize his self-controlling mechanisms without the necessary knowledge and skill to do so. Furthermore, before it can be expected that an individual can perform in such a complex culture as ours, he must be made familiar with that culture and its meaning for him.

Of course our ultimate goal is to work in the direction of the self-controlled or the self-disciplined individual. It is convenient to think of this process as an evolutionary one. When youngsters first come to the elementary school, they are dependent individuals. That is, for all practical purposes, they are completely dependent upon the adult world for their care and sustenance. In addition to the care and sustenance necessary for physical existence, there are elements of care and sustenance of a psychological nature. They look to the adult world for confirmation of their behavior. They look to the adult world for a sense of security, love, and affection and for information. They look to the adult world for opportunities to explore their environment so that it can become more meaningful to them.

Now as children proceed through school it should be our objective to be instrumental in their making a transition from this state of virtual dependency to one of greater independence in thought and action. This seems to be the true spirit of discipline as it applies to the elementary school. This means we must teach them to accept the natural consequences of their behavior, and in the process teach them to weigh the consequences of their behavior before action is taken.

There is no question but that the goal of the self-disciplined individual is exceptionally idealistic for attainment within the elementary school years. In fact, in our society it is almost impossible. One sees that children of twelve, thirteen, and fourteen years of age in our society are not allowed to be independent in thought and action, if he only takes into account the fact that they are considered legal minors at those ages. Therefore, we must in the elementary school be willing to recognize that this goal can only be attained by degrees. However, this should not be a deterent for us in working toward that ultimate end. In the process of helping children develop greater self-control, a teacher will have to impose many external controls. In all probability the imposition of the external controls is one of the greatest sources of discipline problems for elementary school teachers. It should be helpful for the beginning teacher to keep in mind constantly that there must always be some element of external control as we move toward internal control with children. Furthermore, it is the teacher's responsibility to see that the educational program of the school goes on. Very practically this means that a learning environment must be maintained, and if maintaining this environment means the use of external adult control over child behavior in the classroom, then that control must be established by the teacher.

Summary

By way of summary and conclusion in this chapter, instead of repeating the highlights of what has already been discussed, an attempt will be made to offer beginning teachers some suggestions of a very practical nature that stem from the foregoing discussion. There is no significance to be attached to the order in which these suggestions are listed.

1. *Avoid "either-or" situations.* Whenever a teacher establishes a "do-this-or-else" situation with a child, the teachers usually loses. The loss may be delayed but it will come.

2. *Always give a child an out.* It is good psychology to allow a child to be able to withdraw graciously from a situation that he has created that has turned out to be unpleasant. In many cases this will be more effective than any other kind of corrective measure.

3. *Discuss feelings and difficulties with children rather than*

threaten them. Giving youngsters opportunities to unload their feelings and describe their difficulties to you as an adult, and as their teacher, constitutes good psychological therapy. This may be the first time an individual has the opportunity to raise his feelings about his own behavior to a level of consciousness.

4. *Use the group to plan for group action, but permit individual planning for private action.* In most elementary school classrooms more group planning takes place than individual. Sometimes children get tired of being a member of a group and would like very much to plan for some private activity.

5. *Avoid using the group as a threatening device.* Try to remember that the individual who is on trial before his group is a very lonely figure. He probably was a lonely figure to begin with and the act of bringing group condemnation about his head is only going to make the situation worse and create more discipline problems from him.

6. *Avoid using the technique of taking pleasure away from slow learners because they have not been able to get more tedious work done.* It is more difficult for the slow learner to derive pleasure and satisfaction from school work than for children who have greater capacity. Those things he likes to do he should be permitted within reasonable extent.

7. *Keep all rewards and punishments in proper focus with their related activities.* This is an important caution if we ever hope to get children to accept the natural consequences of their choices of behavior.

8. *Try to accept the notion that inflicting corporal punishment (hitting, pulling ears, etc.) is beneath your dignity.* As a teacher you should have greater professional skill.

9. *Try to remember that all behavior is caused.* Each child comes to school with a different set of motives, interests, and values. These are bound to be reflected in school work. Your task as a teacher is to modify that behavior, but before you can do that, you must understand the present behavior.

10. *Maintain your personal dignity in all situations.* This will be difficult to do because children can anger adults. Something gets lost in the classroom when a teacher demonstrates anger. To a certain extent the teacher loses intelligent control over the classroom.

11. *Don't try always to be right.* In the first place you can-

not. There are bound to be children in every elementary school classroom who know something that the teacher does not know. Children will inevitably search for this weakness in a teacher just to see what will happen. Honesty here is the best policy. You and the pupils can study most any subject and become informed. All questions do not have to be answered today.

12. *Have plenty for children to do.* Have plenty for children to do that is challenging to them, that they will be willing to undertake. Many discipline problems in the classroom arise because children are bored. They are bored from lack of things to do or bored from lack of things to do that they consider worthwhile.

13. *Remember your room is only one of an entire school.* It is unrealistic for any teacher to think that a set of procedures can be established in his room, that is completely different from those established in other rooms in the same school. Behaviorwise we cannot expect children to isolate themselves from the other children in the school. In the first place they do not understand why, and in the second place they will resist the attempt.

14. *Help your group establish its own standards of conduct.* Some standards of conduct will have to be established for any classroom, in the light of our democratic principles. Since the children are to be affected by the decisions made, it is psychologically and educationally wise to involve them in decision making about those standards of conduct.

15. *Make routine click.* Get routine matters out of the way as efficiently as possible. Whenever teachers stop in the middle of routine to hold long debates about whether it is being done correctly or not, trouble arises. Keep the routine going if possible and discuss the details afterward.

16. *Stop trouble before it starts.* There are many circumstances in which a teacher can see a situation arising in a classroom and by merely moving over to that general area of the classroom, can stop the trouble. Many fights over the paint brush could have been avoided if a teacher had only observed that two were going to be needed, or had been there to provide a second.

17. *Vary types of activity.* Inactivity frequently produces muscular fatigue. Long periods of time in one seat or one position can produce a tired body and mind. Mix the day's activities with quiet activities, group activities, and activities involving physical motion. A variable day is often a good day.

~~*Ideas for discussion and activity*~~

1. Relate these concepts to discipline:
   security
   responsibility
   recognition
   belonging

2. What do you think of the following "disciplinary" practices?
   Keeping children after school
   Having children write sentences 100 times
   Sending pupils to the principal
   Scolding a child in front of the class
   Assigning more arithmetic and spelling
   Whipping

3. How would you describe your philosophy of discipline to a group of parents whose children were in your classroom?

4. Is the use of external force or pressure in controlling child behavior in a classroom an undemocratic practice?

5. Can a parallel be drawn between external and internal control of behavior and extrinsic and intrinsic motivation? If so, how?

Suggested readings

Association for Childhood Education International, *Discipline*. Bulletin 99. Washington, D.C.: The Association, 1957.
   This is a pamphlet by a distinguished group of writers, containing a group of articles on various facets of discipline.
Dewey, John, *Democracy and Education*. New York: The Macmillan Company, 1916, Chapter 10.
   No student of education should fail to read this chapter on interest and discipline.
National Education Association, *NEA Journal*, 45:339-349; September, 1956.
   A special section on discipline is included in this issue of the journal. It contains several pertinent articles.
———, *NEA Journal*, 47: 367-382; September, 1958.
   This is another issue of the same journal containing a special section on discipline.
Sheviakov, George V. and Fritz Redl, *Discipline for Today's Children and*

Youth. (New Revision by Sybil K. Richardson). Washington, D.C.: Association for Supervision and Curriculum Development, National Education Association, 1956.

This is one of the most quoted references on the subject of discipline. It is worthy of the attention of every elementary school teacher.

Yauch, Wilbur A., *How Good Is Your School?* New York: Harper & Brothers, 1951, Chapter 10.

The book was written to help parents understand schools better. Chapter 10 is a helpful description of what schools should be trying to do as they "make good Americans".

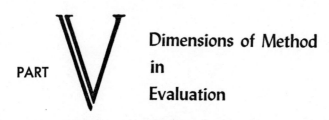

PART $\bigvee$ Dimensions of Method
in
Evaluation

Evaluation often is overlooked as a significant and necessary aspect of the total teaching process. When one considers evaluation as a process of determining whether one has achieved his goals, has achieved them in the most desirable manner, and has made judgment as to the worth of the achieved goals, it becomes the key to keeping the education process dynamic.

The subject of evaluation is one about which a great deal has been written. The applications of evaluation to the various facets of education involve innumerable interpretations. For our purposes here, two dimensions of method are of significance. One is the application of evaluative procedures by the classroom teacher, and the other proceeds from that application to the keeping of records and reporting of pupil progress.

Because of the very close relationship between evaluating procedures and techniques, and those of studying pupils as discussed in Part II, it is suggested that the reader review those chapters.

CHAPTER 15

Applying
Evaluation Procedures

AN IMPORTANT THING to remember about evaluation is that it is a process that is related to the total educational activity and must always be carried out in that light. For the moment let us carry our thinking back to the complete educational activity as represented in Figure 1, page 6.

Note that the process of evaluation is identified principally with the third, or evaluation, level. The evaluation level represents the application of the evaluation process to all aspects of the educational activity including curriculum. It is the application of the evaluative schema provided for in the curriculum. However, it should be noted that evaluation is also applied at the teaching-learning level. In this chapter we are principally concerned with this application. It ought to be remembered that every teacher must play his role in the total evaluative process, and from the classroom he must obtain appropriate data to serve that role.

THE MEANING OF EVALUATION

The term "evaluation" is of relatively recent vintage in our educational literature. It is an outgrowth of the measurement movement of the second and third decade of the present century. The word means many things to different people. For some, measurement and evaluation are synonyms; for others evaluation and appraisal mean the same. Several definitions appearing in the literature will illustrate some of the variations in interpretation.

One of the most frequently quoted definitions is that by Shane and McSwain as they state that evaluation is:

"...a process of inquiry based upon cooperatively prepared criteria, and concerned with the study, interpretation, and guidance of socially desirable changes in the developmental behavior of children.[1]

Thus defined evaluation is a very complex process. More specifically Shane and McSwain list eight steps in the total process:

(1) Isolation and description of the problem(s) to be studied;
(2) Clarification of values bearing on the problem(s);
(3) Development of criteria for study of the problem(s);
(4) Expression of the criteria in terms of the behavior sought in children;
(5) Establishment of situations in which children's behavior can be studied, as the school seeks to modify it to conform with desired citizenship outcomes;
(6) Employment of instruments to gather behavioral data to be studied, in order to decide whether or not children's behavior is being changed significantly;
(7) Analysis of behavioral changes, if significant, to determine whether or not these changes are compatible with the values sought by the school; and
(8) Implementation of decisions reached in view of the findings made by the school staff.[2]

Thomas refers to evaluation as a method of determining how well children are reaching goals.[3] The Southern Association's Cooperative Study in Elementary Education gives the following definition:

Evaluation is more than measurement. It includes (1) stating values and purposes in terms of the needs of individuals and the group, the community, and an ever-changing society; (2) securing evidences that these values and purposes are being realized; (3) interpreting

[1] Harold G. Shane and E. T. McSwain, Evaluation and the Elementary Curriculum, Rev. Ed. (New York: Henry Holt and Company, Inc., 1958), p. 3.
[2] Ibid., pp. 61-62.
[3] R. Murray Thomas, Judging Student Progress (New York: Longmans, Green and Company, 1954), p. 4.

the evidences gathered; (4) redefining values, setting up new purposes, and planning new practices in terms of the modified purposes.[4]

In discussing the purposes of evaluation, Rothney states:

> Evaluating and reporting processes are essential steps in the current guidance, future guidance, and transfer of pupils but they serve other purposes as well. They may confirm estimates of the effectiveness of the teaching that is done and cause us to doubt the value of our instructional methods and materials, enough so that we may undertake their revision or reject them as ineffective.[5]

In the functional sense, evaluation may be thought of as a circular process having three phases. The first phase of the process is that of determining whether the goals toward which activity was launched have been achieved. The second phase is one of determining how adequate the means selected to pursue the goals were. This is the point of questioning the methods and procedures used. The third phase is one of examining the goals for their worth, once they have been achieved. Were they worthy of the effort? Thus these three phases place into operation a cyclical process tending to serve the major purposes of evaluating; namely, to keep the goals, content, and method of education dynamically alive.

Furthermore, this operational concept can be applied under a variety of circumstances. It can be applied to a unit of work in a classroom. Or it can be applied to the efforts of a single individual.

LEVELS OF APPLICATION

There are several levels or points at which the evaluation process must be applied if the full spirit of education is to be fulfilled.

[4] Southern Association's Cooperative Study in Elementary Education, *Evaluating the Elementary School* (Atlanta, Ga.: Commission on Research and Service, 1951), p. 1.
[5] John W. M. Rothney, *Evaluating and Reporting Pupil Progress*. What Research Says to the Teacher Series, No. 7, Department of Classroom Teachers and the American Educational Research Association, National Education Association (Washington, D.C.: The Association, 1955), p. 4.

Wherever educational growth in children is sought in school, to some degree the evaluative process must be applied. This means that everyone concerned with the educational program is an evaluator, but this is specially true of the classroom teacher. Because evaluation is essential to the educational process, the application of evaluation is an important dimension of method..

To the individual

There are two principal reasons why the evaluation process needs to be applied to the individual school pupil. One is to insure that educational growth is taking place. The primary purpose of the school is to produce educational growth in children, and to fail to note that growth and the degree of that growth would be an act of neglect on the part of teachers and school administrators. For example, in all areas of communication, we hope there will be continuous growth throughout the elementary school years. More specifically, we want to observe the growth in reading, speaking, and writing. Such growth can be observed subjectively by teachers in their daily contacts with children, and it may be more objectively observed by use of standardized tests in those areas.

Similarly, we wish to know whether school children are properly orienting themselves to their environment, particularly the social environment. We should investigate and/or observe whether children are developing effective and desirable social and personal relationships with members of their peer groups, are selecting worthwhile goals in their educational and personal development, and are maintaining and improving their psychological stability in the process.

The application of the evaluation process to the individual for these purposes thus accomplishes two very important objectives of elementary education. On the one hand we are fulfilling our obligation as an educational institution to society, and on the other, to the individual as a citizen who lives in that institution.

To the group

Just as there are circumstances in which the focal point of evaluation is upon the individual, so there are needs to direct the process at groups of individuals. A teacher may wish to diagnose the performance of a group in some function in order to check upon his teaching success. For example, a third-grade teacher may administer a standardized test in arithmetic to check upon the degree to which instruction has been effective in developing multiplication skill. Proper study of the results would reveal persistent errors made by the members of the group, which could mean that more attention should be given to that process, or the results might indicate that the teacher should feel satisfied and proceed to the next phase of arithmetic instruction.

Because a group is a group, its function as such needs to be evaluated. If activities are planned by the group, and executed by the group, then they should be evaluated by and for the group. Group interaction techniques should continuously improve as children move through the elementary school years, and in order that the improvement can be appraised, evaluation must take place.

To the process

Whereas the application of evaluation to individuals and to groups is concerned mostly with the results of learning, the act of evaluating processes is directed mainly at method.

We are concerned with the motivation used to impel children into activity, the manner in which pupils worked, the organization of pupils for work, and those techniques used in carrying out the activities. The main questions to be asked are: How effective were we in our work? How could we have done better? Where was my planning weak? Why?

Process evaluation is most effective while activity is in process. A great feature of education is that it should teach people to re-direct their efforts constantly in a more constructive way because of their ability to appraise and reinterpret. For this reason in-process evaluation should be frequent so that pupils can learn to redirect quickly and effectively their efforts in more productive directions. If process evaluation is conducted only at the conclusion of activities, the results can never be used in that same general endeavor; the individuals would have to hope that the next activity would be sufficiently similar so that the results of the evaluation could be applied there.

To the total program

The application of evaluation to the total program is to fulfill the purpose of the evaluative schema in the curriculum. The focus here is upon the total program including the objectives, the content, the methods, and the results. The results of evaluation as applied to individuals, to groups, and to processes, all need to be brought to bear as they can be applied to the total program.

Perhaps it is like saying that one cannot see the forest for the trees, but sometimes we get so involved in some one facet of educational life that we fail to look at our entire operation for the purpose of determining its effectiveness.

Evaluation of the total program leads to curriculum planning. Curriculum planning leads to teaching. Teaching leads to evaluating, and so forth through the cycle again and again. The main thing is to remember that we cannot go through the cycle without evaluation being applied often and at the various appropriate levels.

EVALUATION TECHNIQUES

Most of the techniques of evaluation have been mentioned in earlier chapters, especially in Chapter 4 where techniques of pupil study were under discussion. However, in those cases the points of reference were gaining information for teaching and carrying on the process of teaching. In this chapter we are concerned with these techniques as part of evaluation procedures.

For the purpose of this discussion, evaluation techniques will be approached under the headings of measurement, observation, in process appraisal, culmination appraisal, and over-all appraisal.

Measurement

The arrangement of characteristics of individuals or things in a rank order is a simple form of measurement. Whenever we derive data or scores from individuals on some characteristic or trait and arrange them along a regular continuum, we are measuring. This is what we do when we wish to be very specific in describing our observations.

A characteristic of the measurement process is that it stresses objectivity and tends to reduce subjectivity. For example, in testing one can often hear discussed the question of whether the test under question is *objective*. This question seeks an answer concerning the degree of variation that would be expected if two or more persons were to use and grade the test. If it would be expected that several persons were to grade the same test and get exactly the same grade or score, then it would be claimed that the test was highly objective. On the other hand, if under the same circumstances the scorers got quite different results, the test would be called *subjective*. In other words, the greater the variation in grading or scoring, the greater is the degree of subjectivity in a test. Measurement tends to reduce subjectivity.

In the use of measurement as an evaluation technique we are concerned with four general classes of measure: physical growth, capacity for learning, achievement, and adjustment. To measure physical growth we use such instruments as the scales, the yard stick, the dynamometer, and the X-ray. The intelligence test is the most widely used instrument for measuring capacity for learning. Educational achievement can be measured with the achievement test, and personality tests are used as measures of adjustment.

Most tests that are used for the purpose of determining educational achievement are standardized tests. This means that the authors of those tests administered them over and over again to groups of school pupils with whom they were intended to be used, for the purpose of establishing norms for the tests. In establishing the norms, the authors sought a description of the typical performance of children. For example, in an arithmetic test designed for fifth graders, it would be necessary to indicate where along the scale test, scores for typical fifth graders would fall in accordance with the amount of time they had spent in that grade. The interval between the end of the fourth grade and the beginning of the sixth grade is the norm or normal range for the fifth grade.

In addition to standardized tests for measuring educational achievement, there may be used teacher-constructed tests. The practice of using teacher-constructed tests is not very popular with elementary school teachers. Part of this is because there are so many standardized devices published for use in the elementary school. However, there are many opportunities for use of teacher-constructed devices for indicating educational achievement and for diagnosis of learning difficulties.

In the use of tests as instruments of measurement, there are two inherent risks that always must be taken into account. They are the risks of *reliability* and *validity*. Reliability is that property of a test which indicates the degree of consistency with which results may be obtained by its use. Whenever a test is repeated under similar (or identical) circumstances, the degree to which the results under the two circumstances agree is an indication of the reliability of the test. In other words, to be reliable a test must produce the same (or nearly the same) results when used repeatedly with the same group of persons or an equated group. Validity is that property of a test that indicates the degree to which a test measures that which it is supposed to measure. This is the question of fidelity in measurement; that is, how much trust can be placed in the results because they represent what the results are supposed to be. For example, one of the big questions in using the group intelligence test is to what degree the test is a test of reading ability rather than a test of intelligence. Thus every teacher must question these two risks—the confidence in the accuracy of the results and the faith in the quality of the results of measurements taken.

Observation

The use of observation as an evaluation technique is restricted mostly to social behaviors of pupils. When records are made of observations, they take the form of anecdotal records. Records of observations are useful for evaluation to the extent they can be used to note change, or lack of it, as a result of classroom activity. For example, if a series of units, or activities otherwise organized, had been experienced by pupils, and if they were directed at improving group cooperation, anecdotal records should reveal changes in pupil behavior in the classroom, provided those activities were functionally successful.

There is no real reason why observational techniques should be restricted to social behavior. The technique is equally effective in noting improvement in arithmetic skill or improvement in reading habits. A good teacher will observe and note his observations of all kinds of pupil behavior that may have been caused by the school program. The important thing to do is to try to see the relationship between the classroom activities and changes in boys and girls.

Observation should not be restricted to individuals. It can be applied to groups as well. The very concept of group involves a certain amount of oneness or unity in purpose and action. Several kinds of activities are launched in elementary schools, designed to foster better group effort. In these circumstances it is incumbent upon the teacher to observe group behavior.

Observation as an evaluative technique is highly subjective when compared with the objectivity of some forms of measurement like tests. However, let us not frown upon subjectivity to such an extent that we limit our evaluation to measurement and only to objective measurement at that. A great deal of human interaction is subjective in nature, and we can only deal with it in a subjective manner. There are some ways by which controls can be put upon the use of subjective procedures, however. The use of the behavior journal[6] for making observations of individual behaviors by an entire school staff, which has agreed upon a set of procedures for using these observations, puts some control upon them. The use of the sociogram to indicate changes in social forces in the group is reasonably close to objectivity; it approaches measurement when scores are arranged in rank order.

In-process appraisal

In-process appraisal refers to acts of taking stock of progress during an activity for the purpose of checking upon the adequacy of progress and the quality of process. It is much like the feedback and correction process discussed in psychology of learning. An individual who is following a course of action constantly receives cues from his environment that cause him to change or correct his action in order to proceed more precisely toward his goal. In-process appraisal is used for much the same purpose. Periodically a class or a group within a class should stop their activity long enough to get cues from their actions that will cause them to change their procedures or to confirm their previous activity in relation to the achievement of their goals.

As a process this technique may involve the use of other techniques such as measurement or observation, but the point is one of bringing evidence to bear upon an activity while it is in progress. Group discussion is one avenue of appraisal. Progress reports by members of the class or group will provide information upon which judgments may be made. The class or group needs to bring all of these kinds of information to bear upon their progress so they can make decisions that will confirm their

[6] See page 81.

original choice of actions, somewhat modify that choice, or drastically change the entire procedure. Parenthetically it might be said that this kind of appraisal is not conducted enough in schools. For a teacher it is a most valuable technique for keeping a classroom *alive* in its approach to teaching and learning. Through this process teachers and pupils can periodically redirect their efforts in a more productive reconstruction of educational experience.

Culmination appraisal

Like in-process appraisal, culmination appraisal is a process most useable by pupils and teachers in the classroom. It refers to the use of culminating activities of lessons or units, as a means of evaluating work done. It is a way of describing what the group has done, why they did it, what they learned, and perhaps what and how they might have done better. Teachers encourage culminating activities to help children bring together the results of their efforts in a meangingful manner. The very process itself is evaluative in nature. Culminating activities such as the drama, the project, the mural, oral and written reports, or some combination of these are helpful in making value judgments about learning activities.

Over-all appraisal

Over-all appraisal refers to activities directed at judging the entire school program. Thus no one teacher or any other single individual is responsible for conducting this appraisal. It is a responsibility of many people. Pupils, teachers, administrators, and school patrons all have some responsibility here. The results should lead to a replanning of curriculum in the true spirit of evaluation. However, in this book we are primarily concerned with the evaluation process as a dimension of method for the classroom teacher, and therefore, it must be emphasized that the teacher is a collector of evidence and a means of bringing evidence to bear upon curriculum planning and the improvement of instruction.

Occasionally teachers are asked to participate in over-all elementary-school evaluation in which systematic instruments designed for this purpose are used. When these instruments are used, almost all aspects of the school program are appraised. Three examples of these kinds of instruments are: The Southern Association's Cooperative Study in Elementary Education, to which reference has already been made;[7] a research project of the School of Education of Boston University;[8] and one published by the Texas State Department of Education.[9] Although these instruments have similarity in scope, they differ in format. The one of The Southern Association provides for writing in an appraisal under particular headings or questions. The Boston University instrument provides a system of check-lists under each major heading. The Texas handbook is divided into seven major headings, and under each heading is a description of five levels of practice. The evaluator is to match a school with one of these levels.

In many school communities people prefer to conduct their own appraisal by means created by themselves. An elementary school staff, for example, may wish to plan their own appraisal, create their own instruments, and so forth, because they feel that the job thus done will be more appropriate to their school and that they will profit more from the evaluation. One type of appraisal that is relatively untried in public schools is that of bringing into focus the many value judgments made by parents and other school patrons. We know that this type of evaluation goes on all the time, but so far we have not been able to find some way of harnessing the results. No doubt organization of

[7] Supra, p. 289.

[8] Elementary Evaluative Criteria (Boston: Boston University School of Education, 1953).

[9] Handbook for Self-appraisal and Improvement of Elementary Schools, Rev. Ed. (Austin: Texas State Department of Education, 1948).

discussion groups with these persons would help, and perhaps return reporting from home to school in conjunction with pupil progress reporting would be effective. The opinion survey could be a useful technique.

Whatever the over-all appraisal technique may be, the classroom teacher is bound to be at the hub of the process. The teacher is the one person in the school system who is in contact with pupils, administrators, and school patrons about the education of children. He is the center, if you please, of the educational activity and, therefore, must be a key person in evaluation.

Summary

Evaluation has been defined as a three-phased process of determining whether established goals have been reached, whether those goals have been reached in the most desirable manner, and whether those goals are believed desirable once they have been achieved and examined. Thus defined, evaluation is a basic dimension of teaching method because the process examines method in addition to being part of it.

The scope and significance of evaluation are further indicated because of the levels of application and the various techniques that may be used. It is important that the evaluation process may be applied to the work of individuals as well as groups; it must be applied to the program and process of work activities. At one time or another any or all of such techniques as measurements, observations, appraisal, discussion, creative action, and so forth, may be used in the application of the evaluation process.

Evaluation is an integral part of the complete educational activity. It is the cardinal process in reconstructing educational programs and instructional methods. Because of this, evaluation is a very important dimension of method for elementary school teaching.

Ideas for discussion and activity

1. Look over one of the three evaluation instruments listed in the

suggested readings and report to the class its contents and your appraisal of its usefulness.

2. Can you now distinguish between evaluation and measurement?

3. What are the principal differences between curriculum evaluation and in-process evaluation?

4. How can evaluation be used as a motivational device?

5. How is evaluation related to method?

Suggested readings

Elementary Evaluative Criteria. A Boston University School of Education Research Project. Boston: Boston University School of Education, 1953.
   The booklet is a type of instrument that can be used in elementary school evaluation. Check-lists are used extensively.

Graver, P. A. "Procedural Levels in Evaluating Educational Curricula," *Journal of Educational Research,* 49: 143-147; October, 1955.
   Three types of evaluation level that are commonly used in curriculum appraisal are examined.

Greene, Harry A., Albert N. Jorgensen, and J. Raymond Gerberich, *Measurement and Evaluation in the Elementary School.* Second edition. New York: Longmans, Green and Company, 1953.
   This is a book that could be used as a handbook. It is particularly strong in its emphasis upon measurement. Many tests are identified and described.

Rothney, John W. M., *Evaluating and Reporting Pupil Progress.* What Research Says to the Teacher Series, No. 7. Department of Classroom Teachers and the American Educational Research Association, National Education Association. Washington, D.C.: The Association, 1955.
   Here is another summary of research for classroom teachers. Try to read this one either in connection with this chapter or the next one.

Shane, Harold G. and E. T. McSwain, *Evaluation and the Elementary Curriculum.* Revised edition. New York: Henry Holt and Company, 1958.
   The title is self-explanatory. Chapters 1 and 3 are especially recommended.

Southern Association's Cooperative Study in Elementary Education, *Evaluating the Elementary School.* Atlanta, Georgia: Commission on Research and Service, 1951.
   This instrument is very useful for teams or evaluation groups to use in appraising a total elementary school program.

Texas State Department of Education, *Handbook for Self-appraisal and*

Improvement of Elementary Schools. Revised edition. Austin: The Department, 1958.

The bulletin is intended for use in Texas elementary schools. It is designed for self-appraisal. The contents are listed under seven major headings, and within each, five levels of practice are described.

Wrightstone, J. Wayne, Joseph Justman, and Irving Robbins, *Evaluation in Modern Education.* New York: American Book Company, 1956.

The student undoubtedly will find the chapters in Part Two very helpful. They are devoted to nine major evaluation techniques.

CHAPTER 16

Keeping Records
and Reporting Progress

Eᴠᴇʀʏ ᴘᴏᴛᴇɴᴛɪᴀʟ teacher should be aware of the possibilities of their responsibility for maintaining pupil personnel records and reporting pupil progress to parents. The forms used will vary from community to community and so will the kinds of tasks expected of teachers in connection with their use. Every new teacher going into a community will need instruction about records to be kept and reporting procedures, because no teacher-education institution can provide its students with all knowledge about the entire range of forms and reports they may encounter upon graduation.

Although many of the tasks are mechanical and routine, the acts involved in keeping records and reporting progress constitute a serious dimension of method for elementary school teachers. Some tasks may seem trivial, but they contribute to a greater cause. The act of reporting pupil progress to parents is one of the most vital aspects of the school-community communication. This activity can be one of the best, if not *the* best, method of interpreting the value of a school program. For this activity to be good, the records behind it must also be good.

PURPOSE OF CUMULATIVE RECORDS

There really is but one reason for maintaining pupil personnel

records. That is to reveal the effect of the school program upon
the child. This reason is a big one, and it has many ramifications.
As a corollary to this purpose, these records should serve as a
means of making the pupil's transition from grade to grade and
from teacher to teacher one with a minimal loss of forward
momentum.

Sometimes it is difficult to keep these purposes in mind as
records are maintained, but this is true for different reasons.
Where an abundant system of records is maintained, there may
develop a tendency to accumulate materials that have little value
or have temporary value. In this case the records become so
voluminous that they are difficult to house and use. In other
circumstances the reverse is true. The system of records is inadequate for revealing the growth of children in educational
characteristics. If records are to be used to fulfill their real needs,
vigilance will be required on the part of teachers in their maintenance.

There are legal or quasi-legal aspects of pupil personnel records
that should be mentioned. Certain records may be required by
law or as a means of carrying out the law. For example, the attendance record falls into this category. Attendance records may
be required by law, and they may be a means of carrying out
laws pertaining to school finance. Where schools receive state
financial aid on the basis of the number of children in attendance
at school, the attendance record becomes a means for carrying out
financial regulations. The school attendance record may become
a character reference. In some cases the school record is the
only evidence that a child has lived in a community, and it has
even been used as evidence in cases of criminal prosecution. The
importance of these uses of pupil records demands accuracy and
some attention to detail on the part of those who maintain them.

The principal thing to keep in mind is that schools have purposes for existence, and the curriculum of the school is designed
to carry out those purposes. Classroom activities are sponsored
that are intended to result in educational growth in children. It

is only reasonable that school personnel would exert efforts to assess and record that educational growth; this is a means of demonstrating that the school's purposes have been fulfilled.

KINDS OF RECORDS

The purposes for keeping records spell out for us the general kinds of data that should be maintained. Foremost in importance are data having to do with educational growth. Second would be additional data that would be helpful in helping teachers understand children better and more quickly. Third are any data that must be kept for legal purposes.

Records of educational growth

One kind of information that should go into the permanent record is achievement-test data. As long as they are useful for diagnostic purposes, entire test booklets may be filed. When a test booklet has served its purpose, the profile sheet may be detached for permanent record and the remainder destroyed. This way the bulk of files can be kept reduced.

Since anecdotal records, if kept properly, also reveal educational growth, they should be filed in the personnel file. Some will debate this point by claiming that anecdotal records belong in the teacher's possession only, but it is here maintained that any record that serves the purposes outlined above belongs in the cumulative file. Thus if anecdotal records reveal changes in a pupil's social behavior, his interest pattern, his reading habits, and so forth, those records should become part of his file.

Part of the process of revealing educational growth is the reporting of pupil progress to parents. Records of these reports should become part of the cumulative file. It makes no difference whether the report form is a report card, a letter, or some record of parent-teacher conferences; the record should be maintained.

Diagnostic data for teachers

In order that teachers might be able to use the cumulative file as a device for facilitating and improving instruction, another kind of data, in addition to achievement data, needs to be included. In general, these data are diagnostic in character so that they can provide cues to teachers in the process of providing a learning environment.

All forms of historical data fall into this category. An example would be that information assembled when a child first comes to school, so that the school can understand his previous experience better and thus better adjust the school program to him. The results of physical examinations may be another. Past achievement records may be considered important elements to the extent that they help teachers determine readiness for further school work.

Of great importance to teachers is information about the interest patterns of children and their adjustment to their environments. Some schools will use standardized instruments for this purpose; others will only use anecdotal records; and others a combination of both of these. Regardless of which practice is followed, the information is of value to teachers in the diagnostic study of children and in subsequent teaching.

Certainly any information that will help teachers judge the capacity of children for learning should be a part of the cumulative record. All measures of mental age are desirable. A single intelligence test is not enough to give a true picture of mental age, or intelligence quotient, throughout the elementary school years; probably at least three should be given in order to have a check upon an original measure and to indicate any change that may take place. This kind of information is needed by teachers in judging pupil capacity. Any test of readiness or records that might reveal readiness, such as achievement data, are indications of capacity. The anecdotal record can furnish capacity information in a very functional way. Both achievement data and anecdotal records are mentioned again here only to emphasize that they can be used for many purposes and thus have even greater significance as elements of the pupil personnel record.

Legal records

It is almost superfluous to state that legal or quasi-legal records should be part of the cumulative file; they have to be by their very nature. These include the attendance record, the health record, in some cases the reports to parents, and any transfer records from school to school.

Finally, let it be noted that there is a great deal of interrelationship among the various kinds of records as they are related to purposes. For example, the achievement test is useful for indicating educational growth, for diagnosing capacity, and for legal evidence. Therefore, this interrelationship becomes additional evidence for the inclusion of these kinds of records in a system of pupil personnel records.

The cumulative folder

One of the problems that schools have concerning school records is the matter of housing them. Some sort of folder is needed to keep the various records for each pupil together, and all of the folders have to be housed in some location or locations.

The folder for cumulative records can be of any kind. It may be a simple and plain, tabbed manila file folder with the pupil's name indicated on the tab. The various records can then be placed in the folder in a casual manner or in accordance with an arrangement agreed upon. Or the folder may be one that is designed as a cumulative record itself. This kind of folder has printed upon it spaces and lines labeled for entries of specific information such as height and weight, mental-age scores, achievement-test scores, attendance records, immunization records, and so forth. (Figure 12 on pp. 307-310 illustrates such a

STUDENT CUMULATIVE RECORD

Blue Island Public Schools, District 130, Cook County, Illinois

BIRTH RECORD

Birth Date

Mo.	Day	Year

Birth Place

City	County	State

Verification
Birth Certif. _____
Bapt. Certif. _____
Bible Record _____
Affidavit _____

Sex	Race	Lives With
Male _____	White _____	Parents _____
Female _____	Colored _____	Grandparents _____
	Yellow _____	Guardian _____
	Others _____	Others _____

ADDRESS RECORD

Date	Address	Phone

FAMILY DATA

	NAME	BIRTHPLACE	OCCUPATION
FATHER			
STEPFATHER			
MOTHER			
STEPMOTHER			
GUARDIAN			

OTHER CHILDREN IN FAMILY:

NAME	Sex	Older	Younger	NAME	Sex	Older	Younger

Other Adults Living
With Family (Relationship)

Language (s) Spoken
At Home

Parents Place of Work

NAME	NAME	PHONE

Other Emergency Phone
(Relative - Friend - Neighbor)

NAME	ADDRESS	PHONE

Family Physician

NAME	ADDRESS	PHONE

SCHOOL TRANSFER RECORD

Date Entered	School	From City - State	Remarks

Date Left	School	To - City-State	Remarks

SCHOOL											
Year											
Grade											
Teacher											
Days Present											
Days Absent											
Times Tardy											
LANGUAGE ARTS											
Reading											
Phonics											
Library Reading											
Language											
Spelling											
Writing											
SOCIAL STUDIES											
Geography											
History											
Citizenship											
OTHER SUBJECTS											
Arithmetic											
Science											
Health											
Physical Education											
Art											
Music, Vocal											
Instrumental Music											
Home Arts											
Home Mechanics											
HABITS AND ATTITUDES											
Social Development											
Emotional Development											
Work Habits											
PROMOTED TO											
CONDITIONED TO											
PLACED IN											
RETAINED IN											

EXPLANATION OF MARKS
Grades 1 - 8
A—Excellent, outstanding
B—Very good progress
C—Satisfactory
D—Much improvement is needed
F—Unsatisfactory progress (Grades 4-8)

NOTE: Insert progress report sheets and test booklets on this side of folder at the end of the school year.

NAME ________ Last ________ First ________ Middle

FIGURE 12. *These pages (307-310) represent in order the four consecutive sides of a cumulative record folder. Used with permission of School District 130, Blue Island, Illinois.*

SERVICES, PARTICIPATION, OFFICES, HONORS

	4-5-6	7	8
Athletics			
Music, Vocal			
Art			
Band			
Orchestra			
Safety Patrol			
School Hostess			
School Service			
School Club			

EDUCATIONAL TEST RECORD

DATE	FORM	C. A.	SCORE	G. P.

PSYCHOLOGICAL TEST RECORD

DATE	FORM	C. A.	SCORE	M. A.	I. Q.

310

cumulative record.) Teachers enter data upon these folder-cards and they become the basic cumulative record, although there still may be kinds of information in the folder that is not entered upon it, like anecdotal records or samples of a pupil's work. Whichever kind is used, it is the teacher's responsibility to maintain the record.

Frequently there is much debate about the place of housing cumulative records. Many teachers feel that they should have the folders for the children in their rooms so that they can keep them up more easily and have greater access to them as they work with children. Many school principals feel that the records should be housed in a central location for security purposes because much of the material in the folders should be treated as confidential information. In this case the school office seems to be the most logical selection as a place of housing.

Housing records in the school office seems to be most logical when all things are taken into account. If the school employs clerical personnel, they can be of much help to teachers in the maintenance of the records and folders. There is greater opportunity for constant surveillance in the office than the classroom, and there are many occasions when the school office needs information housed in the files. When records are housed in a central location, all teachers can refer to them; for example, a teacher might wish to see the file of a brother or sister of a child he has in his room, for comparative purposes. When these arguments confront the almost single argument of teacher-convenience for putting them in the classroom, a central location seems to be most desirable.

PURPOSES OF PROGRESS REPORTING

The principal purpose of reporting pupil progress in schools to parents is to reveal to them the effect of the school program upon the child. This is just like the principal purpose in maintaining personnel records in the school, and the two purposes are related.

One is to make a record of growth, and the other is to transmit that information to persons outside the school. The important thing to remember is that the report *should* reveal growth, and throughout the remainder of this discussion reports will be presented in that light.

A second purpose in reporting pupil progress to parents is to help interpret the school's program to the parents. In this respect the progress report is serving a public relations service. People will be helped in understanding public education if they are informed of the kinds of growth that children acquire as a result of their experiences in school. In many cases the actual form of the report indicates what goes on in school, as in the case of the report card that lists the subjects a pupil pursues. However, this is only a limited part of a total program of school interpretation or public relations. Parents can only interpret the school's program by means of the progress report through their children; they will need additional help to see the broad picture of the total school operation.

A third and very important reason for reporting pupil progress to parents is to provide an avenue of communication between the home and the school. This avenue must be a two-way street; communication cannot be established, in the best sense, if information only goes from the school to the home. Teachers can be instrumental in better adjustment of the school program to individual children if they are better acquainted with the home environment and the reactions of persons in the home to the things that are happening to the child in school. Therefore, this purpose can best be fulfilled if the system of pupil progress reporting provides for reporting from the school to the home *and* from the home to the school.

METHODS OF REPORTING

Reporting practices in our schools vary in kind and in detail within any one kind. No doubt much of the variation can be

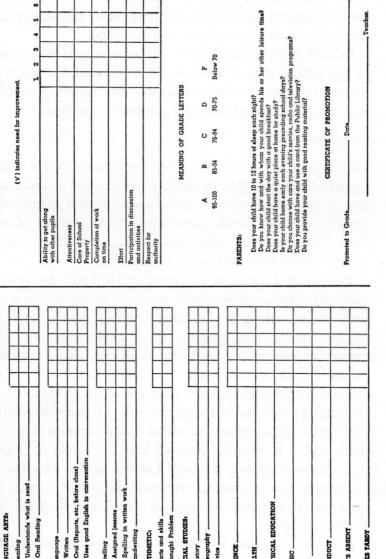

FIGURE 13. *A report card using letter grades. Used with permission of School District 125, Oak Lawn, Illinois.*

attributed to the constant search by professional educators for a way of reporting pupil progress that will satisfy the many needs for these reports and at the same time set up satisfactory communication between the home and the school.

Basically there are three types of progress reports that are used in elementary schools. They are the report card, the report letter, and the parent-teacher conference. Any reporting procedure is a variation of one of these or a combination of them.

The report card

Most anyone who has gone through our elementary and secondary schools at one time or another has received a report card, because the report card is the most commonly used instrument of progress reporting. In the elementary school a number of variations of the report card have been created, but the basic assumptions of the instrument tend to be preserved.

The principal feature of the report card is that it represents an attempt to grade, rate, or classify pupils. The assumption is that such grading, rating, or classifying describes pupil progress. In one sense of the term "progress" this is a valid assumption. Let us use the letter-grade report card as an example. The general procedure with this card is to assign a letter (A, B, C, D, or E) to each subject for which grades are required, in accordance with the teacher's appraisal of the pupil's work. Actually these letters indicate a level of performance rather than an amount of progress made, but it is normally assumed that this rating of level of performance represents progress. Parents usually are willing to accept this type of grading, principally because it is what was used with them when they were in school, and therefore, it is familiar to them.

Many teachers have had difficulty in reconciling the practice of using letter-grades in this fashion with their attempts to solve some of the problems of individual differences. The letter-grade is assigned in accordance with a pupil's achievement; the one

Explanation of marks:
S—Satisfactory
U—Unsatisfactory
I—Improving
?—"Could we work on this together? He seems to need help."

MENTAL APTITUDES

Quarters

	1	2	3	4
Is interested in learning				
Shows intellectual curiosity				
Can express ideas clearly				
Understands the plot of stories				
Follows directions				
Finishes work he has started				
Enjoys singing				
Expresses self through art				

GENERAL RECORD

Half days of absence				
Times tardy				
Conferences with parents				
Kindergarten fees due				
Height of child				
Weight of child				

PHYSICAL HABITS

Quarters

	1	2	3	4
Uses large muscles well (as in throwing)				
Uses small muscles well (as in cutting)				
Responds well to rhythm (as in marching)				
Stands and sits well				
Is able to relax				
Has sufficient physical energy				

CITIZENSHIP HABITS

Seems happy				
Takes suggestions cheerfully				
Can act independently				
Shares possessions				
Volunteers to help others				
Plays well in small groups				

FIGURE 14. A *report card using marks of satisfactory and unsatisfactory. Used with permission of School District 130, Blue Island, Illinois.*

who achieves more gets the higher grade and the one who achieves less, the lower. There is a strong relationship between the achievement of school pupils and their capacities for learning, and as a result, other things like effort being constant, the grade simply describes the approximate ability of the pupil. This means, then, that in assigning grades teachers are prone to give consistently the same grades to pupils in most of their school subjects, and in so doing, are simply saying to the parent, "Your child is an average child as shown by this grade of C." Obviously this practice does not take into account relative growth; in fact it does not reveal growth at all.

A variation of the letter-grade report card is to assign the letters S and U for the various subjects, characteristics, or behaviors. The letter S means that the child has been making satisfactory progress; the letter U means unsatisfactory progress. The philosophy behind this variation is that each child can be appraised in accordance with his own capacity, and this is the principal advantage of this report form. The disadvantages are that again growth is not revealed and that many parents object because the familiar letter-grades are not given. In the latter case they feel that letter-grades make greater distinction and serve as greater factors in pupil learning.

A third variation of the report card is the check-list. This form usually contains a list of characteristics pertaining to social behavior and/or skill performance and understanding, with the opportunity to check each of these items along some scale. In other check-lists the various subjects may be listed just as they are on the report card, but instead of a grade given, a list of behaviors is indicated to be checked by the teacher. The check list has greater possibility for indicating growth than any other form of the report card, but it depends upon which characteristics are listed to be checked.

A fourth variation of the report card is a combination of the features of the aforementioned types. Figure 16 is an example.

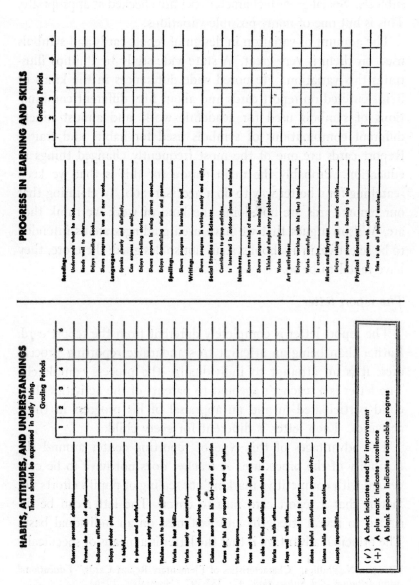

FIGURE 15. A report card utilizing a check-list procedure. Used with permission of School District 85, Elmwood Park, Illinois.

Numbers are used rather than letter-grades for the regular school subjects. Social-growth characteristics are checked as appropriate. This is but one of many possible variations.

The amount of variation in design of report cards and symbols used on them is very great. A state-wide study by Phillips illustrates this variation. He noted wide differences in the kinds of items entered on report cards and about fifty different combinations of symbols used for academic work, and almost ninety different combinations of symbols used for habits and traits.[1] Report cards are one of the most frequently changed things in education. Probably the main reason for this is that we keep searching for a better way to do a necessary job. In claiming that our report cards are not doing the kind of work we think they are, Wilson argues that we have used grading systems intended to be selective, in a school system not so designed; therefore, they have failed to be so.[2]

The report letter

The report letter is completely different from the report card. Rather than being an attempt to standardize reporting procedures, it is an attempt to individualize the process completely. The letter is a teacher's account to parents of the activities their child participated in and an appraisal of his progress in those activities. Each letter is different for every child.

The advantages of this type of reporting center around the flexibility of the procedure. A teacher does not have to be concerned with competitive marking nor scaling of pupil's efforts nor factors that a report card fails to cover. The letter can be designed to reveal strengths and weakness on an individual basis. The principal advantage is that the letter is a means of specifically

---

[1] Beeman N. Phillips, "Characteristics of Elementary Report Cards," *Educational Administration and Supervision,* 42: 385-397 (November, 1956).

[2] Charles H. Wilson, "Our Report Cards Are Failing," *NEA Journal,* 46: 362-364 (September, 1957).

SOCIAL GROWTH

We consider the habits and attitudes listed below as important factors in your child's character development. We shall appreciate your cooperation in helping your child to improve in those characteristics which are checked.

No mark means satisfactory.
√ means improvement is needed.

	Report Periods				
	1	2	3	4	5
Individual Growth					
Is neat and orderly					
Shows courtesy in speech and action					
Listens to assignments					
Completes assignments					
Assumes responsibility					
Uses time wisely					
Shows self control					
Accepts criticism well					
Practices good health habits					
Group Responsibility					
Shows regard for property of others					
Respects rights and opinions of others					
Works well in group activities					
Observes safety rules					

A pupil whose achievement is below his ABILITY should be encouraged to better efforts. A pupil whose achievement EQUALS his ability should be regarded as making normal progress.

EVALUATION IN SUBJECT FUNDAMENTALS

Subjects	Report Periods				
	1st	2nd	3rd	4th	5th
Reading*					
Arithmetic					
Language					
Writing					
Spelling					
Social Studies					
Science					

* The reading grade is based on the level at which your child is reading.

Conduct					

The conduct grade is for the general conduct that typifies good citizenship.

EXPLANATION OF MARKS

1—Excellent work   4—Poor work
2—Good work   D—Failing work
3—Average work   Inc—Incomplete work

A check mark (√) after a grade means that your child is not doing as well in that subject as might reasonably be expected.

SUBJECT	Report Periods				
	1st	2nd	3rd	4th	5th
Health					
Music					
Art					
Physical Education					

Explanation of Marks
S—means satisfactory   U—means unsatisfactory

FIGURE 16. *A report card utilizing more than one procedure. Used with permission of School District 89, Maywood, Illinois.*

transmitting growth information of a quantitative and qualitative nature.

The difficulties of using the report letter are those of the time it takes teachers to write the letters and the problems of language communication in the letters. It takes a teacher many hours to write letters to the parents of each child in the room. Consequently, where they are used there is a tendency for fewer report letters to be sent home than there are report cards. Report letters need to be written in sentences that leave little doubt as to precise meaning, and they must not be clouded with glib generalities. The letter needs to be informative and precise in order to be most effective. Letters are ineffective in areas where there is a high degree of illiteracy or a low level of literacy among parents. So are most forms of reporting, but the letter is especially ineffective in these cases.

In an endeavor to provide for two-way communication between homes and the school, both report cards and report letters sometimes make provision for reporting back to the school by parents. Also, the reports may give the parents an opportunity to request conferences with teachers about their children's work.

The parent-teacher conference

For several reasons the parent-teacher conference is considered the best method of reporting pupil progress to parents. In the first place, the conference provides face-to-face communication. It brings parent and teacher together so that two-way communication can take place. For example, a teacher may present information that the parent does not quite understand. In the conference the lack of understanding can be corrected immediately and without some of the risk of unfortunate misinterpretation. Teachers can show parents the actual work done by pupils and can present graphic illustrations of growth, such as achievement test profiles. The conference also gives teachers and parents the opportunity to compare problems that they encounter in dealing with a child in the school and the home, and to plan means of helping a child make better adjustment to both environments.

The principal disadvantages of the parent-teacher conference are finding time for teachers to hold conferences when parents can be present and getting parents to come to the conference. Where the conference is used alone, complaints are sometimes registered by parents that they do not get enough in writing about their children's progress; consequently, many schools follow conferences with a summary letter at the end of the school year or semester.

REQUEST FOR PARENT-TEACHER CONFERENCE

Dear Mr. and Mrs. ——————————————:

I suggest we plan to hold a conference relating to your child's progress in school at ——————— on ———————————.
                                         TIME   DATE

Naturally, I hope you can come at this time, but if it is not at all possible, please suggest an alternate time and date here:

    HOUR ——————— DATE ———————————

Please sign and return this sheet as soon as possible.

                                         ———————————————————
                                         TEACHER'S SIGNATURE

————————————————
PARENT'S SIGNATURE

FIGURE 17. *A suggested form for arranging parent-teacher conferences.*

Where conferences are held, the first task of the teacher is to arrange for conferences with parents. Ordinarily a school will have some plan for conference time, such as released time for teachers by hiring substitutes, conference days when children are dismissed for that purpose, after-school hours, conference evenings, or some combination of these. Conference times with parents can be arranged by telephone where such services are available. In other cases a form of correspondence can be used. A form card or letter can be created that will indicate to the parent the time that the teacher suggests for a conference, with space provided for the parent to indicate an alternate time. In some schools the plan will be to send these forms to and from the home via the pupils; in others, the school will have a policy of using the mail service for this purpose. Every effort should be made to get both parents to come to conferences even though this is difficult for most fathers.

A teacher must make preparation for a conference. The items to be reported and discussed should be planned in advance and the materials to be shown to parents collected. Among these may be the following:

1. Observed and measured physical development
2. Improvement in social development including attitudes toward peers, adults
3. Progress in skill subjects such as arithmetic, reading, language arts
4. Efforts and progress in acquiring useful knowledge in science and the social studies
5. Interest and effort in the arts of creative living such as music, art, and dramatics
6. Test data to support comments
7. Examples of such things as written work, projects, paintings, or reading lists
8. Any profiles that will indicate the nature and magnitude of educational growth
9. Interpretation of anecdotal records.

This information may be outlined in writing before the conference so that the teacher can proceed in an orderly fashion during the conference. Sometimes schools have a parent-conference form upon which these entries are made prior to the conference. It is also possible to make the conference sheet out in duplicate and place one copy in the hands of the parent at the beginning of the conference, and this then provides the parent with a record of the conference that he can take home with him.

PARENT CONFERENCE FORM

PUPIL'S NAME _____   SCHOOL _____

GRADE _____   DATE _____

TEACHER _____

Notes on Academic Progress

Notes on Social-Emotional Behavior

Interesting Anecdotes

Parent Comments

FIGURE 18. *A parent-teacher conference form.*

In the course of the conference the teacher must insure that the items he wishes to communicate to the parent are understood. Parents should be put as much at ease as possible so that they will feel free to interrogate the teacher about any problem brought up in the conference. Furthermore, an important element of the conference is the opportunity for parents to report to schools their version of the effect of the school program upon their child. Often this is most enlightening.

A record of each conference should become a part of the cumulative file. If a conference sheet is made out prior to the session, it can serve as the record, provided any elements emerging from the conference itself are added to it. Another convenient means of maintaining conference reports and records is in the behavior journal or anecdotal record, because the conference report is really a summary of changed behavior, whether in the form of social behavior or skill behavior.

PROMOTION AND NON-PROMOTION

The establishment of promotional policy is considered to be an administrative matter. However, in a democratically organized school system teachers participate in the formulation of that policy. In any case every elementary teacher is, at some time or another, faced with the problem of whether to retain a child or not. Here the teacher must bring together the results of pupil evaluation in light of the school's promotional policy. If the school's policy is to maintain predetermined grade standards for promotion, then teachers must decide upon promotion on the evidence accumulated as to how well the child measures up to those standards. On the other hand, if it is the policy of the school to promote on the basis of the welfare (educational welfare that is) of the child, the teacher must take into account the child's capacity for learning, his readiness for learning, and the achievement made in the light of this capacity and readiness.

The field of research fails to indicate that any significant gains have been made by retaining children in elementary school grades. In fact the tenor of the conclusions of research is that in the long run non-promoted children encounter more difficulty than those who are promoted under similar circumstances.[3] In coming to conclusions about pupil retention, it seems to the author that it would be more profitable to seek the reasons why children are retained. There probably are only three reasons why a child may be considered for retention. One could be a matter of maturation. Only the passage of time will correct this if it ever can be corrected. A second might be that the pupil lacks ability. Obviously he cannot help this and neither can the teacher; it is an accident of birth in most cases. The third reason could be that the child is a victim of a poor teacher and a poor curriculum. Here again the child has no control over these circumstances. It is these kinds of consideration that make such a moral issue out of promotional considerations. They are a real source of concern for conscientious teachers.

Summary

Every elementary school teacher must participate in the keeping of cumulative records and making of progress reports to parents. The purpose of both of these functions is to reveal the educational growth of children attributable to the school. Records properly kept to fulfill this purpose also become aids to teachers in furthering educational growth.

Cumulative records should contain all forms of records that may be legally required, be desired for pupil study by teachers, be measures of educational growth, and be descriptive of change in social behavior. They no doubt should be housed in some central place where they are readily available to teachers but at the same time maintained as confidential information.

There are three basic forms of the pupil progress report: the report card, the report letter, and the parent-teacher conference. Teachers and administrators must weigh public opinion and their own purposes in progress reporting, to select the form they will use.

[3] For an interesting review of this kind of research, see John I. Goodlad, "Research and Theory Regarding Promotion and Nonpromotion," *Elementary School Journal*, 53: 150-155 (November, 1952).

Similarly, purpose and function must be taken into account in promotional policy.

Ideas for discussion and activity

1. What kind of promotional policy would you prefer in a school in which you teach? Why?

2. Devise a scheme that you would consider "ideal" for reporting pupil progress to parents.

3. To what extent are you willing to accept the notations and appraisals of teachers who have children prior to you, that are filed in a cumulative folder?

4. List the things that should be made part of a good set of cumulative records for elementary school pupils.

Suggested readings

Association for Childhood Education International, *Reporting on the Growth of Children*. Bulletin No. 62. Washington, D.C.: The Association, 1953.
   The pamphlet contains a seires of articles on the many-sided issues of reporting.

Association for Supervision and Curriculum Development, National Education Association, *Reporting Is Communicating*. Washington, D.C.: The Association, 1956.
   The booklet emphasizes the communicative aspects of reporting with suggested principles and procedures.

Goodlad, John I., "Research and Theory Regarding Promotion and Non-promotion," *Elementary School Journal*, 53:150-155; November, 1952.
   This is a thorough review of research and its interpretation for promotional practices.

Goodykoontz, Bess, "A Report on Report Cards," *National Parent-Teacher*, 50: 11-13; October, 1955.
   Controversy in two school systems over reporting practices is described and the rationale of reporting is analyzed.

Martyn, Kenneth A. and Harold J. Bienvenu, "The Parent Conference-Progress Report, Not Psychotherapy." *The Elementary School Journal*, 57:42-44; October, 1956.

The authors criticize some of our practices and then offer a plan for progress-reporting parent conferences.

Phillips, Beeman N., "Characteristics of Elementary Report Cards," *Educational Administration and Supervision*, 42: 385-397, November, 1956.

This is a report of a survey of the use of elementary school report cards. It contains interesting tabulations and illustrations.

Wilson, Charles H., "Our Report Cards Are Failing," NEA *Journal*, 46: 362-364; September, 1957.

The author criticizes the selective grading system that doesn't select. He claims it does not work in accordance with our assumptions for it.

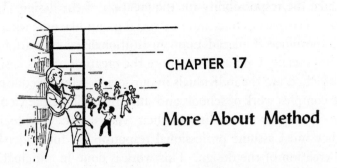

CHAPTER 17

More About Method

THIS BOOK HAS been written about what have been called basic dimensions of method in elementary school teaching. The very assumption that basic dimensions can be identified leads to the inference that there is more to method than these basic approaches. The amount of attention focused upon method, especially in elementary education, would bear this out. Therefore, the purpose of this chapter is to briefly review for the reader the basic dimensions and to point the way toward further considerations about method.

THE TEACHER'S WORK

The total work of a teacher in a modern elementary school involves the performance of many tasks. Some are highly complex; others are quite simple. The point of view taken in this writing has been that these tasks can be arranged according to three distinct, but related, levels of activity. They have been called the three levels of a complete educational activity.

The curriculum planning level

One of these is the curriculum planning level. If we can consider the curriculum to be the design of a social group for the educational experiences of their children in school, then someone must take the responsibility for the creation of the design. In a culture as complex as ours and in a social group like ours wherein such importance is placed upon institutionalized education, it would be socially foolhardy to ignore the creation of this design. Since teachers are the individuals in our society who are educated for the complex work of schools and since they will be the victims of a good or poor curriculum in their work efforts, it is logical that they must assume professional responsibility for leadership in the creation of the design. This work is done in anticipation of what is to come in the classroom, but it takes place before teachers and pupils are assembled in the classroom. Obviously then, teachers must be prepared to work at this level of activity outside of the time that they spend with children in the classroom. Too often we forget that this work must be done, and even more often we forget to teach lay citizens that this work must be done under these circumstances. As a result they misunderstand and are not always sympathetic to our demands for time to do this work.

The teaching-learning level

The second of the three levels of a complete educational activity is the teaching-learning level. At this level of activity a teacher spends most of his time in the classroom with the pupils. It is at this level that method becomes critical to success in teaching. Whereas method is anticipated at the curriculum planning level, method is practiced in the classroom. Most of the dimensions of method presented in this book are related here, and most of the success or failure of a teacher's work is attributed to his performance in the classroom. A teacher works at this level both in and out of school. Preparation for teaching and some phases of evaluation are done when children are not present. However, the large portion of a teacher's time is spent in the manipulation of the classroom environment. Again, few people other than teachers are aware of the time and energy spent in preparing for teaching and in follow-up work.

The evaluation level

Closure to the complete educational activity is accomplished at the evaluation level. Ends, or objectives, and content are selected at the curriculum planning level. Means for achieving those ends are established through method in the classroom, and evaluation determines whether the ends have been achieved and in the best possible manner. Thus through evaluation there is established a basis for new curriculum planning and the cycle can then start all over again. Many features of a teacher's work related to evaluation do not appear to the casual observer. The preparation for evaluating the work of children, the preparation for reporting pupil progress whether it be by report card or conference, the time spent in testing, and the time spent in making anecdotal records do not show to an outsider. A number of the dimensions of method are either in direct application of evaluation procedures or related to them in some way.

The meaning of method

The meaning of method becomes very clear when one examines it in terms of the levels of the educational activity. Like any method, teaching method is a means to an end. The end in this case is the achievement of the objectives established for the school. Since elementary schools are principally concerned with objectives having to do with learning, teaching method becomes a process (means) of arranging subject matter and learners in such a way that the learners can profit from interaction with the subject matter. For such a simple statement, method can become so complex. Interpretations of method range anywhere from a bag of tricks for manipulation of drill behaviors to a psychological and philosophical insight into the stimulation of behavior. But it is because of this range of interpretations that it is possible to identify dimensions of method and place them into categories.

BASIC DIMENSIONS IN REVIEW

From an analysis of the work teachers must perform on the three levels of activity and the role of method in them, four focal points for application of method are apparent: (1) teachers must study children, (2) they must organize teaching materials, (3) they must manipulate the teaching-learning environment, and (4) they must evaluate. These, then, are the areas or categories in which basic dimensions of method can be identified.

Studying children

In order that a teacher may reasonably expect to be able to use method in the sense that it is a process of arranging pupils and subject matter so that the pupils can profit from the subject matter, it is necessary for him to know his pupils well. This means he must study them from as many frames of reference as possible so that he can intelligently make the arrangement.

Three dimensions of method seem basic to this category of effort. One is to understand the purposes for engaging in the activity. Without purpose a teacher will either fail to study children at all or do so in a routine and meaningless manner. A second dimension is the use of techniques of studying children. The measurement movement provided us with many devices that help us understand children better, and growth and development laboratories have demonstrated various techniques for studying growth and development. It takes considerable skill on the part of a classroom teacher to know of and use these techniques in his work. A related but third dimension is the recognition of individual differences. Part of this dimension involves the use and interpretation of techniques, but a substantial part is the understanding a teacher must have of the significance for the classroom teacher's behavior, of the range of individual differences among school pupils.

Organizing teaching materials

Just as a teacher must study his pupils as one application of method, so must he organize materials for instruction. Subject matter for the classroom may be organized in different ways. Two extremes of organization have been identified. One of these is to organize subject matter into the conventional school subjects. The other is to make some adaptation of the experience approach. Each of these carries its own set of basic assumptions and offers certain strengths. A selection of approach must be made that the teacher believes will provide the best learning atmosphere for children.

When the mode of organization of subject matter has been decided upon, instructional materials can be selected. To do a good job of selecting materials a teacher must know instructional materials, sources for the procurement of them, and the rationale for their use. Much psychology of learning is applied in this dimension of method.

Part of the organization of teaching materials is the teacher's planning for his own actions and the actions of his pupils in the classroom. There are involved in this dimension of method such activities as lesson planning, teacher-pupil planning, and arranging the daily program.

The tasks involved in organizing teaching materials are not easy. They must be performed with an understanding of a specific group of pupils and an organized curriculum. They must anticipate group behavior in the teaching-learning process.

The teaching-learning process

The dimensions of method involved in the teaching-learning process are the organizing of pupils for work, directing investigative activities, organizing drill procedures, guiding and pacing activities, and discipline. These are the classroom tasks of the teacher, and they are the ones commonly associated with teach-

ing. It is here that the principles of motivation, practice, learning, and personality development learned by the teacher in
psychology are put to work. It is here that the teacher demonstrates his sensitivity to social forces among children and applies
his knowledge of them to constructive organization of a learning
unit. These are the things all teachers must do. Some may not
participate in curriculum planning, others may not carefully
study children, and still others may never evaluate. But all
teachers must organize children into groups even though it may
only be one group. All teachers face discipline issues. All teachers direct learning activities. Because these areas of teaching are
unavoidable, skill in these dimensions of method is so very basic
to successful teaching.

Evaluation

Two dimensions of method in evaluation have been noted.
One was the application of evaluation procedures, and the other
was the keeping of records and reporting of pupil progress. Evaluation must take place at two levels. The curriculum must be
evaluated in order that the social design may have reasonable
opportunity to fulfill the changing educational needs of the social
group prescribing it. This kind of evaluation, like curriculum
planning, takes place outside of the classroom. The activities of
the classroom may contribute to it, but the evaluation must be
done by teachers and lay persons as part of their responsibility
for the social design they call the curriculum of their school.
Evaluation also takes place in the classroom for the purpose of
giving the same kind of closure to the learning activities of the
boys and girls, that curriculum evaluation should do for the
curriculum. It is a technique of teaching and a process through
which children can learn. Thus the dimensions of method related
to evaluation impinge upon all levels of the complete educational
activity.

ADDITIONAL FACTORS IN METHOD

In training elementary school teachers a great deal of emphasis is placed upon method. It is quite common to find listed in the catalogues of teacher-education institutions several methods courses. There may be at least one general methods course in which the syllabus for the course might resemble the table of contents of this book. There are almost certain to be listed some methods courses in various subject fields.

However, college courses are not the only places where emphasis is placed upon method. Many conferences and workshops are organized around teaching methods. Innumerable in-service training programs have included the study of methods of teaching reading, spelling, arithmetic, social studies, and science.

The search for improvement in method seems endless if the behaviors of teachers in the past reflect the truth. There is no doubt that method is of great significance for teaching, and what have been called the basic dimensions of method in this book are critical to success in teaching. But the reader no doubt will seek further enlightenment. Three avenues are open for him.

He may take additional course work in methods of teaching the separate subjects. Here a direct attempt is made to teach the specific organization of that subject matter so that it will be more meaningful to the learners. Special techniques appropriate to that subject matter will be demonstrated. Particular kinds of instructional material will be recommended. Some of the basic dimensions under discussion in this book will be repeated and strengthened. Sometimes this kind of study will be called the psychology of school subjects. If this be the case, emphasis will be placed upon the results of research in subject-matter organization and teaching techniques. If such additional course work is not available, many volumes have been written on special methods for the various school subjects, and the student of method can read them.

Following his first employment the new teacher may find himself involved in an in-service program for teachers in which special attention is being given to teaching methods. In this case the experience of veteran teachers, study materials, and the occasional use of a consultant become the vehicles for further study.

Occasionally a teacher will find an opportunity to do research in the field of method. There are many facets to method, and we have much to learn. New research is needed, and this is a most satisfying means of further study for the individual who can and will do so.

Beyond our basic dimensions of elementary method there certainly are additional factors in method, but first it behooves us as teachers to learn and accept the principles of teaching that are inherent in the basic dimensions. From them we can develop a philosophy of teaching method that will allow freedom of movement for the classroom teacher to face the many possible, specific situations that are bound to confront him in the course of a year's work. We can never find that bag of tricks that will fit all situations; it is only because we act on the basis of sound principle or generalization that we can teach without fear of being wrong because we may not have used "the right method."

REFLECTION UPON WHAT WE DO

It should be obvious to the reader by now that the job of a teacher is neither a small nor an insignificant one. The acts of planning a curriculum, doing classroom teaching, and evaluating what is done, constitute a very complex network of duties. Furthermore, when one realizes that these tasks are done throughout our entire country for all of America's children, the social significance of professional education appears overwhelming. Public education in America today is considered to be essential to the way of life we have chosen, and this is demonstrated by the continuing demand for more education for more of our people.

No doubt the sphere of influence of public education will grow. This will mean that members of the teaching profession must also grow. We can only grow in our profession as we persistently study our work and reflect upon our problems to the extent that we devise ways and means of solving them. It has been emphasized repeatedly in this book that the basic dimensions of method are not restricted to the things teachers may do with children while they are in the classroom. There are considerations for method in curriculum planning and in evaluation as well. There is much for us to reflect upon, and there is much of our work to appraise, but such reflection and appraisal will give greater meaning to what we do.

INDEX